JOURNEYWELL

Dear Don, What fun to get reacquainted
What fun that you have
with you + know that you have
one of these books of mine. I
look forward to more get-togethers

Trish Hubert

"*Journeywell: A Guide to Quality Aging* is a treasure chest of wisdom, practical tips, and hand holding that invites deep reflection and smart planning. As I read it, I felt nurtured by guidance, wit, and down-to-earth perspectives I quickly came to trust. Herbert addresses every important aspect of aging, from choosing where to live to dealing with health difficulties and preparing well for death. This is not a fast read set of checklists for weighing options, nor lengthy, lofty essays from on high. This is a substantive book that speaks personally to my heart and soul. I'd highly recommend this to those who want a tender-hearted and knowledgeable tour guide for the years ahead. I will be picking up this book often to help me revisit life's important questions, navigate through rough waters, and stay anchored in the center of my soul. Thank you, Trish Herbert, for showing the way!"

—PAT SAMPLES, AUTHOR OF *DAILY COMFORTS FOR CAREGIVERS* AND *THE SECRET WISDOM OF A WOMAN'S BODY: FREEING YOURSELF TO LIVE PASSIONATELY AND AGE FEARLESSLY.*

"*Journeywell: A Guide to Quality Aging,* Trish Herbert's new guide comes at a crucial time as the longevity revolution impacts every facet of our society. Don't miss taking this journey using her powerful step-by-step roadmap to fulfillment, joy and satisfaction."

—MARIKA & HOWARD STONE, AUTHORS OF *TOO YOUNG TO RETIRE:101 WAYS TO START THE REST OF YOUR LIFE*

"Trish Herbert's book, *Journeywell: A Guide to Quality Aging,* is all about wrestling with your destiny and shaping it to your own ends. It's about living fully in the moment. It's also about old dogs learning new tricks. In her eighties, my mom decided to take up Russian. Her friends expressed dismay: 'Such a tough language! You'll be ninety by the time you've learned it!' 'How old will I be if I don't?' she asked. That is precisely Herbert's point: treat every day like a vacation. 'What shall I do today?' and, if the answer is 'nothing,' do it proudly. This is a book that can change your life, maybe even save it—who knows? Above all it's about not squandering your energies on fear and despair, for aging is the universal human condition, and those who have the will to reframe it can find new meaning and spirit in it."

—JUDITH GUEST, AUTHOR OF *ORDINARY PEOPLE*

"*Journeywell: A Guide to Quality Aging* serves as a catalyst to help you ponder what is important to you and how to make your later years as good as they can possibly be. There are stories, questions and exercises, information, and practical tools suggested helping you plan and negotiate the rough spots. It will be helpful not only to older adults, their families, and caregivers, but to teachers, social workers, clergy who want to promote thoughtful discussion about late life issues and opportunities."

—BOLTON ANTHONY, FOUNDER AND PRESIDENT OF *SECOND JOURNEY,* A CORPORATION PROMOTING "MINDFULNESS, SERVICE AND COMMUNITY IN THE SECOND HALF OF LIFE."

"*Journeywell: A Guide to Quality Aging* is an excellent resource for all who desire to improve the quality of the aging process—their own or loved ones'. The book provides exercises, stories and abundant information for a journey we'll all make."

—MARK AND JANET SKEIE, EDITORS, *MAPPING YOUR RETIREMENT*

"This book is a valuable and optimistic guidebook for mindfulness and healthy aging."

—STEVEN MILES, MD, CENTER FOR BIOETHICS, DEPT OF MEDICINE, UNIVERSITY OF MINNESOTA

"Trish Herbert is a wise woman who has examined life and developed superb questions, tools, and insights so that others may truly journey well. She has gifted us with wise guidance on living life optimally with joy and zest . . . may your reading of this book be a blessing in your life."

—GREGORY A. PLOTNIKOFF, MD, MTS, FACP, MEDICAL DIRECTOR, PENNY GEORGE INSTITUTE FOR HEALTH AND HEALING

Journeywell

A Guide to Quality Aging

Trish Herbert

ISBN 10: 1-59298-291-3
ISBN 13: 978-1-59298-291-2

Library of Congress Catalog Number: 2009927794
Printed in the United States of America
First Printing: 2009
13   12   11   10   09   5   4   3   2   1

Cover and interior design by Ryan Scheife, Mayfly Design

Beaver's Pond Press, Inc.
7104 Ohms Lane, Suite 101
Edina, MN 55439-2129
(952) 829-8818
www.BeaversPondPress.com

To order, visit www.BookHouseFulfillment.com
or call (800) 901-3480. Reseller discounts available.

Dedication

I want to dedicate this book to my many teachers and mentors who have been a major part of my journey.

To my family: Peter, husband for 49 years; my children—Molly, Laura, Charlie, and Nelle—who I'm proud are wonderful additions to this world; and now their kids, my grandchildren, who continue to teach me about life.

To my friends—canoeing cronies, Minnetonka Mafia, Carleton buddies, campers at the big-girl retreats, and Dorothy, Norma, Jude, and Wilys Claire—who have witnessed and shared my life. Who would I be without these friends?

To my clients, from years as a psychologist I was allowed to witness life from many angles and learn about the nuances of living.

To my mentors, some who I have known and loved like Kitty Smith and Frank Lamendola, my partners in Journeywell, and others whose writings and modeling have influenced my ways of being like Mary Oliver, Rachel Naomi Remen, Parker Palmer, Joyce Rupp, and Joan Chittister.

To Ann Meissner and Joanne Kendall whose gentle urging and support prompted me to write this book.

Special gratitude to three places, sacred to me, where I escaped to write—Sylvestre's cabin at Blueberry Lake, Oberholtzer's island on Rainy Lake, and our cabin on Lake Vermilion.

And more thanks to my son, Charlie, for the Maud and Henry cartoons in the book, and to Jay Kent for the cover photo of the moonrise on Lake Vermilion.

JOURNEYWELL: A GUIDE TO QUALITY AGING

TABLE OF CONTENTS

Introduction

- If you are looking for a practical guide to help you review what has been important thus far in your life, and what is important to you now…
- If you want to create a lifestyle that fits your values and is emotionally rewarding…
- If you are wondering about the differences between mid-and later life…
- If you want to explore some tools to help you buffer the rough spots that happen to us all thus improving your chances of living your life as fully and satisfyingly as possible…
- If you want to plan for your final days and finish as well as possible…

Journeywell: A Guide to Quality Aging will help you in that process. You are on a journey from the moment you are born. You move through life in cycles of beginnings and endings, experiencing and changing as you go. This is not a how-to-do-aging book. There is no "right way" to grow old. There is no lock-step path. What is "right" for me may not fit for you at all. It is about possibilities and making good choices. *Journeywell* helps you reflect on how to be the person you want to be. It asks you to give some thought to how you can make your last years, whether two, ten, twenty, thirty, or very little time as good as it can be. It asks questions for you to ponder. It provides information and suggestions that have worked well for others and asks you to figure out what might work best for you. Better and worse choices could greatly enhance or complicate your later years. *Journeywell's* goal is to make your own journey easier and more satisfying.

Journeywell provides a framework and an experience for examining your journey. The book does not have to be read from beginning to end: you can scan or choose parts that are personally important or of concern. This book helps you define quality of life for yourself. You are not only who you are today but also an accumulation of all that you have been before. As you grow older, this realization can provide strength and identity. *Journeywell* is also for family, friends, and caregivers—nurses, psychologists, social workers, clergy, teachers, doctors—who may need a catalyst to draw out stories and elicit information, enabling them to understand better the storytellers thoughts, hopes, and feelings.

Journeywell is a common sense guide to help you explore the depth and mystery of your life. What have been some of the choice moments? The good times? The not so good, in fact, the wrenching bad times? How did you get through those times? What tools do you need to get through the rough times around the corner? What are you proud of? Who were the powerful people in your life—teachers, friends, clergy? To whom have you been important? Older persons generally feel the need to take stock of their lives. The more experiences you have had, the more mountains you have climbed, the better the view. Mysteries and wonders of life are slowly revealed. What have you learned? What do you need to do now to make the rest of your life as enjoyable, meaningful, and balanced as possible? Making sense of your journey is a major life task.

Some may think *Journeywell* is "only for really old people and I'm not there yet." Not so. The book is as appropriate for persons who are well into their aging process as it is for persons who are beginning to wonder about their future selves and want to be well prepared. It can be the mechanism for a granddaughter who desires to know her grandparent better; it can spark a couple's conversation about hopes and fears; it can be a discussion catalyst for groups; it could be the means for finishing some personal business you have been putting off; it can be used in a very private way to review what your experiences have meant in order to plan for your future. I invite you to use the framework given in this book to appreciate your life, its beauty and pain.

Late life can be the best time of your life or it can be the toughest … or anywhere in between. It can be a time of great possibilities and freedom or it can be a time of emptiness and sadness. Particular segments of this guide will appeal to you at different times of your life depending on what you are going through or looking for. Instead of accepting the myth of later life being only a period of decline, you can do much to improve your chances of a pleasure-filled rich old age. Examine your options. Do some responsible planning. Program your mind toward health. Expect to have an old age filled with richness and learning.

> *You can't teach a person anything. You can create an environment in which the person can look within, unlocking the treasures of the past and discovering the wisdom there.*

"Old" is often considered a nasty word valiantly avoided by many writers and publishers. The manuscript for my first book had "old" in the original title, and the publishers let me know that this would not do. It is fashionable to use other terms to describe this later period of life whether you are emphasizing the positive such as being a golden-ager, sage, or elder; being in a period of refirement; or even being a "well-der" instead of an elder. On the other hand, there are the negative descriptors … like being a greedy geezer, over-the-hill, past your prime, or sad, lonely, useless souls. Rest assured that this isn't yet another book about the wonderfulness of old age nor about how bad things are. I have seen that this period of life can be a profoundly rich and important time. You have much to say about how yours will be.

Many books overload the positives of aging, in my view, appearing to be rah-rah cheerleaders about an upcoming purely golden age, usually addressing only the very early retirement bonus years, which are often healthy and golden, while ignoring the more challenging times. There are better and worse ways to live during this time. By sharing information and stories about what I have seen work well for others, I am asking you to join with me in a shared venture of figuring out what might best fit for you. When I listen to people's stories, I always wonder how I would be and what I would do, given their set of circumstances. As an older person myself, and professionally a lifelong gero-psychologist, I surely have ideas about how I would like to be. I share with you much of what I have learned with the hope that this will give you and me a jump-start on this next phase of our lives.

Gerontologists have developed many theories about the aging process.

1. ACTIVITY THEORY. Older people should maintain the values of middle age by keeping busy and being productive. This theory is modeled by nursing home social directors who try to keep residents active by involving them in community sing-a-longs, discussion groups, and myriads of activities for the mind and body. This theory is also exhibited by the freshly retired, who proudly announce "I am busier than ever" implying they are okay because they are keeping busy. My perspective is that the activity theory is fine and fitting as long as it makes you feel good to be doing what you are choosing to do; it's for those who are making selective decisions about what they do and with whom they do it. It becomes less satisfying when you're keeping busy just for the sake of being busy. Some retirees choose to be unapologetically self-pleasuring and try diligently to pack into their schedule all that they feel passionately about and want to pursue in their remaining years. The activity theory will not be for those who choose solitude and peaceful living some percentage of the time.

2. DISENGAGEMENT THEORY. Older people withdraw from society feeling they have put in their time and are now content to hand responsibilities over to others. They content themselves doing things they enjoy (such as gardening, baking, reading, listening to music, playing an instrument, playing cards, golf, watching TV, or just puttering around). The disengagement theory also works if it is a choiceful decision. There is a hint of ageism with this theory, suggesting that older people no longer have much to contribute and are supposed to disappear and get out of the way. The very old are a lot more in evidence on the streets and in the town squares in other countries. Where are they in the U.S.? Why are they out of sight or housed in special communities just for old people? Some in this age group do choose to disengage, seek solitude and time for reflection versus the doing, doing, doing busyness that is accepted by most in middle age and carried forth by many into old age. But I fear for the disengaged who are lonely and it is not their choice.

3. CONTINUITY THEORY. This theory functions around the idea that when you grow older you just get "more-so." If you have always been a rather negative person, you will only get grumpier as you age. If you have always been good at coping and able to see the brighter side of things, you will probably make the adjustments that come with aging well. This theory says that you rather seamlessly follow the river of life with no big changes in outlook or personality. The continuity theory seems mostly true. People do get "more-so," but my hesitation is that there's an implication with it that people can't change. This isn't true. At any age, people make choices of great significance. I cannot be a life-long therapist and believe any other way.

4. GEROTRANSCENDENCE THEORY.[1] Gerotranscendence calls for a shift in perspective as you age, from a self-focused, materialistic, rational view of the world to a more worldly perspective. Because of your years and experience, you redefine yourself and become wiser. Gerotranscendent persons become less self-occupied and more thoughtful about what they do and with whom they do it. They think more about fundamental existential questions like "What am I doing here?" "What is this life all about?" There is an increased affinity with past generations and the need to see how they fit into the bigger picture.

The gerotranscendent theory is my favorite because it is based on looking more deeply into yourself and making meaningful decisions, which I encourage throughout this book. My only qualm with it is that, in my experience, not all older people seem to go through this loftier, spiritual way of being, as much as I would wish it for them. Many are not wise. It is not an automatic that you will be wise just because you are older. You must learn from your experiences to become wise. Not everyone spends time with existential angst, nor do they transcend anything, that I can discern. I trust that those people won't be reading this book because *Journeywell* is about asking yourself questions, getting to know yourself better, thus being able to make good decisions that will enable you to have an old age with as much quality as possible.

5. CHOICEFULIST THEORY. This is my theory. Old age can be anything. The above theories have had reams written about them, and I have only briefly described them. One of the above theories might fit for you or a combination of them. The decisions we make have much to do with how our aging experience will go. There's the journey we plan and the journey we take. There are always surprises and choices. This book aims to help you see what some of the choices may be and gives you information, suggestions, and tools to help you along your way. In response to the all-American question "What do you do now that you are retired?" I like saying "I'm a choicefulist." It sounds less snooty than offering a transcendent answer. But maybe Robert Fulgham, author of *All I Really Need to Know I Learned in Kindergarten*, responded better saying "I am a respirateur". . . simply meaning "I am a breather."

Being a choicefulist means that you decide what makes quality for you. It means that the journey is truly yours. It means you can choose to be busy and active doing things that interest you, or you can disengage and withdraw from society if that is what is comfortable and satisfying for you, or you can continue doing and being pretty much who you have always been. You can choose to do the exercises in this book, study the suggestions, and decide what fits for you now. You can decide the best course to follow to enable you to like yourself the most in your final years. At times, the alternatives may not be between better and worse choices but rather between two not-so-good options. Your life is defined by the choices you make every day—small ones and critical ones.

In his hierarchy of needs, Abraham Maslow[2] argued that the factors that drive and motivate people lay on an ascending scale, starting with the basic physiological needs, proceeding to security needs, then social, self-respect, and—if these are achieved—reaching self-actualization. Once a group or order of needs is satisfied, the individual will not be motivated by more of the same, but will seek to satisfy a need of a higher order.

This book is written for those who essentially have their basic physiological and security needs in order. Until you have your basic needs in order—enough food to eat, a place to live, access to healthcare, some feeling of safety and security—you will be less able to focus on the higher level needs of possibilities and growth. We know by now that life gives us many surprises, that there is much we cannot control in our lives, but that there are many different, better or worse, ways to react to what happens. We know by now that it is important to have the information that will help us make good choices. This workbook is a guide to navigating this last period of your life in the most fitting way for your own unique self.

The first chapter, "Who Is This Person Called Me?" has two parts:

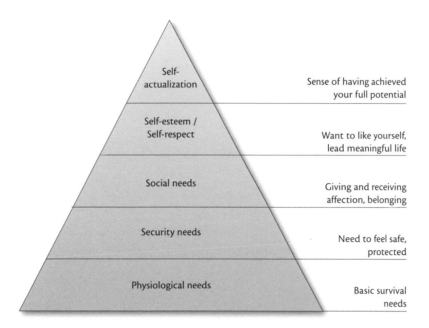

1. "WHO HAVE I BEEN UP UNTIL NOW?" is more than a life review. It is peppered with questions that help you learn from your life story, how you have coped, what your strengths have been, and what you have done that makes you feel good about yourself. It reacquaints you with your past, and helps you see how you have evolved over the years. It's a sort of late-life scrapbook, a way to pass along your story.

By telling your story, you give yourself a chance to shape a legacy that will last beyond this life. Few things are more fascinating than trying to understand a human life—especially your own. Everyone's story is different. Some stories have more sun; some, more clouds. There are ups and downs, losses and rebirths. Some people balk at doing a life review, and don't even like being asked to do it, reporting that it makes them feel old. If this is the case for you, skip to the second part of the chapter and get to the present and future.

2. "WHO AM I RIGHT NOW?" provides a framework for self-exploration. It helps you look at your values, what makes you feel good about yourself, who your mentors are, and how you spend your time. Participate as fully as you want. This exploration provides the compass to guide your journey. It will be up to you to choose which path to take.

The second chapter, "What's Different About Living a Long Life?" generalizes about some of the differences between these two stages, asking you to think about how your values change. It explores the existing barriers that make getting old difficult, both the natural ones and the societal ones, like ageism. It helps you see that this later stage of life is every bit as important as any other stage and that we continue with our personal growth and learning all through life.

The third chapter, "How Do I Make My Life More Meaningful?" helps you clarify for yourself what is truly meaningful to you now, and then gives suggestions of ways you might not have thought of to add still more meaning.

The fourth chapter, "How Do I Make My Life as Good as It Can Be?" looks at the all-important matter of attitude, and how to best care for ourselves.

The fifth chapter, "What Ways-of-Being May Lead to Being Wiser?" suggests characteristics, ways-of-being, that tend to make this time of life richer.

The sixth chapter, "What Are My Responsibilities?" explores what quality of life means to you. It gives information, presents case scenarios, and asks questions in the areas of health care, housing options, and services. I have a fundamental trust that persons have their own answers, and my hope is that this book will be a tool to help you unlock those answers.

The seventh chapter, "Finishing Well," addresses the last part of your life, helps you plan for it, and discusses caregiving, grieving, and what it means to "be present." It looks carefully at the dying process. The chapter is full of scenarios to ponder—stories, questions, and suggestions. What to do? What to say? How do I prepare and plan? How do I want to be treated? What kind of legacy do I want to leave? Many books on aging completely ignore the part of your journey that includes encroaching diminishments, failing health, and death—a very real part that we are all guaranteed. "Finishing Well" helps you sort through the what-ifs of this delicate, but natural, life passage providing suggestions and resources. You may choose to skip this section for now, but know that it is here.

My hope is that *Journeywell: A Guide to Quality Aging* serves as a catalyst to help you think about your next precious years and to be an instrument for emergent growth. You may have retired from work, but you have not retired from life. The emphasis throughout this book is on the "growing" part of growing old. The workbook is practical versus academic. You are asked questions, given information and ideas that have worked for others, and offered tools that could make your journey more enjoyable.

I use the female pronouns more than male to avoid the tiring he/she's. This book began as an update of my first book, *The Vintage Journey: A Guide to Artful Aging,* and includes portions of it, but the project grew into much more and deserved its own identity. The title of this book, *Journeywell,* is meaningful to me because it has been the name of my small company. The content is a bit autobiographical because I share stories from my own life as I encourage you to share yours. This is my journey as well as yours. My son Charlie has added cartoons to emphasize points I want to make and, as a collector of thought-provoking quotes, I offer these further insights for your enjoyment. If the quotes don't name an author they are my words.

USING THIS BOOK

Journeywell is your opportunity to take a pilgrimage into your life. You can choose one of several approaches:

1. Choose someone with whom to share your journey. The experience of sharing expands your privacy boundary. You may experience a sense of legacy and immortality. Your sharing can be done formally, by setting dates for interviewing, filming, or audio recording. Or share informally by picking up the book when you are with another person and finding a question interesting to either of you. Page through the sections on your own, marking parts that interest you. You need not limit yourself to one person or to any particular number of meetings. Pick and choose what you want to talk about and how lighthearted or serious you want to be reflecting on your story. Many a wise son or daughter decide that they have things they would love to know about their parent's life and set up regular times to ask their questions. One of the most empowering ways of being with the oldest old is to not

only having them share her story but to do it reciprocally enabling her to participate and care about your journey, which may double the significance of this process.

2. The book can be used reciprocally. Take turns sharing stories, information, discussing your points of view thus building a mighty bridge between you and this person.

3. You may choose to make the journey a solo endeavor, answering what appeals to you and then giving it, or parts of it, as a gift to someone special. Or maybe you'd prefer talking into an audio or video recorder to permanently record your thoughts and feelings. It could launch you into doing a full family history with the family tree, family photos, a scrapbook, recordings, and stories. With the Internet helping with searches, people are putting together amazing albums. *Journeywell* will provide websites and suggestions. This book is yours, to read and to write in, or to have your listener record your responses to questions. Some stories, some laughs, some lessons learned simply need to be recorded and immortalized.

> *Loving and knowing yourself is wonderfully important, but being truly known and still loved by another, the good and the not-so-good side of you, is exquisite.*

4. You may want to concentrate on one part of the book and disregard the others. You may not feel like looking at your past right now … or looking at your future. But the ideas are here when the time comes.

5. I created this book because I honestly believe that sharing our stories and planning for today and tomorrow are vitally important. Talking and writing are the best ways for us to get to know each other and ourselves. Inability or lack of opportunity to communicate leads to feelings of uselessness and loneliness. Recognizing that you may not have someone with whom to share your story, I encourage you to converse with me even though I cannot be there with you in person. In my effort to make this journey as interactive and personal as possible, I have made myself the other voice in the process by using the opening phrase "Tell me about. . ." and by sharing some of my stories.

6. An unanticipated use of my first book, *Vintage Journey: A Guide to Artful Aging,* was that counselors, social workers, spiritual directors, and teachers in high schools, colleges, and divinity schools found it helpful to start people reflecting on the aging process and their own lives by using the questions and exercises. Every person is a carrier of fascinating stories. When a person dies, there is no way to retrieve the learning and insights of a lifetime unless they have been shared. You already know that people are very different from one another. Some of you may have been "searching" your whole life, pursuing the existential questions, trying to figure out who you are, the meaning of this or that, what this life of yours is all about. Some of you are not particularly seeking self-awareness and are pleased enough with yourself, but simply would like an audience for recalling some of your life's special moments. Share only what you want to share. You may have some wonderful tales in your memory that would be a crime not to pass on. You may have secrets you want to keep, but you may have secrets that aren't so mighty any more; sharing them can be cathartic and

therapeutic. *Journeywell,* however, is not designed to assist people with serious psychological ailments. They should seek professional help.

Journeywell allows you to step back and get perspective on your experiences, to share them and reflect on what you have learned. You will begin to see the patterns and rhythms of your life and gain clarity about those things you would love to do and why. It is a meant to be a communication catalyst. A healthy old age depends on your ability to communicate and on the choices you make. Hopefully, this book will help you better understand yourself and then communicate this knowledge to others. *Journeywell: A Guide to Quality Aging* is a practical, simply written, non-dogmatic tool to help you organize yourself. It's up to you.

Happy Journeying

Chapter 1

Who Is This Person Called Me?

Why do I want to take this journey? The best way to figure out where you're going is to understand where you've been. By deliberately recalling experiences of the past, you, the storyteller, will become aware of the rhythms and patterns of your life and will begin to absorb life's larger meaning and purpose. Telling your story is empowering. It gives a renewed sense of life's significance and dignity. Stories take time, a commodity that is scarce during mid-life. Stories of real life experience, our own and others, are our best teachers, providing a way to pass on what we've learned.

Telling your story is far more than just telling it. It is about making sense of it or, in some cases, finally making peace with it. If your past was mostly painful, think of it as a time you survived. You are a survivor—no longer a victim. Sometimes secrets will come out. This is usually healing because by sharing them the sometimes-mighty power of the secrets are broken and that energy can finally be used in better ways. Only by learning from our stories and our many experiences do we become wise. Only through our stories do we understand who we are. If you choose to take the time to reflect on your life and see it now from a different perspective than you had when you were living it, any one of a number of benefits could occur:

> *The salvation of this human world lies nowhere else than in the human heart, in the human power to reflect, in human meekness and in human responsibility.*
> *—Vaclav Havel*[1]

1. You take stock of your life. By refamiliarizing yourself with what you've done, and what you've learned, you will be able to extrapolate meaning from your own personal odyssey, which can be an extremely healing adventure. Taking stock of your life, recording it, could be the catalyst for a form of legacy for your loved ones. You may uncover parts of your embedded past that may help you understand yourself now, how your values were formed, and with this rediscovered information redesign your future.

2. You have an opportunity for personal integration. In *Childhood and Society*,[2] Erik Erikson and Helen Kivnick provide theoretical context for this process and divide life into stages:

STAGE	PSYCHOSOCIAL CONFLICT
1. early infancy (birth to one year)	trust vs. mistrust
2. early childhood (ages one to three)	autonomy vs. shame and doubt
3. play age (ages four to five)	initiative vs. guilt
4. school age (ages six to eleven)	industry vs. inferiority
5. adolescence (ages twelve to twenty)	ego identity vs. role confusion
6. young adulthood	intimacy vs. isolation
7. middle adulthood	generativity vs. stagnation
8. old age	integrity vs. despair

We want to live a life that matters and want to live it in a way that will be remembered. Erik H. Erikson called this "generativity." We want to feel deep satisfaction when we look back on our lives. We may be a tiny blip in the big picture but a blip that made a difference. Erikson's final stage in the struggle to achieve ego integrity recognizes the importance of integrating and making sense of the various stages and parts of our life, fitting them into a whole. This means acknowledging all of life's experiences, good and bad, and fitting them together into dynamic balance. This reliving of events, the joyful times and the sad times, reintegrates our separate parts. Often it is said that babies are the promise of the world. Yet it is really older people who embrace life, model hopefulness and vigor, who, because they have witnessed much of what life has to give, actually embody the promise.

> *You can't say a decent goodbye to life until you know what it was.*

3. You are given an opportunity to blend your personal history into your present identity. It is important to know who you are now, but also who you've been all along. Your past experiences give meaning and continuity to the present. You are much more than who you are this minute.

4. You will have a written legacy if you participate in the exercises and respond to the questions you choose to answer. See Appendix B for recording your legacy. After you die, you remain in the memories of those who live on. One of the most common regrets expressed by survivors after someone dies are, "I wish I would have asked him…" or "I wish I had told her.…" If you share this written legacy with a spouse, a friend, a son or daughter, or a grandchild you provide an opportunity to let them see who you are in a new way, truly relating as one human to another. What questions do you wish you would have

> *Stories untold are fleeting.*
> *Stories shared are forever.*

asked your parents or loved ones now deceased? By documenting your highs and lows, your memories of special people and meaningful events, a record of what you have learned and what has been most important to you, you will be leaving a wonderful gift to those who follow. Your recorded journey may even become part of their pathway. It can be the vehicle for transmitting your values, your essence, and your hard-earned wisdom to another generation. Something of you will live on. You become the link between the past and the future.

5. You may be propelled into action. Perhaps with the self-awareness that comes from this reflection, you can figure out what you want to change to improve the quality of your life. You have a lot to say about how you age. As it becomes clearer what is really important to you, a sense of urgency may appear. Every moment becomes even more precious.

> *What is past is prologue.*
> *–Shakespeare, The Tempest*

6. You will take an important step toward authenticity by recognizing your difficult periods as well as the joyous times with all the attendant feelings. Your gloomy times are a part of you. Most of us want to be seen, heard, and accepted.

Sharing your painful memories often helps others better understand you and your behavior. Bringing other people into awareness is also useful if it helps you remove a blockage that has prevented you from getting on with life and living fully. Some of you have had smooth sailing; others, rough seas. Most people have some guilt and regrets about events that did or didn't happen. Late life is a time when fundamental truthfulness becomes more important. Self-acceptance evolves. You stop thinking things will be different than they are.

> *Life is a classroom.*

7. You are given a chance to let go of past mistakes and move on. You can't erase mistakes of the past, but you can let go of them and begin tomorrow anew. If unlocking memories proves to be too painful, you have the choice to suppress or divert them again or to seek professional guidance to help you understand and learn from the experience. If, on the other hand, you have painful memories that you've worked through, by no means dig them up again. Old wounds are easy to open up; let them be. Move on with your journey.

> *You gain strength, courage and confidence by every experience in which you really stop to look fear in the face. You are able to say to yourself, "I lived through this horror. I can take the next thing that comes along." You must do the thing you think you cannot do.*
> *—Eleanor Roosevelt*

No matter how old you are, the adage "This is the first day of the rest of my life" is a great way to start the day. The words help you leave behind regrets and unproductive patterns and rebirth yourself. You do learn from your mistakes. Lovingly recalling the mistakes and hard lessons learned can be mightier gifts than sharing the successes and the joys.

You are given a format for finding what brings meaning into your life. This is a quest to find out more than facts and memories. It is a head and heart exercise. By going back to your formative beginnings, you get to matters of the heart, which are often closer to the truth and a source of meaning rather than facts.

> *What we call the beginning is often the end. And to make an end is to make a beginning. The end is where we start from.*
> —*T.S. Eliot, Four Quartets*
> *"Little Gidding"*

This chapter "Who Is This Person Called Me?" has two parts: Who Have I Been Up Until Now? that helps you look at your past, and the second part, Who Am I Right Now? that deals with the present. Decide what you want to focus on. Maybe you aren't interested in your past right now. Skip it until you are, but at least look through the questions because something might grab you, offering valuable information for getting on with your journey. Life review holds the possibility for healing and making meaning. Some people have a very sour feeling about the past and strongly resist life review. Respect this. On the other hand, some people are thick with the unsaid and are bursting to look at this time of their life.

Get yourself a pen, special notebook, and a marker. Look carefully through this section and check questions of particular interest to you. Or place an X on questions you'd rather skip or that aren't applicable to what you are interested in. I encourage you to record your story so it will be available to others with whom you wish to share it. It is an added pleasure for others to actually hear your storyteller's voice,

> *The past sharpens perspective, warns of pitfalls, and helps point the way.*
> —*Dwight Eisenhower*

intonations, and priceless laughter. If you are recording your stories, read Appendix B for tips. You can choose how deeply you want to delve into yourself, how vulnerable to let yourself be. You are the boss. Only you can make sense of your journey. Either write in this book or in a separate notebook or journal. If you have a lot to say, there won't be room here.

PART ONE: WHO HAVE I BEEN UP UNTIL NOW?

Reviewing your history provides an opportunity for personal integration. By retracing your experiences, you develop a sense for the rhythms of change in your life and a sense of what was important and even inspirational. Remembering the good times is uplifting. Recalling how you struggled through times of difficulty expands your appreciation of your own resiliency.

You are your own best teacher. Writing or telling your life story gives you new perspective on experiences that you were so busy having at the time that only now, years later, can you see more clearly what

> *Life can only be understood backwards, but it must be lived forwards.*
> —*Soren Kierkegaard*

happened and what you learned. Reviewing memories, past dreams, hopes, and stumbles can be a therapeutic tool for developing a better understanding of yourself. It can help with emotional reconciliation and finding meaning (which we will discuss in more detail in Chapter Three.) Reviewing memories is especially useful toward life's end when the present has sometimes lost its charm. It can divert from the emotional trials that often accompany dying. It is a time when you can focus on memories of great success or great caring.

Look back at the qualitative evolution of your own life. There are a lot of questions here and far more in Appendix C. You never know what will spark your interest. I remember an old gentleman who was shut down and unresponsive to a care center's staff; he didn't seem to want to recall anything until I pressed the right button, which was "Did you have any pets?" That was the key question to uncorking his silence and prefaced a fascinating life story. Look through the questions here and in Appendix C with a marker in hand. Highlight those that interest you. If you don't have enough room to write, continue in a separate notebook. Pick and choose the questions that interest you.

> *You are your life's best witness.*

INTEGRATING YOUR YESTERDAYS

Family of Origin

Date of birth _____   Time of day _____   Place _____

Your weight at birth _____

What were you told about your birth? Do you know how your name was chosen? Were you named after someone?

Parents

When you visualize your parents, what do you see them doing? Do you know how they met? What do you know about their courtship? What was their ethnic background? Do you have pictures? Did they get along? What did they do for work? What were they especially opinionated about? Did you share their opinions? Do you now?

How did they discipline you? How did your parents compliment you? How did you get along with your father? Mother? What advice did they give? What did they do for fun? Who were their friends? How did they spend their time? What did they argue about? How did you make them happy? Were there any particular instances when you defied your family's expectations?

How do you think they did at parenting? Were they good role models? Why or why not?

What skills did you learn from them? Who do you resemble? What traits do you get from your father? Your mother? Who are you most like? Who were you closest to?

What didn't you ever ask your parents that you've always wanted to know? What was taboo in your household? What were the secrets? What weren't you supposed to question? Was there any alcoholism or drug abuse in your family? How did your parents model "getting old"?

Were there any family traumas that stick out in your memory? How were they dealt with? Were there any periods of economic depression? Were there any natural disasters—flood, fire, hurricane, illness? What happened? How did they cope?

What is your very best memory of childhood? Remember a moment in your childhood, when you felt completely seen and accepted for who you were by an adult. Who was that person? How did it make you feel?

Think about a family keepsake. What do you know about it? Where is it now? What do you think will happen to it?

Describe a rite of passage in your life, a time when you were aware of a big transition (driver's license, marriage, a family divorce, an illness or accident...).

Education

What is your educational history?

Elementary school _____

Next school _____ Graduated _____

Next school _____ Graduated _____

Next school _____ Graduated _____

Next school _____ Graduated _____

Did you like school? What part? Why? What stories do you remember?

What was your family's attitude toward education? Who were your most influential teachers? What did you like about them? What were your favorite subjects? Why? What sports or activities were you involved in? If you had your schooling to do over again, what would you do differently?

Religion

What was your religious background? How active were you in your place of worship? How important was your religion in your life while you were growing up? Describe a typical Sabbath day as a child? Do you remember a particularly meaningful childhood experience related to your faith? Did you think about death as a child?

Work

What was your first job? What did you think you were going to do when you grew up?

What was your most rewarding job? Why?

Were there promotions? Awards? What were the satisfactions?

Military

Have you served in the military? Where did you go? What did you do? What impact did it have on you? How did you view military service then? Now? What lessons did you learn? Were there times when you were afraid?

Relationships

Who were your primary role models (family, clergy, teachers, sports persons)? What did you admire about them?

Tell me about your marriage(s)/special relationship(s)? First date? How long a courtship? Other romances? Tell me about your wedding. How did you know this was the person you wanted? What was the most romantic thing he or she ever did for you? What was the happiest time for the two of you? What qualities did you like best about her or him? Dislike? Did you tell this person these things? Can you now? What would you like to say?

With whom have you laughed the most? With whom have you cried? Describe an especially important relationship in your life. How did it influence you?

Holidays

What were your Christmas/Hanukkah traditions? New Year's Eve? Halloween? Thanksgiving? Easter? Passover? How did you celebrate?

Rough times

Before you begin this section, think about whether parts of your life still feel too raw and painful to talk about. You are your own best guide. Go on to another part of your life for the time being. No need to force anything. If you have already grieved an old loss and moved on, let it be.

Tell me about some of the rough times in your life and how you got through them … a scary time? A hurtful time? Broken relationships? Did you ever have any money stolen from you or your house robbed? Describe the feelings. Have you felt that people have taken advantage of you? What deaths have had the biggest effect on you? Have you been with someone when he or she died?

> *Those things that hurt, instruct.*
> —Benjamin Franklin

How did you cope?

Happy Times

What was the happiest period in your life? Why?

When did you feel the best about yourself? Why?

Did you have a favorite place? A secret place?

Memorable Stories

Think of some great places of beauty where you've been. What's the greatest adventure you've been on? What did you learn about yourself?

Name some favorite pastimes, movies, radio shows, sayings. As a child, who were your best friends? Did you have a gang?

What were your favorite pets? What were your favorite stories about them?

What home remedies do you recall? Do you still use them? What home remedies did you create? What were your favorite foods then? What recipes did you inherit? What recipes are you passing on? Did you have any special victories? Triumphs?

> *When you find what is good for you*
> *and hold fast to it, you become whole.*
> *—Author Unknown*

Remember there are more questions in Appendix C. This may inspire you to make a scrapbook or a DVD (Appendix B). If this whets your appetite for further exploration of your family history, the last part of Appendix B will help you launch yourself into a more extensive search of your genealogy. There are a staggering number of websites and resources to help you with your genealogy, along with information on gathering family memorabilia, photos, letters, and documentation.

PART TWO: WHO AM I RIGHT NOW?

Your stories and experiences of the past are part of who you are today. Integrating them with the present helps you crystallize your understanding of who you are today. This second section gives you the opportunity to describe yourself as you see yourself now. You know yourself better than anyone else possibly can.

Describe Yourself:

Circle five adjectives that best describe you:

happy   content   bored   tired   enthusiastic   achy   apathetic   rigid   old   patriotic sensitive   lucky   opinionated   indecisive   resourceful   caring   introverted   extroverted sentimental   stubborn   easy-going   sick   healthy   loving   creative   fulfilled   sad boring   religious   wise   learning   active   humbled   interesting   cheerful   complaining lonely   grouchy   busy   sexy   cynical   nasty   depressed   productive   poor   well-off satisfied   searching   funny   growing   regretful   interested   free   patient   impatient jealous   angry   curious   appreciative

Talk about the five adjectives you chose in more detail.

Are your choices mostly positive or negative?
What adjectives would others choose to describe you?

What term best describes what you consider your essence to be?
How many people know the "real" you?

What do you like most about yourself?

What don't you like about yourself? What ideas do you have about changing this?

How do you celebrate? Express joy? Happiness?

How does your family deal with hard times, negative feelings? Do they…

    Try to act as if nothing is happening?

    Discuss issues calmly and openly?

    Cry, emote, talk about situations?

    Divert with humor?

    Yell and swear at each other?

    Sulk or stalk out?

    Erupt into violence?

What does intimacy mean to you? How important is intimacy in your life?

How comfortable are you about expressing negative feelings?

Intimate, positive feelings? Say more.

How do you rate your ability to listen (circle one)?   **Excellent   Okay   Poor**

Are you experiencing resistance or tension in your life right now? What is it about? What would you have to do to let go of it (see Chapter Seven, Part 5, "Letting Go, Forgiveness")?

What makes you happy/satisfied now?

What part of your life stresses you the most? Job, finances, health, relationships, school, the world (or community), something else, or just everything? Say more about this.

How does your body respond to feelings of anxiety?

Religion/Spirituality

Tell me about your religion/spirituality and its role in your life? How do you practice/celebrate it?

Do you believe in God? What is your image of God? Do you believe in a Higher Power? Has this changed for you over the years? Do your beliefs help you deal with any fears you might have? How important is it to you that others think the way you do? If you have children, do they share your faith? Who/what influences you the most in your spiritual journey? What about your religion/spirituality helps you the most?

Interests

What subjects do you feel passionately about? (Possibilities may include greed, dishonesty, gun control, immigration, inaccessibility of health care, homelessness, abortion, premarital sex, extramarital sex, global warming, euthanasia, unfair taxes, pornography, suicide, test tube babies, nuclear waste, exploitation of the environment, violence on the streets, and tense racial/ethnic relations.) What are your hot buttons?

What messages did you get from your family about the importance of any of the following? Appearance? Family? Money? Marriage? Patriotism? Church or synagogue? College? Grades in school? Career? Cleanliness? Diet? Environment? Discuss how you have changed over time.

Are your political views similar or dissimilar to those of your parents? What or who has influenced your politics?

RELATIONSHIPS

Family

Please expand your definition of family to fit for you. It does not have to be family by marriage or blood relationship. The American Home Economics Association defines family as two or more persons who have commitments to one another over a period of time and share resources, responsibility for decisions, and values and goals.

If you have children, tell me about them.

Names _____   Birthdays _____

Where do they live now?

If you are divorced or widowed, how old were your children when that happened?

When did each child leave home?

Did you enjoy parenting most of the time, some of the time, or not too much?

Did you find parenting more enjoyable when the kids were very young, during their teen years, when they were young adults, when they became adults, or all of the time?

Who of your children is most like you now?

Who best understands the way you think and feel?
Was there much sibling rivalry among your children? If so, do you know why?

What were some of your toughest times as a parent? How did you handle them? What did you learn?

When you have contact with your children now, who does the initiating (you, your child, both)? In what ways are you proud of your children?

What do you like the most about your relationships with your children? Grandchildren? Great-grandchildren? What are the disappointments? How could you make it better?

In what way do you think that you model "getting old" for younger people that might influence them most positively or negatively?

How much inclusion in your children's lives do you want?

❏ a great deal   ❏ some   ❏ not much

Do you want to know about your children/grandchildren's:

	Yes	No
Marital happiness?	❏	❏
Relationships?	❏	❏
Problems with their children?	❏	❏
Successes?	❏	❏
Jobs, financial problems?	❏	❏
Jobs, successes?	❏	❏
Adventures, trips?	❏	❏
Other?	❏	❏

Would you say that your family of origin was:
   ❏ sincerely affectionate toward one another
   ❏ moderately affectionate
   ❏ not good at displaying affection but you felt loved
   ❏ not good at displaying affection because it wasn't there

Would you say that your present family is:
   ❏ sincerely affectionate toward one another
   ❏ moderately affectionate
   ❏ not good at displaying affection but you feel loved
   ❏ not good at displaying affection

Would you like to change this?

Do you talk with your family about your:

Feelings	Often Enough	Not Enough
Differences of opinion	❏	❏
Fears	❏	❏
Projects, interests	❏	❏
Opinions about current events	❏	❏
Opinions about pending decisions	❏	❏
Finances	❏	❏
Health	❏	❏
Future plans	❏	❏
Feelings for them	❏	❏

Are there things you regret doing or have avoided discussing that you feel that you can discuss now?
It is important to acknowledge these … perhaps apologize, and forgive yourself or those involved.

Acknowledge what you have learned and would perhaps do differently, and then let it go. (Information on how to do this is detailed in Chapter Seven, Part 5)

Friends

Who has been your friend(s) the longest? What have you been through together?

Do you have different friends for different needs? Hunting? Fishing? Shopping? Eating? Having fun? Philosophizing? Who are they?

Who do you go to if you want to be listened to and understood? Do you prefer to be alone or with others? Say more. Is it easy for you to get close to another? Is it easy for you to show affection with friends? Has this changed over time? What would you like more of from a friend?

Retirement

People retire for many reasons. Some get sick and have to retire. Some are forced out of a job unexpectedly. Some know it is coming and plan for it, and some don't plan at all. Some retire from one career and start another. People's reaction to their retirement varies. Some love their new freedom. Others find that their self-esteem and identity were totally tied to their job and are in a quandary. They miss their workmates, the status, the structure. What do you miss? What's good and bad about retirement? If you are retired, were you reluctant or eager? What are the major adjustments? What are you excited about doing?

Relationships change after retirement. It is important to communicate about this, about role expectations, time management, etc. If you are married, or live with someone, do the following exercise separately and then compare your expectations.

Expectation	*My View*	*Partners View*	*Both of us*
Prepare and have meals together			
breakfast			
lunch			
dinner			
Handle the money matters			
Be the cook			
Be the clean up person			
Be the social director			
Keep the house, condo, apartment in good shape			
inside			
outside			
Want to travel as much as possible			
Plan vacations, holidays			
Communicate with family			
Spend more time together			
Maintain independence from each other			
Exercise together			
Have personal space within home			
Pray, meditate, share thoughtful time together			

What retirement interests will you pursue with your partner?

What retirement interests will you pursue alone? What do you suspect might be your problem areas?

Retirement calls for negotiation of expectations. Talk. What would be fun to do together? What would you appreciate help doing?

A favorite support group that I once facilitated was for women who were adjusting to their husband's retirement. It was truly entertaining and proved helpful to the participants. Many felt their space had been invaded. Private time became an issue. The husband suddenly wanted to know where she was going, who she was going with, who she was talking to on the phone, etc. Approaches for alleviating the situations were discussed, and the next week the outcomes were reported upon … sometimes with positive results, sometimes not. The commonality of concerns and support of the group made an often serious situation lighten up considerably.

A Typical Day

Describe a typical day in your life right now.

How much time do you have alone?

❏ Too much   ❏ Not enough   ❏ Just about right

Who do you talk to regularly?
What do you want to do more of? Less of ?

What's your favorite part of the day? Why?

Has this changed over the years? Say more.

Home/Community

What does "home" signify to you?

What do you like best about where you live now? Are you active in your community? How?

What are some material things you own that are important to you? Tell me about them.

Leisure Time

What are some of the ways you use your leisure time?

What are your favorite television shows?
     radio programs?
     Internet preoccupations?
What music do you like? Be specific

What have been some of your favorite movies?

How do you exercise?

What sports do you like to watch?

Are you satisfied with how you spend your time? If not, what would you like to change?

What do you enjoy most? Why? How has this changed over the years? What did you used to like to do? Are you competitive?

Oppression

Oppression is about being confined, restricted, or discriminated against by individuals or societal structures solely because you belong to a particular group or category of people. In the United States, this happens to some degree to all, although less so for young, educated, able-bodied, white, Christian, heterosexual males. If you are part of an oppressed group because of age, race, gender, disability, religion, or sexual orientation, consider these questions. What particular experiences of personal exclusion or prejudice come to mind? If you experienced oppression as a child, how did this affect you? If you have retired, do you ever feel like people treat you as if you're less important? How does that make you feel? Have you ever been sexually harassed? What were some of your most hurtful experiences? How were you supported? What are your feelings about any oppression you have experienced? What have you learned?

Fantasy Questions

Pretend you are talking to your fairy godmother. If you could have anything you want, what would you ask for?

If you could be more like any one person, who would it be? Why?

If you had a month or six weeks to live and an unlimited budget, what would you do?

What one personal possession would you like to keep, if you had to choose?

Humor

Who is the funniest person you know? Say something about him or her.

Who do you know who has the best laugh?
Name three things you had fun doing as a child.

When was the last time you had a good laugh? What was it about?

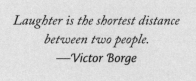

Laughter is the shortest distance
between two people.
—Victor Borge

Is your sense of humor, your spirit, more activated around certain people? Who?

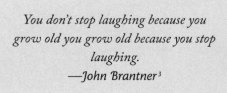

You don't stop laughing because you
grow old you grow old because you stop
laughing.
—John Brantner [3]

CONCLUSION

Who is this person called me? This chapter has given
you a framework for reviewing your life and figuring
out the answer to this question. It also grants you permission to indulge yourself in some valuable introspec-

"Wow! I have really lived!"

tion that will help you discover what relationships and experiences have shaped you and what you truly
value. Perhaps you were able to recapture some pure pleasures of childhood. Notice the many roles you
have had, all the things you have done, the losses you have survived. You are made up of all these things.
Your story is unique, yet filled with threads of universal truth.

Now you can move on to think about creating your best possible future. Taking this time to get
reacquainted with yourself is a magnificent gift that only you could have given yourself. If you have
shared your story and insights with another, the process of discovery can be doubly rewarding. Your written and shared experiences then become an important legacy, a way to be remembered. Perhaps this time
spent looking at your past and within yourself will help you to affirm your life, to see how the parts fit
into the whole, and to bring clarity to what is most life-giving and important to you.

Reviewing your life story is a pathway to accepting yourself. You may have always wanted to be a
little more like someone else you admire, more self-assured, more articulate, more athletic, more creative.
But something happens as you age. Those ways of being become irrelevant; you are able to look at your
own fairly amazing life and think, "This is who I am. What a fascinating life I've had." Soak up your
beautiful and thought-provoking stories, revel in your good memories, and appreciate your ability to learn
from the difficult times and the hard decisions that you have made. You often evolve to an age when you
can accept who you were, accept who you are now, and have a good notion of how you want to be during
your remaining time.

Congratulations. You are a survivor. You can marvel at life's complexities and mysteries. Your many
years of living give you a fresh perspective unavailable to you when you were younger.

Celebrate Your Journey

Chapter 2

What's Different About Living a Long Life?

This chapter briefly describes what "old" means. Then it discusses the barriers to aging gracefully in our society. Natural things happen that make this a challenging time, and our culture imprints us with negative notions and expectations about late life that add to this challenge. A section called "Things change; We change" reflects on how different our society is today than it was when we were younger. Most of this chapter looks at the ways mid-life is different from later-life: how our values may change, how we may become more spiritual, how the things that are important to us are likely to change over time.

WHAT IS "OLD"?

The older we get, the harder it is to generalize about what we, as an age group, are like, about what we are doing or thinking. We are most alike when we are born. As we accumulate experience, we grow less and less alike. There are books and books on what happens in utero, the first year, the terrible twos, the teen-age years. There are fewer books speculating on any verifiable path for young adults who are already less homogenous. By old age, it is even more difficult to make generalizations. Physical transformations occur at these times that are more dramatic than any seen since puberty. Big things are happening to our bodies—usually an accumulation of many years of wear and tear. Weird things happen that no one talks about, like the mysterious migration of body parts. In men, hair appears to fall off the top of the head into the nose and ears. In women, pubic hair disappears and reappears one-by-one on the chin and other places. Men's rear ends seem to migrate to their belly area. Women's breasts migrate toward their waists.

The older you get, the more experiences you have had and the more variables exist for the interpretation of those experiences. Old age can be anything—dependent on our genetics, on the beliefs dictated by our particular experiences, and on the powerful, often subtle and hidden messages given to us by our society.

One categorization of old people says:

Young healthy 60–75 year olds—the go-go group

The less-able 75–85 year olds—the slow-go group

The 85+ year olds—the no-go group

The go-go's have been given bonus time and can truly stretch middle age values and "doings" if they choose to and are healthy. They have unlimited choices. Choices become different as a body changes, but one can always find ways to create a life that is as good as it can be, whatever the situation. The slowing down that takes place with increasing diminishments is not all bad. As long as you remain on the fast track, you are less inclined to take the time to delve into the reflection needed to be sure that you are spending your energy in ways that match your wants and values.

The notion that "old" is always twenty years older than whatever age you are now is as true as anything because "old" is subjective and in the eye of the beholder. The exceptions are of those over 85 or 90 who, physically, often have a harder time denying it. To a young person old age is a foreign country with an unknown language. This is a huge group. If you begin identifying the notion of "old" at the age of 65 going to 100+, you are dealing with is a 35+year age span. No one would put a newborn in the same category as a 35 year old. It is important to recognize the ridiculousness of making generalizations about this group.

Early in my career I had to learn and relearn about the dangers in dealing with such a large category. Once, I was visiting a 95-year-old woman who was living independently in her own home but was having difficulty managing. She complained that her sons, Frankie and Jimmy, just weren't helping her enough … with the shoveling and raking and errands. I was mulling this over when I left and ran into Frankie coming up the walkway. He was in his 70s and was using a cane!

On the other hand, there is no way to get around having to make some generalizations in order to offer thinking points. Read autobiographical books that describe aging from the inside like Malcolm Cowley's *View from Eighty*, Florida Scott-Maxwell's *The Measure of my Days*, or any of May Sarton's wonderful books *Journal of Solitude, Recovering: A Journal, As We Are Now, At 82, Encore: A Journal of the Eightieth Year*. May Sarton[1] says, "the joys of my life have nothing to do with age. They do not change … flowers, the morning and evening light, music, poetry, goldfinches darting about." She glories in being able to take more time with them.

The overriding theme of this book is as its title suggests: Journey well. Every one of us is unique. Every one of us has our own definition of what quality of life is and what gives our life meaning. Cicero said, "Life is a play with a poorly written last act." We have much to say about our last act. We have choices to make that will influence how well we maneuver that part of our journey.

Now, when you think of the term "old," what words come to mind? Are they mostly positive or negative?

A. BARRIERS TO HEALTHY AGING

1. Natural things happen that make aging a challenging time

Physical decline starts at the age of thirty at a rate, according to various journals, between 0.5 to 2% per year. You lose physical capacity gradually and this accumulates. Your eyes and ears aren't what they used to be, and you usually have less resilience and energy. Your rebound capacity slows down after illness or accidents. One person said, "you know you are old when everything sags, dries up or leaks."

Gravity takes a toll. One day when I was standing on my head in yoga class (but evidently not following directions), my teacher said, "Trish, can't you see what I am doing?" And I had to respond, "No, my cheeks are hanging over my eyes." Gypsy Rose Lee said, "I have exactly what I had twenty years ago. It's just lower." A friend said recently, "Everything has fallen down and is pressing on my bladder." Many of us can relate to that.

More time is spent looking for things. There's more walking into a room and wondering what you meant to do there. One friend said that she had cleaner clothes than ever because she kept going downstairs to do something that she couldn't remember so she put in a load of wash. Diseases take root and mysterious aches arrive. Physical transformations are sometimes dramatic and sometimes subtle. What changes have you noticed?

Things happen. Even though we are, as an age group, healthier than ever before, we do die of something, at some point. I talk about better and worse ways to go through that process in the last chapter called "Finishing Well." Late life is a period of accumulated losses. We deal more with health issues, our own and those around us. We lose loved ones to death or relocation, either way a loss. Sometimes we feel like we lose our identity when we retire; we often have to adjust our dreams and our lifestyle. We know to expect surprises by now, but they are, nevertheless, surprises.

If you love and care for people, you will not escape pain. If you don't love and care for people, you never really live.

There are better and worse ways to meet the challenges that naturally come with living a long life. Suggestions about how to deal with the hand you are dealt come in the next chapters … how to take care of yourself, to communicate well, to deal with your feelings, to grieve, to let go, to find meaning, and to live as fully as possible. You know yourself better than anyone. Pick from the suggestions and ideas that fit for you.

When thinking about your own old age, what are you most apprehensive about?

2. Society imprints us with negative expectations about late life

The structure of our culture does not expect much from the older population, although this notion is changing rapidly. Historically we have not been challenged to grow and become more. The expectation has been to decline, to fade and become less. If this is our expectation, our chances of doing precisely that, increase. Program your mind consciously toward health. Intend to be healthy. We can't know just how much decline is directly related to self-fulfilling negative expectations, but there are an increasing number of studies that should make us wonder.

Ellen Langer[2] experimented with relatively lucid but forgetful nursing home residents requesting that they remember staff names and activity schedules. She rewarded their correct answers with chips redeemable at the gift shop. She gave them a reason to remember and they did. They perked up remarkably. Your body knows what you think. That's why you blush when you even think about certain things. One friend, after watching a *South Pacific* video, noticed an internal uplift that lasted for days and she couldn't stop singing the tunes.

There are many variables besides your beliefs and attitude that figure into how you will age—your genes, your predisposition to some illnesses, and the mighty influence of how you take care of yourself. Sometimes it feels like there is no justice. We know people who escape disease with lousy health habits, while others with healthier lifestyles don't. The best bet remains that it is smarter to play the odds; if we have a lifestyle and attitude programmed for health, we usually have better life quality in general. Plus we have the satisfaction of having no regrets if something happens.

AGEISM

Ageism is alive and well in our society. It is aimed more at the old-old than the young-old. Ageism is the term used to describe a societal pattern of widely held devaluative attitudes, beliefs, and stereotypes based on chronological age. Any -ism is the need of one group to feel superior over another. Ageism is really the only –ism that is still on top of the table, not under it. The media and advertisers make it hard to feel good about how you look when the continual emphasis is on avoiding wrinkles, baldness, white hair, and so on. Older people, like any oppressed group, are asked to accept societal standards and assimilate. Just as nonwhites are pressured to "look" white, gay and lesbians are more accepted if they look straight; young women are asked to adopt male rules in the business world, and old people are driven to look young and adopt standards of middle age. Most of the stereotypes of older people are pejorative, one extreme being the infantlilizing "poor dears" while the other extreme is the "greedy geezer" view. I see this attitude changing, and it will change more rapidly as the baby boomers hit retirement.

Ageism is a pervasive attempt by the young and even the young-old to distance themselves from even thinking about this later, less-able stage of life. Ageism is fear based. Most people recoil at the notion of being like those old folks they see in wheelchairs in the halls of nursing homes. They can't even fantasize being like that some day. A major societal norm is to deny death and dying. Our need to control is behind this denial. We evidently want to believe that humans have no limits. We could start turning this denial around by incorporating the notion of the naturalness of death into our conversation, by moving toward normalizing the reality and inevitability of diminishments. These would be important initial steps to taking better care of those people in the nursing homes who could one day be us.

Is looking your age getting to be taboo? Multitudes of products and services are trying to forestall or reverse aging. Our society appears to let market interests define how we should look. The anti-aging industry reinforces the notion that old age is repugnant, that how you look in old age is to be avoided at all cost—and cost it does. We now have teeth whiteners, hair coloring, hair growing, moisturizers, face lifts, eye lifts, Botox injections to paralyze muscles below your frown lines, and Restylane injections to fill up sags and reduce wrinkles. Wrinkles are now a choice if you have enough time and money.

Because there are more choices in this anti-aging climate, people are weighing in and making choices that fit their value systems. Many I talk to report a sort of consensus: moisturizers, hair coloring, and teeth whitening, yes; surgeries or laser solutions, no. But many, if they can afford it, go for whatever they hope will "help." Variables play into decisions. Some older working people are thinking that their job calls for a more youthful appearance. Most report wanting to "look as good as I can," and in this society that usually means looking younger. Looking young is different than wanting to be as healthy as you can be, which involves caring for your skin, eating healthy, and exercising. Nicholas Perrione[3] asserted in his book, *The Wrinkle Cure,* in a variety of descriptive ways that "wrinkled, sagging skin" is a disease and you can fight it. We are familiar with the ads: "regain your youth!" "Crows feet? Wrinkles?

For only $19.95 you can rid yourself of this ugliness!" … followed by a testimonial from people who have had their lives turn around due to miraculous product.

What are your thoughts on trying to look younger?

You rarely find anyone singing the praises of older bodies. On occasion, people write of the stories reflected by their bodies … the journeys they have taken with them through large and small, in-shape and out-of-shape times, the stories behind every scar. Karl Marx, writing about his wife, said, "There are many females in the world, and some among them are beautiful. But where could I find again a face whose every feature, even every wrinkle, is a reminder of the greatest and sweetest memories of my life?"

Nora Efron[4], in her book *I Feel Bad about my Neck,* writes with humor, "Oh, the necks. There are chicken necks. There are turkey gobbler necks. There are elephant necks. There are necks with wattles and necks with creases that are on the verge of becoming wattles. There are scrawny necks, loose necks, crepey necks, banded necks, wrinkled necks, stringy necks, saggy necks, flabby necks, mottled necks. There are necks that are in amazing combinations of all of the above. According to my dermatologist, the neck starts to go at forty-three, and that's that. You can put makeup on your face and concealer under your eyes and dye on your hair, you can shoot collagen and Botox and Restylane into your wrinkles and creases, but short of surgery, there's not a damn thing you can do about a neck. The neck is a dead give-away. Our faces are lies and our necks are the truth. You have to cut open a redwood tree to see how old it is, but you wouldn't have to if it had a neck."

> *Thought for the day: There is more money being spent on breast implants and Viagra today than on Alzheimer's research. This means that by 2040, there should be a large elderly population with perky boobs and huge erections and absolutely no recollection of what to do with them. (Source: Internet)*

Ageism is often harder on men than on women because women, unfortunately, have had to deal with discrimination due to gender during their lifetimes. Retired men have never had the experience of being mysteriously less respected by younger people for no apparent reason. My friend Lloyd was enraged when he and his son went to buy a car, and the salesman focused conversation only on the son, assuming, even when told otherwise, that the younger male was the "with-it" customer.

Ageism comes in many forms. We have *infantilizing and patronizing*, especially with the old-old, when well-meaning helpers do things for them that they could do for themselves. We have *tokenism* with Picasso and Grandma Moses being exceptions to what the rest of us are like. We mostly *assimilate*, that is we try to look and act younger than we are. How many aging women have had a hairdresser say something like mine did … "I can see some white popping out in your hair here, honey. I think it's time to start the camouflaging!" or a few years later, my doctor suggesting that I would look ten years younger if I had my eyelids "fixed!" We lose what I call our "right to folly" when people start making judgments about things that seem crazy to them even though we have been doing things like that our whole life. A man I know bought a convertible, and made some investments that his sons

> *Don't turn us into wrinkled babies.*
> *—Maggie Kuhn*

deemed poor judgment … when it was perfectly consistent with a multitude of other decisions he had made during his life.

DOCTORS DEFEAT "OLD AGE"! That was an actual headline. Think about it. Ageism is manifested throughout our society's skewed value system. Working for money remains highly valued while volunteerism is undervalued. Volunteering means giving from the heart and receiving inner rewards, whereas working for pay has practical motives of survival, achieving power, and overt rewards. I think that we are seeing a slight change in attitude; inner rewards and meaningful "doing" are beginning to trump working for money … even though many of us would agree with Joe Lewis.

> *I don't like money actually, but it quiets my nerves.*
> —Joe Lewis

If there is, indeed, a shift toward valuing volunteerism, older people would feel more prideful and less like they are headed for obsolescence when they retire. If we, as a society, shift to the bigger picture of thinking more cyclically, of taking turns, of interdependence, of needing enough but not more than necessary, of appreciating pure giving for the sake of the deeper rewards we will see the idea of getting old as an exciting time of possibilities and growth.

The chronological age of the discriminated-against group has risen in the last few years. The sixty and even some seventy year olds can pass at looking and acting youngish enough, and are often able to keep pace with younger people, thereby not feeling the impact of ageism as much as those over eighty, who can't help looking old because they are old, and usually can't help being slow because their bodies are telling them so. In fact, it is often the young-old who appear to have the most internalized ageism … not wanting to be grouped with "those old folks." They like to perpetuate the illusion of unlimited longevity and can as long as their health and energy holds out. They probably have more lessons coming. Although we do have much to say about our health, many "who do everything right" have severe health issues. We continue to realize that we have less control than we think. Those who choose to maintain the values of middle age never experience the wonderful gentle values and ways of being talked about in Chapter Five.

I know I am ageist. I have to work on appreciating the face in the mirror. I find myself routinely startled at photographs of myself. I do appreciate the evidence of rich experience in other people's faces; I see beautiful faces full of stories. But I have a harder time with my own. Our society's image of beauty is the image of youth. We are groomed to want to look young. It is deeply ingrained.

It's hard to keep pace with your face as you age. When you look in the mirror what do you see? What do you think and feel?

Who is this face that keeps looking at me?

Your body, how it looks and what it can do, and your inner view of yourself seems to be constantly out of whack. I, for one, am not only a bit surprised at the face in my mirror, but have to remind myself over and over again what my body can now realistically do. I have a persistent memory of a body that can still hop into canoes and sailboats and play racquetball. Not true. My body has a rude way of reminding me that I don't hop, nor do I bounce up steps any more. Betty Friedan said, "I am perpetually surprised when I pull on a sweater to see my mother's arm coming through the sleeve."

What experiences of incongruence or ageism like this have you had?

We get scared. Our memory often does become sluggish, and this becomes a worry. Is this in the normal range? We like to think that our brain is like a computer, so stuffed with knowledge that it just takes a little longer for accurate retrieval. But normal benign senescence, as it is called, is a wee bit frightening and annoying to most of us.

The good thing about our growing fears and lowered expectations is that they are a set-up for making this period of life a pleasant surprise for many. I can't count the number of older people who appear flabbergasted by how delightful they find this time of life to be.

What are your expectations for your old age?

What have been some of the pleasant surprises?

B. FEEL GOOD ABOUT THE AGE YOU ARE

May Sarton[5] thinks about her body this way in *On Coming into Eighty: New Poems*

"FRIEND OR ENEMY"

*I can look at my body as a old friend who needs my help,
or an enemy who frustrates me in every way with its fragility
and inability to cope. Old friend, I shall try to be of
comfort to you to the end.*

*I don't feel old. I feel like a young man
who has something wrong with me.
—Dick Cavette*

Be proud of the age you are. Gloria Steinem, in response to the meant-to-be flattering statement many of us have received, "You certainly don't look like you're forty," said "This must be what forty looks like." This response is good for any age. Some people retain amazingly youthful looks into old age. It doesn't mean they are better people. It simply means they are examples of the great variety of ways people can age. Maggie Kuhn, the founder of the Gray Panthers, when introduced by President Gerald Ford as a "young lady," responded, "Mr. President, I am not a young lady. I've lived a long time. I'm proud to be an old lady." A conference I attended long ago with Maggie as the guest speaker had us add our age to our nametag when we were signing in. It was interesting how undone many of the signees became at this invasion of privacy.

So when someone says, "I can't believe you are a grandma … or a great-grandma" or "you don't look that old," simply respond "This is what it must look like." You will be doing your part in changing the embedded stereotypes people have. Malcom Cowley[6], in *The View from 80*, says "We start growing old in other people's eyes, then slowly we come to accept their judgment." As a result, old people begin to believe that "you can't teach an old dog a new trick," and that it is too late to change so why try. Over-caring people who assume that older people need to be protected often infantilize them. Over-protection soon makes them feel incapable and pretty dead while still living. One of your tasks is to learn how to moderate over-caring people effectively and graciously so that you can remain in charge. And then, when you are in need, to let them know in a gentle but assertive way what you can and cannot do and when you do need some help.

It's true that aging isn't for sissies. Humor helps. Phyllis Diller is quoted as saying, "There must be more to life than just eating and getting bigger" and "I'm at an age where my back goes out more than I do." You can see these remarks as funny (which I choose to do) or disturbing, because they reinforce the negative stereotypes of aging. The message of a birthday card can be insulting to one person and hilarious to another. The secret to giving cards is knowing the person and matching the card with him or her. It's part of the balancing act, which I will talk more about in a later chapter.

If you have thoroughly bought the "looking younger is better" and have the money, I say "go for it." Face lifts, tummy tucks, and Viagra uplifts do make some people feel better about themselves. In her eighties, my husband's aunt was in a fairly deep depression after her husband died and seemingly snapped out of it when she had a face-lift, finally feeling some control over something. On the other hand, even Nora Efron[7] acknowledges, "What I know is that I spend a huge amount of time with my finger in the dike fending off aging."

I've noticed a certain phenomena occurring. At some point people stop denying their age and start bragging about it. Maybe they are proud of how well they are doing considering what they figured they'd be like at that age. Maybe they want people to know why they look the way they do. Everyone's body ages in its own way. In addition to how it was programmed, it has to deal with the multitude of abuses it has undoubtedly been dealt—maybe smoking, drinking, binging or dieting, wearing ridiculous pointy heels, playing football, or other potentially destructive behaviors.

The stereotypes are changing. We are part of the generation of pattern breakers. We are modeling the many ways sixty, seventy, eighty, and ninety plus year olds can look and act. When I was sixty, I still liked to do adventurous white-water canoe trips. I learned not to feel complimented if people let me know that I was different from other sixty year olds. Of course I'm different. We are all different, and that is what is important to see. This is the way *one* sixty year old is. If you want to be an exception and not join forces with other people in your age group, how will our age group reflect the spirit of people like you? My message is *don't even try to stereotype this huge age group.* To accept the compliment, I would be feeding the tokenism. I am not an exception. We are simply all different. Acknowledge, Gloria Steinem style, that this is the way one woman acts at this age and, in the big picture, she is one of many women.

The young exhibit some dread of growing older. But their viewpoint is changing as they observe more older people as lovers of life, freed of the mid-life struggle-for-survival chains and, at last, able to grow into their best selves. They are seeing that aging can mean something substantial. A quiet sort of modeling is going on. We learn by experience and by observing. It does no good to preach and shout about the joys of aging, nor is it anything but a waste of energy to spend time complaining about how you look. It takes the modeling of obvious enjoyment of life to quietly and unobtrusively reverse the myth of life after sixty as being a downhill course. There is something contagious and heartening about witnessing the resiliency and strength of persons going through times of loss, of witnessing delight at ordinary things like a walk down the street, the beauty of flowers, the bantering of small children. That modeling communicates a gladness about life that cannot be missed. If asked by a young person how you feel about being old, how would you respond?

Things change

As children, we created our own summer day,

drank water from a garden hose or kitchen faucet,

were thrown in back of a station wagon on a mattress

for trips to the cabin,

spent hours outside making forts in the snow,

were gone from home for hours playing,

greeted strangers with a happy "hello,"

rode in the back of a pickup or on running boards,

hung out with friends,

understood the words of songs,

didn't lock the doors to our homes,

ate whatever tasted good,

played pick-up ball games in neighborhood

biked and made up games,

didn't think about food values,

did whatever the doctor said.

As adults, if our joints went bad, we were out of luck,

if our eyes clouded up, they stayed that way,

if politicians were found doing shady things,

we were shocked,

if we had coffee spilled on us, had car accidents

If we lost kids for awhile in supermarket or park

✔ no organized activities

✔ no bottled water

✔ no car seats

✔ no TV, computer games

✔ no worries by parents

✔ no suspicion

✔ no sense

✔ no text-messaging

✔ no chance

✔ no fear

✔ no guilt

✔ no school-sponsored sports

✔ no long practices over mealtimes

✔ no nutritional information

✔ no questions asked

✔ no replacements

✔ no cataract surgery

✔ no longer shocked

✔ no thought of lawsuits

✔ no big panic by parents

Time brings change. Many of us had so much less fear, more wholesome fun, more trust, more responsibility, and more time for creativity. Time and experience changed us. Now we are less naïve, have more knowledge, and find that technology has both added and subtracted quality in our lives. We treasure the gains and mourn the losses. Make your own list. Have fun.

What has changed for you? For the better? And for the worse? What do you miss?

How have your beliefs changed?

Your notions about value-laden subjects change with the times, with your increase in knowledge and experience, with societal influence. Many people claim that they don't change. This simply isn't true. With new knowledge and experiences, you change, whether admitted or not. Think of how much more environmentally aware we are now. El Nino, global warming, recycling, nuclear waste management, water privatization. Car emission standards were not even in our vocabulary not so long ago. Think of what we are learning about diet, what's good for us and not good for us. Things change; we change. Only two things in this life are certain. We will die and things change. This acceptance of impermanence is very helpful when we look at our emotions. For instance, first depressions are often the worst, because we don't know that things will ever be better again. That's why teenage depression is so scary. As older people, we have experienced broken relationships and loss, and survived; new rough times don't carry quite the danger, because, no matter how terrible we feel, we have the deep-down knowledge that we can survive this.

How have your feelings about the following subjects changed over time?

	Then	Now
Appropriate age to marry	❏	❏
Appropriate age to have children	❏	❏
Premarital sex	❏	❏
Extramarital sex	❏	❏
Divorce	❏	❏
Working mothers	❏	❏
Asking for what you want	❏	❏
Respect for elders	❏	❏
Meaning of health	❏	❏
Meaning of old	❏	❏
Meaning of success	❏	❏
War/patriotism	❏	❏
Politics	❏	❏
Physician-assisted suicide	❏	❏
Trust of public officials	❏	❏
Fear for own safety	❏	❏
Diet	❏	❏
Risk-taking	❏	❏
Meaning of beauty	❏	❏
Funerals	❏	❏
Cremation	❏	❏
Homosexuality	❏	❏
Environmental awareness	❏	❏

The previous exercise points out the necessity of continuing to discuss with those close to you how you feel about issues and what is important to you. Notice how some values remain constant; others change over time. Accumulated experiences over time allow us to see that we are one teensy part of the cycle of life, of a bigger picture—that we are part of a planet, as well as part of a community, city, state, and country. For much of our mid-life, our focus is on ourselves or immediate world—our work, children, family, and friends. With the bigger picture that aging brings, we are able to see ourselves as part of the greater whole.

> *He that has seen both sides of fifty has lived to little purpose, if he has no other views of the world than he had when he was much younger.*
> —William Cowper

Differences between mid-life and later-life

The generally accepted message in our society says that mid-life is when we are at the peak of our power. It is the time when external accomplishments are valued, the time when we often have a family to provide for so we do what we have to do to succeed and survive. In this stage, the pressure is on. It is time to produce, to earn money to support our family, to be responsible, to compete, to achieve, and to provide opportunities for our children to thrive. Busy, busy, busy; do more; keep active. This prevalent way of thinking gets embedded in us and is not conducive to good feelings about ourselves as we get older and have less energy.

We also see mid-life people become frozen with stress, benumbed by the rush, the culture-imposed voice within them feeding their fears of not making it, worrying about the future, and we observe that they are unable to pause for very long to enjoy the present. Many of us grew weary of this pushing ourselves, the pressure, the schedules, the chauffeuring kids one place and another, yet felt we had no choice but to keep at it. Many of us dreamed of the time when we wouldn't have to run through life any more. Whoopee! This time often comes when we are older and retired. An increasing number of older people are appreciating leaving that more frantic pace behind and embracing different values, gentler tasks.

Many of us were groomed with negative stereotypes of old age and are accustomed to dancing to our parents' or society's script, which says that old age is a past-your-peak or over-the-hill time of life. One of the frightening things about these burned-in beliefs is, that there can be a premature psychic dying, a withdrawal from vital involvement in life. Jung[8] talked about people erroneously clinging to the tasks and values of the first half of life not realizing that the second half has a different set of tasks and values. He says, "We cannot live the afternoon of life according to the programme of life's morning." Our views and desires change.

In later life, we can, often have to, walk, slow down, and carefully decide what we want to do next. It is a time full of choices. We become choicefulists! Our life becomes our own. It is no longer shaped by our jobs or by other people. With a reduction in rushing, we free up our minds and feel more peaceful. We find that we much prefer the freedom of self-initiated study versus other-imposed assignments given to us. Many of us are reconsidering the so-called truths and myths we live by, recognizing that perhaps life doesn't have to include this breathless, stressful push to triumph over obstacles that so many of us bought for so long.

Younger people observe the speeded up, often crazy, lifestyle of mid-life and feel a little envious at the modeling they are witnessing by older adults who are inviting them back to simplicity, inviting them to rethink the need to accumulate material goods in favor of appreciating life's quieter rhythms and simpler pleasures (like reading a good book or talking with a friend). Later life gives us time to find the rhythm that best fits us. Some choose to keep pushing, cramming in

I used to go for the handsome guy....

Now I go for the guy who can drive at night.

one adventure after another, and others choose to slow down or are forced to slow down. Aging can be anything. It's time to treat ourselves to those things we want to do.

If you are retired, how would you evaluate your lifestyle now? Are you more or less active? Is it a comfortable pace for you?

Studies find that it is the young who most fear death. They know at some level that they are mortal, but death seems a long way off so they are able to ignore it. There is a foreboding about death that remains as we age, and it seems that only when faced by our own or another's dying does this foreboding ease up. We begin to truly accept that we are, indeed, mortal. When that acceptance happens, all sorts of good things can begin to occur. Our focus turns to living … living right now. It is freeing and more peaceful to live in the present. Once we are old, we lose the dread and fearful thoughts about old age and get into the realistic living of it. We start living the cliché: "Be grateful for the gift of another day."

As older adults, we know ourselves better. We've seen our patterns again and again. We know our self-doubts, our shadow sides, and are less likely to dwell on those facets. Either we don't have the energy, or we have decided to not be so hard on ourselves. We can no longer abuse our bodies without consequences like we did when we were younger. If we drink too much, partake in haphazard diets, deprive ourselves of sleep, it takes a toll. We aren't as resilient. Our standards change.

Problems need to be solved or lived with at any age. In mid-life, the typical problems are "making it" economically, getting ahead in a career, parenting, and relationship problems. In later life, we find ourselves adjusting to accumulated losses—from loss of friends and family to our own stamina and health.

In later life, we know what things matter to us … like reading the paper in the morning with a cup of coffee, taking a walk, tending to our garden, and having a good conversation, or learning something new and interesting. Even though our experiences are unique to each of us, common values like caring, seeking justice, appreciating beauty, the things we do that bring out our best, lift us up to be the people we want to be. The increased sense of mystery and wonder we feel points to an experienced truth that cannot be fully explained or proven.

We are more easily awe-struck as we age. A youngster may be full of innocent wonder at the beauty of a flower or how a worm wiggles, but this appreciation carries none of the sophisticated depth displayed by a person who has lived a long time and now chooses to be enchanted by these wonders. An old person returns to being charmed by the laughter of children, the beauty of a butterfly or a red-winged hawk, the flickering of the sun's rays, and the many miracles like conception and birth. We are restored to an innocence that disappeared or at least was submerged during mid-life. One of the glories of living a long life is this restoration of meaning to wonders of nature with the added perception of their enormous value.

Many of the changes we see as we age are part of a natural developmental process. It is important to discover our own uniqueness, to become independent persons, to be responsible in mid-life. The next vital stage of development is seeing how our independent, unique self fits under the larger umbrella of interdependence, the natural giving-and-receiving cycle of being human. Our society has so lopsidedly glorified the importance of the concept of independence and control that the natural diminishments that occur in the later stages of life often feel humiliating and difficult for persons to accept. What part of growing old most frightens you?

Old age is often a time of far less facade. We have learned that what is ultimately important is liking who we are and perhaps acting in a way that will leave our earth a little better. Earlier it might have been expedient to look confident; in older years it is okay to feel humble, without answers. In fact, being without answers is seen by many as a sign of wisdom. Opening to the grandness and mystery of life seems to be accelerated by life crisis, because it's during these times of trauma that what is truly important becomes clearer.

There seems to be a strong almost gravitational pull toward acquiring things and materialism during our mid-years, a feeling that whatever we have is not quite enough. As I write, however, more and more young people are looking twice at or defying this norm—choosing, or being forced by economic necessity, to live more simply, to respect and honor the earth's gifts instead of abusing them. The acquisitory norm present in mid-life seems to dissipate quite naturally when we get older. We had been seduced into thinking that we wanted to accumulate, that we needed more—more money, more stuff, more skills, more tasks. Guess what? They often brought more stress and dissatisfaction. Many of us not only get over the need to acquire more things but, in fact, often want to get rid of things now deemed unnecessary. "Stuff" isn't where it's at. What's valued is peace of mind, our health, the feeling that we can contribute in some way, the appreciation of having people to care about, and the ability to continue to learn and grow.

What stuff are you ready to get rid of? (Make a plan for it.)

> *I am dying but otherwise*
> *I'm in very good health.*
> *—Dame Edith Sitwell*

Choiceful solitude becomes more important. An evolving older person has a new understanding of fundamental existential questions—often a feeling of cosmic communion with the spirit of the universe, a redefinition of time and space, of the self and relationships to others. We become less self-occupied and more selective in our choice of activities. An increased feeling of affinity with past generations and a decreased interest in superficial social interaction often occurs. The mystery dimension in life is accepted, and the appreciation of the ordinary increases. There appears to be a movement away from ego-centeredness in favor of seeing ourselves as a link in the chain of life where the chain is what matters.

Is alone time important to you? How do you like to spend it?

> *It was just stuff. I still have my family*
> *—the refrain of several Katrina victims*

There are nine requisites for contented living:
health enough to make work a pleasure;
wealth enough to support your needs;
strength to battle with difficulties and overcome them;
grace enough to confess your sins and forsake them;
patience enough to toil until some good is accomplished;
charity enough to see some good in your neighbor;
love enough to move you to be useful and helpful to others;
faith enough to make real the things of God;
hope enough to remove all anxious fears concerning the future.
— *Johann Wolfgang von Goethe, German poet*

We discover that we don't need more; we just need enough—enough money, enough comfort, enough health, enough companionship, enough choices, enough love. We have to make decisions about wanting "more." How much more money should we spend on space exploration? No matter how far we go, there will always be farther to go. How long do we want to live? Scientists are spending lots of money experimenting with chromosomes of mice and fruit flies enabling them to live longer. But can scientists ever know about the quality of life of fruit flies? Are they asking the right questions? Perhaps our older population will lead us to asking the right questions, helping us see what's enough and what kind of long-range quality we truly want.

What are your questions?

Now that people have healthier lifestyles, and if they get very sick can reasonably expect to be made well or better, we are living longer. For the most part, the changes in medicine have been wonderful. Older people are healthier longer. Generally, a person who is eighty today is comparable physically to a person who was sixty-five years of age thirty years ago. Years of quality living have been added to our lives.

With these added years of living, families find themselves dealing with dynamics that did not formerly exist. Adult children are finding that they have to work on parental relationships and be honest about their feelings because they are no longer "saved" from this dynamic by their aging parents' early departure from their lives. The added time gives either older and their adult children a great deal more to avoid and deny certain subjects, or the opportunity to make some changes for the better, complete with all its pain, suffering, joy, wonder, and tenderness.

In mid-life, society often sets our agenda. In retirement, our time is no longer structured for us; we are responsible for our own schedule. This is much appreciated by some and troubling for others who discover a surprising lack of self-discipline. They may have grown comfortable with being programmed and now feel guilty when there's empty time in their day. They may choose to fill this time up or reframe their thinking and start appreciating this precious time. In our younger days, most of us got caught up in the competitive world; now that we are older, we are finding emancipation from it. The task here is to be able to distinguish between doing for the sake of just doing and "satisfying doing," the kind of doing that is indistinguishable from "being."

What is satisfying "doing" for you? How can you pattern more of this into your life?

It seems that after the younger years, the spiritual path for many evolves from the stage of "looking for answers and assuredness" to a stage where most folks have either found their "answer" and attempt to live accordingly or are better able to tolerate ambiguity. Two examples of famous men in history who evolved from an all-knowing scientific point of view to appreciating the wonder and mystery of life were Ludwig Wittgenstein and Alfred North Whitehead. Both changed their view of science from the rather rigid and self-assured positivism of their younger years to a more pragmatic attitude in mid-life and finally to a transcendent outlook in their old age. Earlier in their lives, they were convinced that with sufficient research, everything could be given a scientific explanation. Then they moved to thinking that maybe everything was not explainable. In later years, they accepted the idea that some things may have very unscientific explanations or no explanation at all. These two men came to appreciate life's mystery and complexity.

There is preciousness to living your life in your own rhythm, following your own instincts: eat when you are hungry, sleep when you are sleepy, get up when you feel rested, do a great many things that can't be described as anything in particular, set no goals, do nothing. During mid-life whatever is natural to our body rhythms may have been knocked out of us by our jobs and the urgency of getting things done. We ran, ran, ran, got up to a clock, went to work by the clock, worked maybe fifty weeks of the year, forty-to-sixty hours a week, with one to four weeks vacation. In retirement we can find our own rhythm again. It's there waiting to be rediscovered.

What rhythms suit you? What patterns help you feel centered? What "ruts" do you love?

SUMMARY CHART

VIEW FROM MIDDLE AGE	VIEW FROM LATER LIFE
Attitude of "more is better"	Enough is enough, or even less is better
External accomplishments valued	Inner work more important
Control/independence of major importance	Control/independence still important but balanced with the freeing ability to "let go"
Do what you "have to"	Do what you want to

VIEW FROM MIDDLE AGE	VIEW FROM LATER LIFE
Deadlines set by others	Choose how to spend your time
Focus on self and/or immediate world (work, family, friends)	See self as part of greater whole
Time demands of work and family don't allow time for other desired activities	Time to pursue desired activities
Façade necessary to present best self, to "fit in"	Time to be real, no need for an artificial persona
Physical body usually resilient	Physical diminishments occur, less bounce-back, more aches
Physical peak and productive peak	Spiritual peak
Acquiring things feels good	Giving things away feels good
Fear of loss of power and control	Fear of loss of power and control
Important to look confident, to "know"	Okay to feel humble, know a little less, wonder a little more
Society sets your agenda: need to produce, earn money, perform	You set your own agenda
Job and role provides identity	Time to create your own relevance
Rewarded by pay raise, recognition	Rewarded by feeling good about yourself
Time to be serious, responsible	Time to reclaim sense of awe, lightheartedness
Look for "answers," assuredness	Tolerate ambiguity, uncertainty, affirm importance of questions
Worried about future	Focus on present, live spontaneously
Feel immortal (even though you know you are not)	Feel mortal, notice encroaching diminishments
Feel stressed, fatigued	Time to nap
Health often taken for granted	Health often becomes a focus
Feel negative and fearful about old age	You are there, know that it can be anything

VIEW FROM MIDDLE AGE	VIEW FROM LATER LIFE
Problems are "making it," getting ahead	Problems are adjusting to losses such as the death of loved ones and your health problems
Parenting full time	Enjoy the good stuff about grandchildren, then send them home
No safety net for health care or financial emergency	Medicare and Social Security
Emphasis on "doing"	Choiceful "doing" and "being"

In order to find life meaningful, it is important to believe that our later years are as valuable as our earlier ones. It is a time of continued growth and can be a time of great deepening. The summary chart is full of generalizations. You obviously can have relationship problems and losses at any point of life. More young people are not allowing themselves to get caught up in the harried life and are balancing themselves well, living simply. And there is no clear dividing line between mid-life and early old age. Old age is not an entity unto itself; it is the next stage of development. There are positives and negatives at every age.

This discussion is not about finding fault with other stages. It is not wrong to value productivity when you are supporting a family any more than it is wrong to luxuriate in the liberation from the pressure of having to prove yourself. There are not two sides to this. It is necessary for a younger person to learn how to be independent, to be responsible and take care of herself or himself. You cannot learn the value of healthy interdependence unless you have learned to be independent at an earlier developmental stage. Persons who are older adults today were productivity-oriented and proponents of competition when younger. They still may be.

Which of these generalizations apply to you? Which don't fit? What is different in your view about mid-and later life? Which views seem better? Which views worry you?

The summary chart may suggest to mid-lifers what their future selves may be doing and thinking. In the final analysis, this is really about one person struggling with the different stages in his or her life and being in partnership with these different parts. It is important to affirm this later stage of life and encourage the accompanying ways of thinking and being that promote self-appreciation. A major hindrance to positive aging is continuing to equate only paid work with self-worth thus diminishing the value of worthy avocations such as reading, traveling, volunteering, and caregiving, or the small deeds like being kind to your next door neighbor. Life is likely to become meaningless and empty for those who can't expand their thinking about what constitutes basic self-worth. It is important to attribute new, positive meaning to getting older and to question and stop tolerating the deeply ingrained societal adoration of youth and negativity toward age. All stages of life have merit and problems. The stress of supporting yourself and/or family during middle age is as big a problem as is adjusting to losses of various sorts in later life. The values

You are different when you are older. Some things are better; some things are worse.

IS FASTER BETTER? by Stevie Ray's Productions[8]
(permission granted)

In the movie, Robinson Crusoe, Crusoe grew tired of just sitting around enjoying the island fruits, swimming in the ocean tide, and laying on the sunny beach. He captured a man he called "Friday" from a local tribe to "educate." He taught him the English language (of course he wouldn't learn Friday's) and strove to teach him how to be civilized. Friday had already helped build everything they needed for shelter, food, and water.

Not being civilized like the England-born Crusoe, he didn't know that life was still incomplete. Civilized nations know that life is not meant to be enjoyed, it is meant to be conquered.

Crusoe decided that they would have their own mini-Olympics. First he set up a race. he said, "We will both run to that tree. The better runner wins."

"Wins what?" asked Friday. "The race, of course," replied Crusoe.

"Why do we race?" "Because we want to know who the better runner is."

"Why?" "It's important to know who is best at things."

"Isn't it enough to know that we are both good?" "No. Now stop asking stupid questions and let's begin. We are going to see who the better runner is … Ready, Set, Go!"

The two men started running. Crusoe, with his arms and legs pumping madly, gulping for air as his face grimaced tightly. Friday ran almost as if he was dancing, his legs flying and arms swinging in the wind. A huge smile on his face. Crusoe got to the tree far ahead of Friday and hunched over gasping for breath as he waited for his opponent to arrive.

When Friday finally made it to the tree he said, "I win!" "Are you mad?" Crusoe cried, "I was here long before you. How can you think you won?" "You said the better runner would win the race. I saw how you ran. You ran as if a wild boar were chasing you. You strained every muscle and you did not enjoy one bit of your running. Now you stand there hardly able to breathe and in pain. I let my body be happy while running. I let my legs run beautifully like they were made to do, not jamming them into the ground like you. I let my arms swing out so they could enjoy the run as much as my legs, not punching the air like you. I breathed the air deep so my face could smile. You looked like you were going to faint at any moment. Clearly I am the better runner because I enjoyed it." "But I got to the tree first." cried Crusoe, "I am the faster runner. I win."

"Ah, you did not say the 'faster' runner would win, you said the 'better.' Besides, what good is getting to the tree first if you can't enjoy yourself when you get there?"

of middle age such as the importance of work, money, security, having a skill, and achievement set the standard for our society. Yet when reflecting on what has been important at the end of life, people are more likely to rank higher their relationships, loving and having been loved, and contributing.

Perhaps it will be older people and the many enlightened younger people who will lead us out of the fast-paced, me-centered, divisive atmosphere caused by the mid-life competitive values to a slowed down interdependent community valuing cooperation and caring, tending to our earth and each other. We are all in this together.

SPIRITUALITY AND AGING

Many of us become more spiritual as we age. The older we get, the easier it is to look at the grand picture, recognizing that we are a small part of something larger. The term "spirituality" is synonymous with religion for some, but I see spirituality as more of an umbrella concept that includes religion, yet is far more encompassing and inclusive. Religion is often the bridge to the spiritual, but as Dr. Rachel Naomi Remen, a doctor and favorite teacher of mine, said, "Sometimes religious people get stuck rigidly on the bridge instead of crossing over it." Psychological health often comes under the umbrella of spirituality. Psychology focuses more on self-examination, on an individual's pain, or fears, or behavior patterns, on areas of stuckness with the goal of helping the individual cope better. Psychology and spirituality come together when they look at the essence of a person, help in the quest for wholeness, and look at the unanswerable existential questions: Why am I here? Why did this happen to me? What does this mean? Spirituality goes beyond interest in the self; it is the deepest sense of belonging and participation. It is about how we are connected to each other, to the Earth, to God, to a Higher Power, or to a common consciousness.

In this day of the Internet, television coverage of world events, and for those fortunate enough to be able to travel, it becomes harder to have a narrow view. Boundaries that have divided cultures and races stretch and loosen. As I write, America has elected a black man to be president of the United States, a thought unimaginable up until now. We are being asked to think outside of ourselves. We see change. We feel change.

What are some of the changes you have witnessed in your lifetime?

As part of this shrinking earth, many of us feel more connected and see our responsibility toward preserving it. We wake up to the fact that more resources are being extracted from our earth than it can replenish. We learn about recycling, about stopping the use of products that are harmful in the long run, and we become more open to alternative ideas of energy production.

What specific habits have you changed?

Older people have seen more astonishing changes by virtue of their years. It is easier to see the "whole" when we are living closer to the whole of our life. There is a shift in awareness about what is important. Many of us move away from thinking things out there will make us happy and get back to looking within and appreciating the ordinary—the earth, air, water, sounds, tastes, smells, wonder of a good night's sleep, and thankfulness for the parts of our bodies that are functioning well. There is a movement away from focusing on what we have and what we do, to what we have to do to like ourselves.

Think about what you do or have done that generate(s) pleasure and gives the immeasurable inner peace of thinking, "I like myself for having done this!" or "Oh, I'm really glad that I did that." Think of specific instances.

Old age is a time of deepening. We understand more. Our physical body may start to cause some restrictions to our freedom helping us become more self-aware. We can see that we are participating in the cycle of life. We are forced to let go of the control we thought we had. Our capacity for love and compassion deepens. We can accept our own and other people's foibles more easily, and we appreciate eccentricities. We see the beauty of things at a new depth.

Our capacity for spirituality increases, and we may become wiser. Wisdom as we age is not an automatic. We have witnessed and experienced a lot, a prerequisite for wisdom, but wisdom requires learning from those experiences. Having more years, we also have more variables for interpreting these experiences. Remember, we are less alike when we are old than at any other time. We have been in relationships that have evolved and become more complex than we ever would have dreamed. We are better able to see their complexity and identify more patterns—good ones and not-so-good-ones. No one lives into old age without encountering setbacks, experiencing loss and disappointments. Facing and recovering from these traumas give

You can become more when your body is becoming less.

us the raw material for our greatest learning. Few get through life completely unscathed, and the grand majority learn from these experiences and grow. The seeds of wisdom, the learning that occurs as a result of life surprises, cannot be taught "virtually" to young people. It appears to be hard to push this process, to receive the in-depth learning any other way other than through real experience.

The theme remains constant. Old age can be anything depending on our genetics, our beliefs dictated by our particular experiences, as well as the powerful, often subtle and hidden messages given to us by our society. By making thoughtful choices, we have much to say about how rich this time of life can be. Some of the negative stereotypes attributed to older people are true. Many older people become more rigid, closed to new ideas, stuck in their ways. If the main theme here is "aging can be anything," that includes the cheerful, the grumpy, the complainers, the stoic, the flexible, and the inflexible. We are a combination of many characteristics whether we are in the realm of our narrow small self (often brought about by little things like whether our big toe hurts or not) or our higher, grander self. We have choices about how to be. By the time we are old, we have come to see the many facets of ourselves more clearly, warts and all.

Do you know people ten or twenty years older than you who seems to be aging admirably? Why do you think so?

The more evolved agers remain open, go with the flow, and let go of the hindrances that keep them from growing. But there are those who choose to remain totally self-involved the majority of the time. They choose to be interested only in "me" and claim to know what is not only good for them but often for the rest of us; these are the "stagnant agers." Often they have closed down out of resignation, fear, or anger, and they think that society "owes them." Their choices of action may be the same as evolved elders but they have different motivations. They may disengage from participation in social activities—not to pursue a quieter contemplative way of being—but because they are angry, have unresolved issues around all sorts of things, or are basically depressed and think that they have outlived their usefulness. Or they may remain active because they are desperately stretching the middle age "doing" years when they felt better about themselves.

Death is always standing close by reminding us to live each moment.

A more transcendent older person chooses to do things because she wants to, because she still finds it stimulating. We all have anger to some degree, but thriving older people can let go of it. In fact, spiritual growth can be measured by how quickly we let go of those negative feelings that suck our energy. The stagnant ones hold on … and on. The question to ask ourselves is, "what is motivating us to do what we do?" Some people exercise because they love it and it helps them feel good; others because they think they have to and hate every minute. Some continue working for pay because they find it stimulating and fulfilling, getting their identity and social anchorage from what they do, while others continue working because "by gum, I'll prove I can still do it." Some walk through beautiful woods and see nothing; others walk through the same woods and are in awe. A transcended individual travels to learn, to appreciate other cultures, to be an ambassador of good will; a stagnant individual travels with her/himself as the focus and becomes the "ugly American." Some choose to serve others because they identify with a person and see it as a chance to be of service to a fellow human being, whereas, others help people because they feel "better than them" or "feel sorry" for these poor souls.

What are some examples of this stagnant versus evolved behavior that you have witnessed?

There is no one template for aging well. We will all do it differently. Some persons want to complete tasks, retain control, avoid pain to the extreme, be in charge; others want the opposite, to drop unfinished tasks, to yield control, and to live with, and hopefully learn from, pain—to "let go and let God." Many of us lean to one way of being but still flex and flounder. We may have a notion about how we will be but never really know until we are faced with a new test. Being "old" isn't imaginable or interesting until you are there. As you know, there is a wide spectrum of variables between the stagnant type of older adult and the more growth-oriented type, and most of us bobble along somewhere on that spectrum.

CONCLUSION

There is a dread of growing older expressed by many of the young and young-old who find it hard to imagine a lifestyle different than the one they have. But as they observe older people as lovers of life, freed of the chains of the mid-life struggle-for-survival, and seemingly growing and enjoying this later time of life, their attitude will change. For many, growing older is a time of moving forward, a richer and deeper way of looking at life. The values that often come with this way of being are feminine values, more relational, more about caring and appreciating. We have learned through hard-earned experience that life doesn't always give us what we want, and this awareness helps us appreciate what we have. It is said that we have three peaks in our life: we peak physically, productively, and then spiritually

THREE PEAKS OF LIFE

Physical (age 30)	Productive capability (age 30–55)	Personhood (65+)
Birth		Death

Your personhood, your spirituality, your wholeness comes in later life because you have experienced so much and can now see with a wider lens. You see the bigger picture, the patterns and cycles that you couldn't have seen when younger. Some people peak spiritually at a much younger age because of their particular life experiences. There are many broad minded, balanced, wise ones who have endured some hard times and learned depth lessons earlier.

Older people are modeling different values. Our view of what later life might be like is changing. There is less dread of getting old and, with the boomers hitting this age group, this new view will become more prevalent. The boomers will demand respect, and their numbers will force the younger generations to reevaluate their expectations about this time of life. They will no longer think that the delightful, thoughtful, peaceful and happy-seeming old people they see are exceptions to the rule. There will be too many of them. It appears to do no good to preach and shout about the joys of aging. It takes the modeling of an obvious enjoyment of life exhibited by many elderly to reverse the myth that life after sixty-five is a downhill course. I'm not referring to just the young-old, but also to the old-old. There is something very contagious and heartening about witnessing the resiliency and strength of persons going through times of loss, about witnessing a gentleness and lightness and delight in ordinary things, a kind of gladness about life.

Many mid-lifers are already looking at themselves and recognizing that they have to slow down. They are looking at their hamster-wheel lifestyle, blood pressures, stress, the increasing amount of depression, and the relentless pressures of society. They are looking forward to the choices that come with retirement, the opportunities to do and be more of the kind of person they want to be. The behavior of a species changes when a critical mass is reached. "The Hundredth Monkey"[9] allegory applies to what I think is happening in our world, and it is our older people and many wise younger ones who are leading the way. Your energy and modeling feeds into everyone's energy. You could be the hundredth monkey. Your every little caring gesture feeds into the critical mass needed for change.

The emergence of an awake and aware, wise, and growth-filled older generation is modeling a rebirth of gentler values, of caring and appreciating, that can reestablish equilibrium and psychological health to our society. Instead of a downhill slide, we begin to see an upward arc.

Never doubt that a small group of thoughtful, committed citizens can change the world. Indeed, it is the only thing that ever has.
—Margaret Mead[10] *(permission granted)*

Chapter 3

How Do I Make My Life More Meaningful?

Chapter One of this book, "Who Is This Person Called Me," helped you to become reacquainted with yourself. By pulling together the many components of your own unique story, recognizing its complexities, you have the context for planning for your future. You are better able to see your individual experiences as part of a whole. Life is a process. It is always changing, and you continue learning as you move through it. In *The Will to Meaning*, Victor Frankl[1] says that life is full of meaning and that you can discover and learn great lessons by studying your life patterns. He says, "Remember what I have said about life's transitoriness. In the past nothing is irrevocably lost but everything is irrevocably stored. People only see the transitoriness but overlook the full granaries of the past in which they have been delivered and deposited, in which they have been saved, their harvest."

WHAT'S MEANINGFUL TO ME?

Meaning-Making Questions

If you were asked by a child to tell about the most important thing you have learned in your life, what would you say?

When you find what is good for you and hold fast to it, you become whole.
—*Author unknown*

What was the best period of your life? Why?

What was the worst time of your life? Why? Did you know it at the time? What did you learn?

What do you think was the best thing you ever did for someone else?

If you could have anything in the world, what would it be?

If you could give anything in the world to someone else, what would you give? To whom?

When you think of your parents or your grandparents, what do you wish you had asked them?

Are you holding any stories that your family would like to know? Think of some of them.

What projects have given you the most pleasure?

What can you do for a three-hour stint and enjoy so much that you don't even notice the time?

At what have you worked hardest (social causes, career, friendships, marriage, parenting)?

What are you proudest of?

Think of a person whom you greatly admire? A person of great integrity? Give an example of how you saw this person demonstrate this way of being.

Tell me about a world event, a happening that changed you. How?

Reflect on your answers and see if you find some common threads, some direction that would be interesting to pursue. Your next move toward self-renewal is to make time to do more of the things that make you feel full of life. You can find answers to many of life's perplexing decisions by asking this one question: What do I need to do that will help me like myself the most?

VALUES CLARIFICATION

What's meaningful to you is based on your values. This is an exercise that can clarify for you why you think the way you do now. Do this exercise on your own, or when you are in a group—which can often be more fun and informative. Look at your life through the eye of decades, asking yourself pertinent questions. The following is one example of many possible approaches to this exercise:

DECADE	ROLE	WORLD EVENTS	VALUES	PERSONAL HAPPENINGS	FRIENDS	WHERE DID YOU LIVE?
0–10						
10–20						
20–30						
30–40						
40–50						
60–70						
70–80						
80–90						
90–100						

What are some other questions that would interest you? Suggestions:

What were your turning points? (major losses? major moves? new jobs? illness? accident? financial setbacks?)

What new innovations were being discovered during this time period?

Was it a mostly good time or difficult time for you?

Who or what had the biggest influence in your life during this decade?

Our values are formed and imprinted at a very early age. What are some of your family-of-origin rules or sayings? Unwritten or even unsaid rules? Some of mine were:

Winners never quit; quitters never win.

Do as I say, not as I do.

> *An old gentleman answered the question "What's your goal in life now?" by quickly saying ... "I want to be the kind of old guy who was missing for me when I was a kid."*

Don't ever let me hear you complaining.

Anything worth doing is worth doing well.

If you are bored, be bored in another room.

Celebrate anything. This could mean getting a clean bill of health from the doctor, the house wren returning to her nest, or the first flowers peeping up in the spring.

No hugs or kisses unless leaving on an airplane. Make your own list of family adages:

Which of these messages do you still agree with? Which have you chosen to discard? You carry with you your mother's lineage and your father's lineage. Your children carry yours.

20 THINGS YOU WOULD LIKE TO DO.

What new things do you want to try? What tried and true things that you know give you pleasure can you do more of now? Dream!

1. _____
2. _____
3. _____
4. _____
5. _____
6. _____
7. _____
8. _____
9. _____
10. _____
11. _____
12. _____
13. _____
14. _____
15. _____
16. _____
17. _____
18. _____
19. _____
20. _____

Prioritize these. What comes first? Do you need more education? Planning? Information?

Think out of the box. Try new things. Set goals for yourself. My husband is a birder and spends endless wonderful time studying his bird books and making lists. In addition he explores forests and wetlands looking for new species. I decided that I wanted a project of my own and came up with the idea that it would be fun to swim in the natural waters of every state in my lifetime. This goal has led to explorations of a different sort and many adventures, and at this writing, I am proud to report that I only have Oklahoma and North Carolina to go.

Most people's souls are hungry for purpose, for meaning, for knowing that somehow they have made and are making a difference to someone or something. Vitality depends, in part, on the supply of meaning in your life. A sense of purpose does not mean you have to save the world or think in lofty terms about meaningfulness. Being kind and caring to one other person is purpose. Realize that it takes many people doing small things to make up a much greater force of caring. You don't have to think in terms of a capital P—Purpose … small little purposes do just fine.

You do have a reason for being here. People who have a goal or a project, or exude purposefulness, may more easily know they are living their lives fully. Those of us who continue to learn about subjects that interest us, tend our gardens, care for our cat or dog, help out our bodies by diligently caring for them, attend to someone who could use our help, or even give a kind glance to a person who just might be in need of it are exhibiting a reason for being here. What you do and who you are matters. You become a part of a force for good. All of our hearts working together make a giant heart.

PEAK MOMENTS

Life can be transformed, changed completely, in a moment—a moment that forces you to view things differently. What happened? Your peak moments are those precious times when you know that "life doesn't get any better than this,"—when you stand in awe of nature or a work of art, when you know that you've truly connected with another person, when you have achieved a personal victory, or when you have completed a job "well done." For some of you, peak moments may occur when you feel fully known, accepted, and loved by another—or when you give and receive love simultaneously. Such moments may have occurred when you witnessed your child being born, when you caught that enormous fish, when you got that hole in one, when you viewed a waterfall or a rainbow, or when you felt safe enough to have challenged someone and come out of the encounter feeling proud of yourself.

> *Nobody grows old by merely living a number of years; People grow old from lack of purpose. Years may wrinkle the skin. Lack of purpose wrinkles the soul.*
> —*author unknown*

Once upon a time, there was a wise man who used to go to the ocean to do his writing. He had a habit of walking on the beach before he began his work. One day, as he was walking along the shore, he looked down the beach and saw a human figure moving like a dancer. He smiled to himself at the thought of someone who would dance to the day, and so, he walked faster to catch up. As he got closer, he noticed that the figure was that of a young man, and that what he was doing was not dancing at all. The young man was reaching down to the shore, picking up small objects, and throwing them into the ocean.

He came closer still and called out, "Good morning! May I ask what it is that you are doing?" The young man paused, looked up, and replied, "Throwing starfish into the ocean."

*"I must ask, then, why are you throwing starfish into the ocean?"
asked the somewhat startled wise man.*

*To this, the young man replied, "The sun is up and the tide is going out.
If I don't throw them in, they'll die."*

Upon hearing this, the wise man commented, "But, young man, do you not realize that there are miles and miles of beach and there are starfish all along every mile? You can't possibly make a difference!"

At this, the young man bent down, picked up yet another starfish, and threw it into the ocean. As it met the water, he said, "It made a difference for that one."

—Reilly[2]

Perhaps the moment occurred during the simple exchange of a supportive glance, when water caressed your body as you swam, when you heard rain on the roof of a tent, when long ago you nursed your baby and it looked up at you and smiled, when you ran through a meadow with the wind in your hair, or when you snuggled close to the warmth of a person you love. They are the little moments of grace when you've felt awe, reverence, tenderness, or pride. They are those moments when you feel gripped by feelings of contentment, happiness, and a sense of being connected to all things. Sometimes these holy moments are times of deep mystery, times that offer no explanation that fit into your sense of reality. Your mind is forced to expand. These moments shift you from your isolated self to an expanded notion of "what is." After someone

Yah, I like being in the moment ... 'til it sucks; then I like to find some good moments in the past to think about. It helps my balance.

*Sweet glimpses of perfection ...
I am alive!*

close to you dies, certain memories become peak moments and are immortalized. Those meaning-filled moments suspend your sense of time. List some of your peak moments from the past. Maybe you would like to write more about this experience in prose or poetry. How did they affect you?

Some of these moments just happen. You up the chances of having more of these moments by putting yourself in situations where they more easily occur. "Follow your bliss" says Joseph Campbell in *The Power of Myth*. "Follow your bliss" speaks to taking action versus simply appreciating little bursts of grace that just happen. Following your bliss requires you to pursue actively those things that give you great pleasure. Once you recognize what it is that makes you feel vibrantly alive, you can use this awareness as a source of guidance in your life. Perhaps you need to seek out more time in nature. Maybe it is when you give love that does not require reciprocity, or become aware of a mysterious sense of knowing that you are much more than just yourself and are connected somehow to everyone, everything. Such moments may be sustained or fleeting, but they allow you to witness what bliss is for you, to understand yourself a little better. They can help you direct your journey. What more do you need to do to feel this aliveness?

These moments can't be taken from you. They are timeless events, points where measured time touches eternity.

NOTICE WHAT'S HAPPENING AROUND YOU

Try not to let any precious moment go unappreciated. Notice with your senses what you are seeing, hearing, touching, smelling, or tasting. Observe your thoughts. Name your feelings. This can be the most meaningful time that you can spend with yourself. One old friend said: "I was sitting in my favorite chair just kind of doing nothing, drinking my cup of coffee when a beam of light bounced off a crystal hanging in the window sending an array of rainbows and patterns all over the room. I had never seen anything so beautiful." Sitting and staring and noticing allow you to soak up the beauty all around you. You can learn to make even trivial-seeming acts luminous and vital: making tea, digging in the dirt, singing in the shower, sipping your coffee, watching the squirrels in the backyard, looking at the stars, taking a bath, feeling the warm sun on your back. Notice every detail.

Lie down with your belly to the ground,
like an old dog in the sun. Smell
the greenness of the cloverleaf, feel the damp
earth through your clothes, let an ant
wander the uncharted territory
of you skin. Lie down
with your belly to the ground. Melt into
the earth's contours like a harmless snake.
All else is mere bravado.
Let you mind resolve itself

> *The moment one gives close attention to any thing, even a blade of grass, it becomes a mysterious, awesome, indescribably magnificent world in itself.*
> —Henry Miller (with permission)

in a tangle of grass.
Lie down with your belly
to the ground, flat out, on ground level.
Prostrate yourself before the soil
you will someday enter:
Stop doing,
Stop judging, fearing, trying.
This is not dying, but the way to live
in the world of change and gravity.
Let go. Let your burdens drop.
Let your grief-charge bleed off
into the ground.
Lie down with your belly to the ground
and then rise up
with the earth still in you.
—Nancy Paddock[3] *(permission granted)*

Think differently when you are taking a walk. Be a part of everything you see. When something interests you, stop and absorb the beauty, think and feel your connection to the whole. As you walk in the woods, consider imagining what it would be like to be a pine tree, standing firm and tall. Feel the sun, the breezes. Feel the wind through your needles, the little bird visitors on your branches. Hear their sounds. Become the birds. Flitting from branch to branch, busying yourself with finding food, mindful of predators but enjoying life, singing your song. Or become an eagle, soaring high above. How must that feel? Watch sea gulls protecting their babies. Consider the age-old ground you are standing on, the history it has. Perhaps it was in the path of glaciers or witnessed beginnings of life and births and deaths and more births and deaths. Feel the harmony. As you walk, walk with beauty. See it. Feel it. Smell the earth, the pine needles, the natural decaying matter. Feel yourself in every movement. Hear each sound. Smell. Experience oneness with all life, the fluidity—dust to dust.

INDULGE YOUR SENSES

LISTEN to the call of the loons, other bird sounds. Play music that gives you pleasure whether it be opera arias, jazz, or hymns. Sit quietly and just listen to the sounds around you … that are always there if you just listen. List your favorite sounds:

FEEL the wind. Give hugs or warm handshakes. Make an appointment to have a body massage. List the ways you appreciate touch:

Every moment missed is a moment unlived.

SMELL the lilacs, newly cut grass, your favorite lotion, the wonderful smell of bacon wafting from the kitchen. Think of smells that conjure up certain memories or people: One scent can lift up a memory from childhood. What smells bring to mind certain things or people?

SEE the wonders of nature, the sunrises, sunsets, the woods, the creatures, water in its many forms, small children laughing and playing, beauty in the world. Read any of Mary Oliver's poetry books to help you get into the mood of appreciation. I have a bumper sticker that says, "What would Mary Oliver see?"

TASTE with mindfulness. Slowly, slowly concentrate on every bite. Recall memorable delicacies or great feasts you may have had in your lifetime. What tastes or smells automatically remind you of specific times in your past?

AT BLACKWATER POND

At Blackwater Pond the tossed waters have settled
after a night of rain.
I dip my cupped hands. I drink
a long time. It tastes
like stone, leaves, fire. It falls cold
into my body, waking the bones. I hear them
deep inside me, whispering
oh what is that beautiful thing
that just happened?
—Mary Oliver[4] (with permission)

Think what your day would be like if every time something wonderful happened, you responded in this way!

FIND PLACES THAT LIFT YOU UP

Plant yourself on a bench by a lake or in a park and people-watch. Go to a local farmer's market. Sit by the ocean and marvel. Visit a church with beautiful stained glass windows. Spend an afternoon at a children's museum.

What places hold positive energy for you? How often do you get to each one?

APPRECIATE THE ORDINARY

Why is it that when you are in the middle of life you don't or can't take time to appreciate the splendor of what's going on? When my children were little, I remember pausing long enough to ponder why my mother took such pure, unadulterated joy in playing with her grandchildren, chuckling and thoroughly appreciating all of their remarks. I was at least aware enough to acknowledge to myself that "she probably knows what life's all about." Then, I went on my hurried way. Choose to take the time and know that the simplest things are, indeed, the most profound.

When is the ordinary quite extraordinary? Looking at a flower? Making yourself a cup of coffee in the morning? Receiving a kind glance?

I remember Sunday evenings, as a child, listening with my family to favorite radio shows, playing gin rummy or cribbage, and eating popcorn. These moments were ordinary. I was not so enchanted with them at the time, but the memories have become sweet and extraordinary. When my mother, much later in life and in the middle stages of Alzheimer's, didn't know where she was, didn't know my name, didn't know or care what was going on in the world, she could still marvel at the "leaves wiggling on the trees," the squirrels dashing about, could ooh and ah at a baby placed in her arms. Was she still teaching me that basic lesson about the simplicity and profoundness of life?

Developmentally, we appear to move from the simple awe and curiosity of a child to not even having the time to appreciate the ordinary as a middle-aged "fast track" person. Thankfully, we seem to return to an appreciation of simplicity again. This late life appreciation is much more sophisticated and hopeful. We now choose to attribute meaning to the simple things with a deeper perception of their enormous value.

List those ordinary things that give you extraordinary pleasure. Once you name them, your appreciation will be enhanced every time you experience them.

> *Normal day, let me be aware of the treasure you are. Let me learn from you, love you, bless you before you depart. Let me not pass you by in quest of some perfect tomorrow. Let me hold you while I may, for it may not always be so.*
> —Mary Jean Iron[5]

This is a note I received from a dear friend around her ninetieth birthday:

Dear Trish,

Thank you for your note and family picture. I so treasure the update. You asked me how I am. Quite well I think. It strikes me as funny that I say I feel so well when to look at me you might wonder. I have gotten quite unsteady on my feet, my hearing is so bad that I have my TV blasting so that the kids laugh when they come to visit. My cancer is still with me but being decently managed and relatively peaceful at present. So being able to say "quite well" takes on an amazing slant. No one could have made me believe that I—the real me—who, even though it definitely includes my body, am obviously much more than just that, could have adjusted to life's maladies and truly feel quite serene and pleased with myself.

I was thinking last week how I used to wonder with alarm about how my mother occupied her time after my father died. Even though she didn't complain, I couldn't figure what she did all day and suffered for her boring, lonely seeming life. I encouraged her to move in with Elizabeth or Lucy, two of her many widowed friends who lived alone in their relatively big houses. She said to me then and I remember thinking that this was, perhaps, wisdom—"I want to live alone. I am not lonely. I know that you can't understand this because you are at a time of life when you need people around. I felt the same at your age. Now I prefer being alone, doing what I want to do when I want to do it."

> *The invariable mark of wisdom is to see the miraculous in the ordinary.*
> —Ralph Waldo Emerson

I'm now older than she was when she said that to me. I think of it often and I do understand it, dear mother. Life evolves in such an interesting way. Getting old isn't better or worse than being young; it is just different. I seem to be entertained by the very simple. I love watching the birds at the feeder and the squirrels scampering around. I love listening to my new music system. Mary gave me a fancy CD player that makes me feel like I'm sitting in an orchestra pit. I love my oatmeal and brown sugar in the morning. I enjoy the morning crossword puzzle and listening to public radio. I most of all treasure my family and friends and the memories of those no longer around. I simply don't seem to need much to entertain myself. Yet life seems quite wonderful and profound. Life sends us on quite a frantic path to ultimately teach us the simple pleasures, don't you think?

Much love, Sarah

Think more about the simple pleasures you've enjoyed in the past or are enjoying right now, pleasures that are special to you so that every time you do them you are aware of their significance. Not major events but simple pleasures … digging in the dirt, singing in the shower, reading the paper, doing your morning sudoku, feeding the birds, treating yourself to an ice cream cone. Name some of your simple pleasures?

How do you reinforce their importance?

The first step is doing what you just did—naming these extraordinary-ordinary pleasures. The next step is writing about them, talking out loud about them, concentrating on their importance to you. Plan your time so you can have more of these balancing pleasures. You can mold your consciousness.

HOW MIGHT I ADD MORE MEANING TO MY LIFE?

We yearn for a life that has mattered and continues to matter. We know by now that it is usually not money, acquisitions, or power that satiates this hunger. It is when life has meaning that we feel purposeful and happy. Happiness is a by-product, not a goal. We have compiled our own unique experiences and can now reflect on them and see what we have learned. Our busy middle years, as discussed in Chapter Two, often left little time for reflection. Many of us were so busy bringing the bread home or caring for children we never took the time or perhaps had the inclination to wonder about life, to reflect on what is important.

The only constant at any stage of life is change. We are on a journey and always in process. Mid-life crises occur among those who believe that the momentum of life is always in a forward and upward direction—more relationships, more security, more money, more happiness. Few of us were properly prepared for the many obstacles in the road; we had to learn the hard way that life is also about what happens on the journey—the surprises. The trick is to enjoy the journey, moment by moment, instead of always anticipating getting to what-

> *A long life makes me feel nearer truth, yet it won't go into words, so how can I convey it? I can't and I want to. I want to tell people approaching and perhaps fearing age that it is a time of discovery. If they say "Of what?" I can only answer, "We must each find out for ourselves, otherwise it won't be a discovery."*
> —*Florida Scott-Maxwell*[7]

ever "there" is. In a lecture, Joseph Campbell defined "mid-life crisis" as finally making it up the ladder of success only to discover the ladder is against the wrong building.

The section that follows will help you avoid "old age crisis" by asking you to pause and reflect on whether you are at the right building. What has been most important to you? Life is like a good book—the more you get into it, the more things start to fall into place. Perhaps you will be able to see not only the uniqueness of your journey but also how your journey connects you with other people. This section isn't about finding "ultimate meaning." You can, however, find little clarifying meanings that move you in that direction. The search itself provides meaning.

Time becomes more precious and an ever-greater gift. No one lives a perfect life. The fact is that having to survive imperfections and losses helps us discover the depth of our being. When we are living the lows, it is hard to embrace the notion that it is a learning experience. Still, most of the time, we do learn and change. Change is an exciting constant and forces our reality, our goals and dreams, to be altered.

CARING BEYOND YOURSELF

We know by now that having plenty of money doesn't guarantee happiness. People in the United States and Europe may be wealthier than were their parents, but studies show that they are not happier. Instead there is more depression and anxiety reported than ever. What's this about?

The fast-paced life wears well with some but causes unbelievable stress on others. Stress at any age takes a toll. Gentler values like being kind and caring beyond ourselves equates with basic healthy well-being. We know that doing good things for others makes us feel good. Now research is backing this up. I liked the direct response of one eighty-year-old lady contemplating what gives her life meaning. She said, "I try to take care of myself, keep myself alive, and tend to the little flock of people I care about." On further inquiry, I found she did just that. She exercised, took meals to a cousin, drove different friends to the doctor and to the store, checked up on some friends by phone … kept herself busy tending to her flock. She thanked me several times after the workshop, saying she always felt that the mere question "What gives your life meaning?" was a little intimidating. Now she appreciated figuring out a response that meant something to her. It is therapeutic to come up with an answer for yourself, for those other times when you wonder. Not one of us is going to change the world, but we can do our little bit every day to move beyond focusing on ourselves and become part of the gentle but forceful critical mass tipping the scale toward enduring good. Think baby-steps—little p, not giant P—purpose.

> *"They recognize that they now have more of their lives behind them than ahead of them. And such indisputable arithmetic can concentrate the mind. After decades of pursuing riches, wealth seems less alluring. For them, and for many others in this new era, meaning is the new money."*
> —*Daniel Pink*[6]

You probably know people who let their ailing bodies and illnesses dominate their every moment. Nothing else seems to exist for them. You can choose to not be that way. I visited with two delightful women, ages eighty and eighty-one, who were so wrapped up in world issues, so full of vigor and enthusiasm, that only in passing did their annoyance with their physical problems emerge. One had had cancer for seventeen years, had recently had a pump installed to directly inject chemicals into her liver, and seemed to pay little attention to the subject except to mutter, "What a bother it all is." The other, also in passing, laughed at how she has to strap her head into some sort of traction contraption every morning, worried that someone could burst into her apartment and think that she was attempting to hang herself.

Why is an illness for one person so preoccupying and for another merely a bother? Could it be that, even though these women methodically take care of their bodies as best they can, their major interests and curiosities lie outside themselves? Or is it because they just don't have the accompanying pain that preoccupies others? Perhaps the latter, but even persons who have considerable pain choose how they react to it. Well-being is greatly enhanced if you can move beyond self-absorption.

> *Believe, when you are most unhappy, that there is something for you to do in the world. So long as you can sweeten another's pain, life is not in vain.*
> —Helen Keller

> *A young man said to a very old man,*
> *"What is your greatest burden as you grow old?"*
> *The ancient one replied,*
> *"That I have nothing to carry."*
> —Asian Saying

A woman whose scoliosis was so severe that her spine was on her side under her armpit, seriously scrambling her organs and causing abnormal functioning, had made herself the jewel of the care-center where she lived. Unlike many of her buddies there, she worked well with computers and became the email queen by writing to the other residents' various grandchildren and great-grandchildren. She was an inspiring example of a person who was fully healed in the wholistic sense. Her body remained broken, but her mind and spirit were thriving.

Brown[8] studied 423 older couples for five years, asking them what kind of practical and emotional support they gave family and friends and what help they could count on receiving. During that time, 134 of the people died and it was determined that those who didn't provide any support to others were twice as likely to die as those who helped friends and family. This controlled study took into account the functional health of the giver, age, education level, income, and other variables. This study suggests that we would be better off flip-flopping our current emphasis on how older people need to be supported and figure out how to get them to be of service and support to others. One good example of this is a telephone "grapevine" that has homebound elders calling other homebound elders every morning to check on their well-being.

EXAMPLES OF WAYS SOME OLDER ADULTS HAVE CHOSEN TO MAKE THEIR LIVES MEANINGFUL

They:

- **CONTINUED LEARNING.** They took classes, attended Elderhostels, went to college or graduate school. Agnes got her Ph.D. in American history at age ninety-two from the Union Institute. She had collected and saved political buttons her whole life and used them for her thesis.

- **FOLLOWED THEIR CURIOSITIES.** They traveled, made pottery, quilts. They painted, worked with stained glass, created new recipes, embroidered, sang, danced, sewed, and did woodworking. Billy was caning chairs at the age of eighty-eight.

- **VOLUNTEERED** for their church, schools, clubs, hospices, hospitals. Phyllis, age eighty-nine, visits the "old folks" in the nursing home every Wednesday. John works the information booth at the airport. Peter and Larry work with immigrants from foreign countries who want to become U.S. citizens and need to learn to speak English better. Dave spends three hours each week recording books on tape for the blind. Some care for children or adults in need (visit and run errands for people who need help, make phone calls to people who are homebound and need to know someone is interested in them, deliver Meals on Wheels).

- **PASSED ON FAMILY HISTORY.** They investigated family history, wrote journals, created photo albums, shifted family films to DVDs. At age seventy-five, Bill traveled to Norway to do research his family tree.

- **TAUGHT OTHERS THEIR SKILLS.** Joe, eighty-three, a retired banker, helps people manage their money, volunteering at a bank and in a high school.

- **FOUND NEW HOBBIES.** They took up fishing, golfing, collecting antiques, bird watching, gardening, bridge, spider solitaire, crossword puzzles. Helen became an avid bowler in her seventies.

- **PICKED UP OLD HOBBIES AGAIN.** Chuck dusted off his old trombone and joined a local band and is having fun.

- **FOUND A NEW JOB, A NEW CAREER.** Bob, a retired dentist, worked as a salesman at a major discount store.

- **BECAME SILLY OR BIZARRE.** They cleaned their house in the nude, slept in their backyard under the stars, did secret acts of kindness, thought of clever ways to express their caring, set fun goals.

- **PRACTICED "COMMITTING RANDOM ACTS OF KINDNESS AND SENSELESS ACTS OF BEAUTY."** They created meaning by practicing this sort of guerrilla goodness.

- **WORKED FOR A CAUSE.** They did something about what they passionately believed in. Esther started lobbying the legislature on gun control at age seventy-eight.

- **WERE OF SERVICE.** They were only limited by their imagination. Some served as tutors or mentors at local schools, read to the sight impaired, greeted people in hospitals, joined the Peace Corps, worked with Jimmy and Rosalynn Carter's Habitat for Humanity. I spent three weeks in Xian, China, helping teenage students with their conversational English through Global Volunteers, which has a wide variety of programs going in many countries. It is easily one of the best things I have ever done for myself. The Experience Corps, operating in many states, through a program called Seniors for Schools, found that 88% of elementary school students markedly improved their reading skills in a year with tutors. And this kind of volunteering is always a two-way street with the older volunteers reporting much satisfaction and feeling more of a connection with the community.

Besides the obvious psychological and spiritual benefits of doing good, it is now well established that there is a physical pay-off to being a helper. Allan Luks and Peggy Payne in *The Healing Power of Doing Good* report that helping others gives the helper a "helper's high." A "helper's high" involves physical sensations that strongly indicate a sharp reduction in stress and a release of the body's natural painkillers, the endorphins. This initial rush is followed by a longer-lasting period of improved emotional well-being. What you have always known has now been proven clinically; when you focus on things outside yourself there is actual physical relief from aches and pain. Once again, you don't have to think big; you can be of service in small ways like alleviating the pressure on your son or daughter by babysitting grand children. We will all do it our own way. Say hello to people you see. Be friendly to your neighbors or to strangers. Send flowers anonymously. Listen to another. Encourage someone to be all they can be. Write some friendly notes to people or send an uplifting email. When you are making a wonderful dinner, make extra, and deliver it to someone.

> *If we are in a position to affect the happiness or suffering of others, we have ethical responsibilities toward them.*
> —*Sam Harris*[9]

OPPORTUNITIES GALORE

Many older people have the health, time, money, and experience to attend to the world's ever increasing needs. They are often less driven by wanting to make money and are more interested in finding meaningful ways to contribute to making this world a better place for their grandchildren. They want to feel necessary.

> *Check out Appendix D for a marketplace of opportunities, resources, and possibilities.*

There are an increasing number of intergenerational programs linking different age groups. Generation United is a coalition of more than 185 intergenerational programs that brings young people together with older people to work for a common goal like preserving wildlife, or kids helping older people learn about computers, and older people teaching kids about history. Elders Share the Arts in New York City combines teens with homebound elders to make collages out of their life stories, which are then displayed at an annual Living History Festival. Colleges, like Worcester State College, are creating programs for their students and community volunteers to teach English to immigrants. Southern Illinois has a program called "Vets on the Net" pairing kids with retirees as email pals.

Check to see what colleges in your area are doing, or suggest that they might start a program. OLLI (Osher Lifelong Learning Institute) is located at 120 universities and colleges across the country calling themselves "Health Clubs for the Mind." OLLI offers a wide variety of intriguing and interesting classes for older adults. Environmental Alliance for Senior Involvement in Virginia teams older people with grade school kids to work on organic gardens together; they have more than 500 projects in all fifty states. The USA Freedom Corps (*USAfreedomcorps.gov*) coordinates many volunteer programs besides the Peace Corps. *Americorps.org* builds affordable housing, mentors and tutors young people, teaches computer skills, runs after-school programs, and helps communities respond to disaster. *Citizencorps.gov* helps communities to become safer and better prepared for times of emergency. Learn-and-Serve-America links classrooms with community service. *SeniorCorps.org* uses skill and experience of seniors to help in the community. It coordinates the Foster grandparents program, Senior Companions, and RSVP (retired senior volunteers). These are but a few examples that show this mushrooming arena of opportunity for older adults who are seeking heartwarming volunteer work. The world needs what we have to give.

Some retirees decide that it's time to start a second career, to pursue a dream. Your second career is likely to last about half as long as your time before retirement, perhaps longer. Some do fee-for-service work; others do temporary work. Many pursue another career, but want a not-so-big-job that leaves time for other things. Some decide to go back to the part of their former job they most enjoyed.

I, for one, love volunteering, listening to people, and helping them sort out what's going on with them, without taking a note—a refreshing change from my former paid work as a psychologist, doing testing, supervision, tangling with insurance companies, and being buried in paperwork. My income isn't needed any more for our children's college education, and I am no longer dependent on receiving medical benefits. Some companies are recruiting older workers, finding them to be more reliable in attendance and better workers. Borders Bookstores offer benefits to part-time employees who work as little as one day a week; they are developing a "passport" system allowing these employees to work winters in the south and summers in the north. We are bound to see more and more innovative ideas as the boomers retire.

Have any of these suggestions whet your appetite? What do you think you would like to do?

Meaning comes in many forms. This chapter has hopefully led you into an exploration of what is meaningful to you, helping you to become aware, labeling what you are already doing, and offering suggestions and possibilities of what you might choose to pursue. Many older adults miss out on the opportunities out there. You may report that you are "doing fine, thank you!" and you may be, but I encourage you to explore other fulfilling possibilities that might make this time of your life even better.

When retirees, or anyone whose role has changed, are no longer focused on careers, they often flounder, some for the first time, and wonder about their identity, asking, "Who am I now? Why should I get up in the morning?" or the wistful "I went from being a Who's Who to a Who's He!" When your role changes and you don't have a set plan, you may find that you have a new sort of time-management problem, with either too many choices on your hands or too few. Believe that you're on the threshold of an exciting new chapter in your life. It's time to reinvent yourself.

> *Twenty years from now, you will be more disappointed by the things you didn't do than by the ones you did. So throw off the bowlines. Sail away from the safe harbor. Catch the trade winds in your sails. Explore. Dream. Discover.*
> *—Mark Twain*

Chapter 4

How Do I Make My Life as Good as It Can Be?

How might I best deal with my feelings and work on developing an attitude that will enhance this period of my life? What kind of a toolkit can I create that will get me through the ups and downs? How do I take care of myself, maintain a healthy lifestyle, and learn how to balance myself better? You will find your own answers. I ask questions to help you explore your options and give suggestions that have worked for others. This is the time to choose what you might want to do differently. What is living fully? One of the criteria for enlightenment and living life fully is to accept the inevitable and cyclical nature of grief and loss. If you love and care about anyone or anything, a certain amount of pain is guaranteed to come with it. This fact places people in a quandary throughout life. You toddle along measuring your thoughts, saying to yourself, "I shouldn't get into this relationship or take this risk, because I'll get hurt." Yet, when you start overprotecting yourself from hurt and backing away from caring, you lose the joy of truly living.

So, caring often gives you pain. Ironically, caring again is the best way to heal. If you choose to "live fully," this means keeping your heart open. Healing means choosing to move toward love and kindness and continuing to learn, versus closing yourself off from any potential for fear of the accompanying pain. Dwelling on missed opportunities, bad choices, and poor relationships blocks any movement toward peace of mind. The point at which you stop resisting and trying to control a situation is when healing begins to occur. It is when you stop fighting the past and learn to let go that extraordinary growth and completion can occur.

You have questions, fantasies, dreams, and hopes, and they change and are moderated all the time. You may have fantasized the man in your life to be tall and muscular and then found yourself with a not-so-tall, not-so-muscular fellow who seems just about right. You may have fantasized that you, or a child of yours, would be a major league athlete and it didn't happen. You may have been terrified of growing older because society paints old age so grimly, and now you find aging quite liberating and satisfying. You may have thought you would live into old age with the person you married, but it hasn't worked out that way because of divorce or death. You are forced to set aside the old dreams, readjust, and go on. Journeys are like

> *Every moment missed is a moment unlived.*

this. Questions change. Realities change. Just when you are halfway there, you discover that the goal has changed. With new experiences, your world becomes different. Wonderful things happen and tragedies happen and you are never the same as before. Life is about changing and adapting.

This chapter discusses the many ways to work on your attitude and take care of yourself. It discusses feelings—what to do with your own and how to react to others. It shows you how to ask for what you want. We will look at research and learn from the experiences of others who have developed attitudes and ways to care for themselves that enable them to thrive and live fully.

ATTITUDE

There are many things we can't control in our lives. Our parents give us our DNA. We can't control what other people do, natural disasters, and the many curves that life throws in our direction. On the other hand, we can choose to live a healthy lifestyle, we can do much to influence our attitude, and we can

> *I haven't changed anything but my attitude and everything has changed.*
> *—a client*

develop tools that will help us play the hand we are dealt the best we can. Attitude is huge. Our minds can be very useful tools, but can be our enemy as well as our friend. How we look at things can make all the difference in our quality of life. One afternoon, I visited two women in their mid-eighties. They both initiated the conversation with the same simple statement: "No one came to visit

me today." One woman was bereft, felt unloved, uncared for, and miserable. The other followed the sentence with, "Isn't that terrific! I had the morning all to myself."

Think how your attitude would be influenced, like mine was, when I heard my old friend, Emil, who was approaching the end of his life, wake up, and say…

Hot Damn! I got another day of life!

and then he went on to speculate how he could make the most of his day. I think my life changed in that moment. Have you ever had the good fortune of witnessing someone with an attitude like this that simply blows you away? Tell me about it.

A lighter way of looking at things can be learned. This isn't about a Pollyanna attitude or denial. Bad things happen and we need to work through the pain of the grieving process, letting the sad or mad feelings surface before we can get on to living life more fully again. Attitude is an ever-

It takes a conscious and mighty effort for some of us to see the positive side of things.

changing, dynamic process, and when we make it work for us, it can be our most priceless possession. Attitude is never static. Many of us arrive at a practical place where we see that our choice in difficult times is simply to be miserable and stay miserable or to make the best of the situation. Coping isn't so much heroic as practical; there is no better choice.

Tell me about some times when you have had to cope.

Congratulate yourself for this challenging work.

Often, our attitude and reaction to things that happen to us are what people remember most about us. Attitude seems to transcend other physical and personal traits. A person with a positive outlook on life is the one who has a gleam in the eye, an aura, a sparkle that shines through. On the other hand, we know people who seem to walk under a gloomy cloud, whose worst fears seem to happen. Similarly, the lighthearted, positive people appear to make good things happen. This is no accident and it isn't magic. We can cause good things to happen to ourselves. When we have a positive outlook, we get the added bonus of creating a ripple effect, a presence so desirable to others that we are invited to share their special experiences.

LEARNING FROM RESEARCH

Many studies now verify that our spiritual and mental attitudes affect our physical health, giving valuable scientific support to what we already knew. We have seen that we're more likely to get sick after a period of stress. We know that there is something to kissing an "owie" of a small child that makes him/her actually feel better. We know that our heart races when we just think about something that excites us. We know that laughing makes us feel better. Now we have fancy words for it. Laughter sparks our healing endorphins. Every cell in our body communicates to other cells by way of psychoneuro-immune chemicals. This is why our hearts race, and why we blush when we are embarrassed. There is literal power to thinking healthy thoughts and expressing our feelings. We've always known intuitively that our mind, body, and spirit are not separate. Now more studies are proving it scientifically.

In her book, *The Balance Within: The Science Connecting Health and Emotions*, Esther M. Sternberg[1], M.D. describes the physiology of stress, the interaction between the immune system and the nervous system, how the mind influences the body and the body influences the mind to make our mental and physical health better or worse. Now we know why placeboes work. Every day scientists understand more about how our brains work. Every moment thousands of chemicals and cells are interacting and changing in our bodies. New technologies are allowing scientists to measure changes of thousands of genes at a time, all in a single microchip. This "is akin to the difference between looking at the musical score for a symphony and playing all the notes on the page, or choosing a single note—the same throughout the piece—and playing it alone.... It is only by hearing all the notes together, and hearing them change against each other, that the real sound of the music emerges[2]."

Scientists are exploring how perceptions of events that are colored by your emotions and life experience can influence your immune responses. They can design ways to modify your emotional responses

It is just as easy to help yourself to a bit of heaven as to a chunk of hell, and a good deal more intelligent.
—*Jerome Ellison*[3]

in ways that might help prevent or change the course of some diseases. All of this has multi-faceted implications. Once there is an understanding of the biological basis for various kinds of stress, a variety of coping strategies that could prevent that stress can be found. Multiple factors contribute to getting an illness—our genetic makeup, diet, lifestyle, toxicity of our environment—but our attitude also contributes. And, no matter what causes our ill health, our ability to make the most out of whatever is given us is definitely related to our attitude.

We are so acculturated to swallow what our society has put into our minds about aging that we have no idea what percentage of how we behave is based on how we think we are supposed to behave. If we believe that old age is about declining and becoming less, what percent of our decline is due to this belief? Some studies verify this fear. In one study Ellen Langer[4], effectively reversed the biological age of a group of elderly men over seventy-five years old by systematically taking them back to a time when they saw themselves as young and vital, asking them to talk, act, dress, and behave as they did in their mid-fifties. They went to a country retreat for a week, which was made to be similar to what they would have experienced at that age. Music from that era was piped in. Impartial observers judged the men to look and behave more like fifty-five year olds than seventy-five year olds after that week. Objective physiological measures taken before and after the retreat verified that they had "de-aged." Their posture became more erect, stiff joints loosened, IQ scores improved, and fingers straightened … all because they imagined themselves young again.

Candace Pert's[5] research shows that a negative attitude undermines your immune system. Results indicate that you simply can't afford to be depressed. Depression makes your body sick. What to do or say to remain positive varies from person to person. For example, here's a rationale that worked for John with the help of a therapist. John figured out that his hatred of Joe was making him dysfunctional and preoccupied. Not only that, it was really a victory for Joe. When competitive people realize that they are using up valuable energy resenting, hating, or being victimized by their obsession with another and that the only way they are going to emerge victorious is to let go of it, matters are simplified. One day in my office, John, after years of simmering, said resolutely, "I'm not going to let myself go under. I'm going to start letting go of these destructive feelings and concentrate on making the most out of my time. I'm beginning to see that, if I succeed at this, I will have truly won." And he proceeded to do so.

S. Kobasa's and M. Puccetti's[6] 1983 research showed that people with a combination of three attitudes were least likely to become ill:

1. Persons who view tasks they face as challenges or opportunities.
2. Persons who feel they have many choices.
3. Persons who feel that they have a purpose for living.

Revenge is living well despite what may have happened to you.

People with these attitudes exhibit "hardiness," which is "three times more powerful than social support and exercise put together in determining who gets sick in times of stress."

You can manipulate your brain. When you nurture it with positive, hopeful thoughts, your mind eventually comes to believe what you are telling it. There is truth to, "Fake it until you make it." Your brain is not necessarily your friend. It cannot always be trusted. It hears whatever it is told, and your body reacts accordingly. You can befriend it by intentionally feeding it believable thoughts that lean toward the positive. Feelings are honest. They are barometers of what you are thinking. It is your thoughts that can be controlled. You can choose your thoughts and attitudes and thus your way of being.

In his book, *The Biology of Belief*, Bruce Lipton's[7] research says that your parents provide you with your important gene blueprints but that their parenting skills, the environment of your early years, affect the expression of these genes. Messages received in childhood such as "you are stupid and won't amount to anything" move to the truth column and become deeply embedded. We become hard-wired early. That's why parenting classes and early childhood education are so important. But the important news is that, at any age, *we can rewire ourselves.* How we think undeniably influences our biochemistry. Our cells may be the gene blueprints, but a cell's life is influenced by its physical and energetic environment, which means that energy-based complementary approaches to healing need to be given their due. We become a co-creator of our lives when we come to believe this, not a victim of our genes. We are no longer a feeble biochemical machine controlled by our genes. We've discovered that we have a powerful influence on how the cells in our body respond.

Lipton talks about how we cannot afford to be as fearful as our society has groomed us to be—fear of terrorists, strangers, the food we eat, the pills we take, the asbestos in our cabinets, etc. We only have so much energy, and it's important not to give it all to the fear mode, which causes a sustained adrenaline drain sapping our ability to protect ourselves. We have to balance the toll that fear takes with positive, loving, fulfilling thoughts that rebuild our immune systems and life-enhancing energy. Biofeedback, meditation, and mindfulness training help us to be aware of what is going on in the moment, making it more difficult for harmful programming to take over. It is more than just common sense to say that our attitude makes a difference. If we believe negative things, our cells know it. We can change the quality, the thrust of our lives, by changing what we believe.

All this research is good news for aging brains. Psychoanalysts had led us to think that by early childhood our brain patterns were fairly set, but today's research is showing that we can change, that we definitely can "teach old dogs new tricks." Our emotions affect our mind and body; we are not captive to our genes. If we change our thought patterns and figure out ways to reduce stress, we can rewire ourselves so that the genes that give us a predisposition to certain diseases can be kept from expressing themselves.

TRAITS FOR SUCCESSFUL LIVING AT ANY AGE

Ability to see holiness in everyday things
Ability to lighten up—be optimistic
Willingness to be vulnerable
Something to look forward to
Compassionate intelligence
Ability to express feelings
Ability to give and receive
Genuine interest in others
Awareness of feelings
Good listening skills
Willingness to risk
Celebrative spirit
Clear boundaries
Lifelong learner
Sense of purpose
Sense of wonder
Sense of humor
Playfulness
Enthusiasm
Sensitivity
Flexibility
Resilience
Curiosity
Courage
Hope
Joy

> *Live in perpetual astonishment.*
> *—Theodore Roethke*

TECHNIQUES FOR WORKING ON MY ATTITUDE

Positive Self-Talk

It is hard not to feel good if you have the above traits and attitudes. A basic psychological premise is that you "feel according to how you think." So it follows that, if you want to feel better, you need to learn to put more positive thoughts into your head.

> *You can live as if life has meaning and you are a part of the web of life; or you can live as if life is chaotic and you are a victim of its whims.*
> *—Joseph Fabry[8]*

Recognizing the kinds of thoughts that you habitually think is an important awareness step enabling you to begin to change any negative ones into healthier ways of thinking. The media makes it difficult by subtly and not so subtly filling you with the negative thoughts about aging we've discussed. Learn to counteract any catastrophic statements you hear or find yourself muttering with less extreme statements. If you want to look forward to a satisfying old age, stop emphasizing the negative and blaming everything that goes wrong on aging. For example, so often you hear people say, "I'm feeling old" whenever they feel sick. When you are sick, you are sick, not old. Watch your words. They matter. Here are some examples:

> *You can't have true splendid fullness until you're at least seventy years of age.*
> —John Brantner[9]

HARMFUL SELF-TALK	POSITIVE SELF-TALK
Retirement scares me silly. My whole identity was tied into my job. Now what will I do?	It's so exciting to think of all the things I can do now.
When people grow old, they become more fault-finding, rigid, and irritable.	Some people become rigid, others soften, loosen up, and seem to relax and enjoy life more.
I didn't sleep very well. I have a headache. This is going to be an awful day.	I'll take it easy. It'll feel good to have a relaxed day. I'll take a walk. That always feels good.
Oh no! My face is getting so wrinkly.	I've smiled for every one of my wrinkles!
I can't stand getting old.	I guess that's better than the alternative.
I feel so tired and run down and have some new aches in my leg. It's another one of those things that happen to when you get old.	I feel unusually tired and weak. I'm going to make an appointment with the doctor to see what's wrong.
I can't find my keys. This is it…I've got Alzheimer's.	I can't find my keys. What a pain. I periodically pull stunts like this.
Nobody gives a hoot that I'm so lonesome. People don't really care.	I'm having one of those days. I'd better call somebody for coffee. I always feel better if I do something.
I'm so stupid. I can't even understand these insurance forms.	These forms are really complicated. I'll go get some help.
My daughter hasn't called all week. I'm such a burden. I must have done something wrong.	I haven't heard from Mary. She is really busy. I sure miss her. I wonder if she is free for lunch.
What a mess I am. I look like an "old bag."	Well, I'll never win a prize but I like this old body. It has served me well.

Positive thoughts seem natural for some and totally foreign to others. With a little effort you can change your negative thinking.

OLD AGE, I DECIDED, IS A GIFT.

I am now, probably for the first time in my life, the person I have always wanted to be. Oh, not my body! I sometimes despair over my body, the wrinkles, the baggy eyes, and the sagging butt … but I don't agonize over those things for long. I would never trade my amazing friends, my wonderful life, my loving family for less gray hair or a flatter belly. As I've aged, I've become more kind to myself, and less critical of myself. I've become my own friend. I don't chide myself for eating that extra cookie, or for not making my bed, or for buying that silly cement gecko that I didn't need, but looks so avant-garde on my patio. I am entitled to a treat, to be messy, to be extravagant. I have seen too many dear friends leave this world too soon; before they understood the great freedom that comes with aging. Whose business is it if I choose to read or play on the computer until 4 AM and sleep until noon? I will dance with myself to those wonderful tunes of the 60&70's, and if I, at the same time, wish to weep over a lost love … I will. I will walk the beach in a swim suit that is stretched over a bulging body, and will dive into the waves with abandon if I choose to, despite the pitying glances from the jet set. They, too, will get old. I know I am sometimes forgetful. But there again, some of life is just as well forgotten. And I eventually remember the important things. Sure, over the years my heart has been broken. How can your heart not break when you lose a loved one, or when a child suffers, or even when somebody's beloved pet gets hit by a car? But broken hearts are what give us strength and understanding and compassion. A heart never broken is pristine and sterile and will never know the joy of being imperfect. I am so blessed to have lived long enough to have my hair turning gray, and to have my youthful laughs be forever etched into deep grooves on my face. So many have never laughed, and so many have died before their hair could turn silver. As you get older, it is easier to be positive. You care less about what other people think. I don't question myself anymore. I've even earned the right to be wrong. So, to answer your question, I like being old. It has set me free. I like the person I have become. I am not going to live forever, but while I am still here, I will not waste time lamenting what could have been, or worrying about what will be. And I shall eat dessert every single day. (if I feel like it)

—*author unknown*

AFFIRM YOURSELF

Healing is about getting to know and like yourself. There are several ways to work on this. While it's important that you insert affirmations into your mind, make them believable. If the statements you choose are impossible, such as, "I am tall, slim, and athletic," (when you are five feet tall and weigh 150 pounds) don't bother saying it. Affirmations must have some semblance of possibility for your mind to take them seriously. You can waste enormous amounts of energy when you're hard on yourself. You are your own worst critic and your negative self-talk can do some deep damage. Each thought directs your path and is responsible for how you are feeling. You can change your feelings by ridding yourself of negative beliefs and replacing them with affirmative thoughts. Suggestions are:

I can make this a great day.
I have choices.
I am changing and that is good.
I can ask for what I want.

I can choose where to direct my energy.
I can make someone else feel good today.
I will get through this.
I will be totally present with the person I am with today.
I am a strong, capable, caring person.
I can enjoy this moment.

Before you get out of bed in the morning, get in the habit of focusing on something positive and good in your life. Identify one activity that gives you pleasure to pursue that day. Then get out of bed and start your day with an upbeat attitude and a plan for the day. Make a list of your own personal, helpful, and hopeful self-talk. Put your list in an accessible place for those times when you are feeling unsure of yourself.

Your beliefs become your thoughts
Your thoughts become your words
Your words become your actions
Your actions become your values
Your values become your destiny.
—Mahatma Ghandhi

REFRAMING

One person walks through a forest and sees nothing. The next person can walk through the same woods and have a peak experience.

> *Old age, to the unlearned, is winter; to the learned, it is harvest time.*
> —Author Unknown

Nossrat Peseschkian [10] relates the story of an Asian king who had an anxiety-provoking dream. He dreamed that all his teeth fell out, one by one. Disturbed, he called in his dream interpreter. The dream interpreter listened sorrowfully to his dream and disclosed to the king, "I have bad news for you. You will lose all your relatives one by one, just like teeth." The interpretation aroused the anger of the king. He had the dream interpreter thrown into a dungeon. Then he had another dream interpreter come. This one listened to the dream and said, "I am happy to make a joyful interpretation. You will live to be older than all your relatives, you will outlive them all." The king was overjoyed and rewarded him richly. The courtiers were amazed at this. "You actually didn't say anything different from your predecessor. But why was he punished and you rewarded?" The dream interpreter answered, "We both interpreted the dream the same way. It depends not only on what one says, but also on how one says it."

You give yourself power when you learn to reframe your thoughts in a positive way. It is an on-going job to neutralize the negative messages received from society in general and sometimes from persons such as doctors and clergy, who are in positions of authority. For example, the informed consent documents that you are asked to sign prior to an operation are frightening to many. If you read the chemotherapy protocol that often accompanies the diagnosis of cancer, you will probably find only intimidating, technically vivid descriptions of all that could go wrong. It is important to be given information, but it takes courage to sign up for procedures after you've read a list of possible side effects and have not been given one balancing word of encouragement or hope … like you will be healed or comforted, or that the complications listed are rare. Ask your doctor for a balancing statement to help you reframe.

As your body changes and you can't do some of the things that formerly gave you pleasure, you need to be creative and substitute new activities that now suit you better. Hunters become bird watchers or photographers. Runners become bikers. I found that beating a drum has the same exhilarating effect on my soul as did slamming a racquetball in earlier years and my joints are happier. What you find satisfying changes. There is a lot more of enjoying the moment.

What adjustments have you had to make?

Many professional and family caregivers experience quiet satisfaction aware when doing "whatever can be done" for someone they love. Even the pangs of grief and loneliness after a major loss are compensated for by the awareness that you would not trade those present feelings for never having loved at all. Reframing enables you to adjust to life situations by changing your actions and by rethinking the words you use, substituting more life-enhancing and hopeful words and concepts.

EXAMPLES	DESTRUCTIVE	REFRAMED
Wheelchair, cane, walker, hearing aids	Symbol of deterioration of body	Helpful tools, enabling mobility and maintenance of independence
Person with illness	Victim	Living with a disease, a resilient survivor
Independence	"I won't accept any help."	"If I accept help, I will be able to be independent longer."

What examples of this do you see?

Often people with health challenges are unable to move beyond old burned-in notions about how they "should be" and refuse to use adaptive living aids of any kind. We see deaf people without hearing aids, vision impaired people refusing to wear glasses. We see people with bad joints refusing to use a cane, or more impaired people refusing to use wheelchairs or walkers. Embarrassment, vanity, or blockheadedness can literally be the kiss of death. They are one fall away from being far more dependent. Attitudinal impairments disallow independence.

For older people, maintaining independence is a priority. Many choose to live close to their families and dread the time when they might have to lean on their children or others for any sort of help. Our society stresses the importance of independence, which, although a natural and necessary developmental stage, is overplayed to such an extreme that it makes the normal changes and increasing diminishments and dependency that often comes at the end of life seem mortifying and degrading. Instead of feeling comfortable with asking for help when one's physical capabilities diminish, many elders feel distressed and saddened and their self-esteem plummets.

BECOMING MORE ASSERTIVE

Another important and closely related technique for attitude building is communicating assertively. You have much to say about making your life as good as it can be. Using an assertive approach gives you your best chance.

> The real voyage of self-discovery consists not in seeking new landscapes, but in having new eyes.
> —Marcel Proust

What does it mean to be assertive? Assertiveness is in the middle of the spectrum of responses between non-assertiveness (passivity) and aggressiveness. Learning to be assertive is a critical component of self-care. Passive people let things happen, have victim tendencies, and wonder what happened at the end of their days. Aggressive people blast through life and wonder why they have no friends. People who are able to assert themselves feel confident and capable. It is the assertive ones, who have learned the art of give and take, of balance, of listening and hearing, along with being able to clearly communicate their thoughts and feelings, who have the likelihood of having the life they want. The following table helps describe the differences among assertive, aggressive, and passive people.

PASSIVE	ASSERTIVE	AGGRESSIVE
Avoids conflict	Communicates directly	Controls, dominates
Recognizes the rights of others	Recognizes own rights as well as the rights of others	Recognizes own rights only
Lacks confidence	Is confident	Acts confident, cocky
Builds up resentment and anger	Deals with anger	Acts out anger in attack mode
Has little self-respect	Is respected by self and others	Generates feelings of hostility
Is hard to get to know	Promotes authentic relationships	No one wants to get to know this person
Voice soft and wimpy	Voice well modulated and firm	Voice strident

In addition to being passive, assertive, or aggressive, two other response categories are often used. Some of us are socially compliant, which is one step up from being passive because a decision is made to not respond assertively. The other is passive-aggressiveness, which is an indirect, dishonest, double-meaning response—often expressed through humor. Recipients of this behavior find it much more difficult to handle than pure, blatant aggressiveness.

TEST YOUR ASSERTIVENESS

Response Categories: 1) Passive; 2) Socially Compliant; 3) Assertive; 4) Passive-Aggressive; 5) Aggressive. One example of each of the categories is listed for each scenario. Identify each category and circle the response closest to your own.

1. You question the treatment the doctor is suggesting. You:
   a. Say nothing, do what doctor says.
   b. Challenge doctor's competence and demand an explanation.
   c. Ask doctor for more information: give your opinion; request feedback; if not satisfied, seek a second opinion.
   d. Go along because the doctor has been right before.
   e. Ask doctor how much money is in it for him or her.

2. The person you visit is lonely. She wants you to spend Sunday afternoons with her. This is inconvenient, but you are aware that she views "No" as a personal rejection. You:
   a. Feel there is no choice; you visit on Sundays.
   b. Explain that Sunday is inconvenient—refuse in an understanding manner. Say you will call before you come.
   c. Say, "Forget it, maybe I shouldn't come at all."
   d. Say you'll come, but plan to have someone call and cancel.
   e. Try to come some Sundays.

3. You've made reservations at a restaurant with two friends. At the last minute, another friend arrives and asks to come along. You don't want to include her. You:
   a. Invite her along.
   b. Tell her that you have been planning to be with your other friends that night and would prefer making plans with her for another time.
   c. Say, "Lots of nerve. You should have called first."
   d. Allow her to come, but ignore her all evening.
   e. Invite her along so you won't hurt her feelings.

4. Your partner, friend, or spouse continually interrupts and appears not to be listening to what you are saying. You feel angry. You:
   a. Say, "It hurts and makes me mad when you interrupt all the time. You've been doing it a lot lately. Please be aware of it and stop."
   b. Do nothing.
   c. Say, "You would learn more if you would listen more."
   d. Excuse him or her because this behavior is not usual.
   e. Jokingly say that it must be difficult to carry the full burden of the conversation.

5. You are waiting in line to get into a popular movie. This line is one hundred feet long, and as you get up to about five feet from the ticket booth, menacing motorcycle riders butt in line right in front of you to grab the last tickets. You:

    a. Back off.

    b. Tell them in a loud voice to get to the back of the line.

    c. Choose to be quiet to protect your physical health.

    d. Ask them politely to go to the back of the line.

    e. Kiddingly say, "I wish I were a macho stud."

Response category rating of each question: Categories: 1) Passive; 2) Socially Compliant; 3) Assertive; 4) Passive-Aggressive; 5) Aggressive

    1. a—1, b—5, c—3, d—2, e—4

    2. a—1, b—3, c—5, d—4, e—2

    3. a—1, b—3, c—5, d—4, e—2

    4. a—3, b—1, c—5, d—2, e—4

    5. a—1, b—5, c—2, d—3, e—4

Are you assertive? The intent of the above exercise is to aid you in understanding what is meant by being assertive and to demonstrate that, even though assertiveness is the preferred response ordinarily, the dynamics of the situation (as in question #5) affect your response. Few parents escape the delicate "walking on thin ice" feeling when dealing with their adult children, without recognizing that it is often best to keep their opinions about child raising, etc. to themselves, to back off and let their children learn their own way.

It's part of the great balancing act:

When do I want to be assertive? When do I just let go of this annoyance?

ASSERTIVENESS WITH YOUR DOCTOR

Always have a list of questions for your doctor. Ask. Ask. Ask

If the situation is a delicate one, bring along another set of ears with a pen and paper to remember what the doctor says. Often your ears stop hearing if your heart and brain are staggered by startling information. If you need to see a specialist, ask your regular doctor who he would want to see if it were him or a family member. If you need surgery, ask the surgeon how many times he or she does this particular operation. There is impressive evidence correlating the number of procedures a surgeon has done and mortality rates. Similarly it is important to pick a hospital that has a high volume of the kind of surgery you are having. You might ask if there are less invasive procedures available and, if it is an elective surgery, if it would be better to wait for something new on the horizon.

Boundary Setting

Setting limits with others is a form of assertiveness. Learning to say "no" to requests or demands that go against your core is a symbol of self-respect and self-caring. Congratulate yourself. Claiming your boundaries and setting limits is always a delicate proposition, but it's a way to teach people how you wish to be treated. If you continue to accommodate others and don't make boundaries for yourself, you soon lose the respect of others. Here are examples of what some people found worked for them:

1. "I don't like the way you're talking to me"; "I feel unjustly attacked and really frustrated"; "I'm going to hang up the phone now. I'll call back tomorrow and see if we can do better."

2. Learn to initiate rather than react:
    "This is what I'd like to do…"
    "I've decided to organize my life a little more. Could you please limit your calling to between 8:00 and 9:00 A.M. or 5:00 and 6:00 P.M.? That would be a big help."

3. Don't assume that people know what you need. Ask clearly for what you want. Often older people I counsel feel that their adult children are insensitive to their needs. On further inquiry I find that when their kids ask them on the phone "how are things going, or how are you?" the parents respond with an "okay" or "not so bad" but still blame them for not recognizing what is really going on. It is helpful to make a list that says specifically what is needed and ask directly. Faulty communication is often at the base of the problem. Even when you are sick, it's important that you, or someone who knows you well, be assertive.

4. You need to be direct. Hints aren't enough. Use a good assertive approach like John did: "I could use some help on my yard. There are some things I can't do anymore. Could you help out for a couple of hours this weekend? I'd really appreciate it." Or "I love your visits. You are so easy to be with. You take my mind off things and make me laugh."

Everyone outta here 'cept for the dog.

Hosp. Bed 3A124

5. In a support group, say, "I need some time to talk today."

6. As a friend and visitor to a chronic complainer, say, "I want to know how you are feeling and what adjustments might be made to help you feel better, but I'd like to spend most of the time talking about other things. How about fifteen minutes on what's wrong and then switching subjects?" You are the visitor and can choose to take care of yourself. You can leave if he/she chooses not to change.

7. Avoid toxic people if possible. If they are people you can't avoid, practice assertiveness or develop the socially more compliant skill of letting their behavior roll off you. Work on changing the tone of the situation by pausing, remembering the good things about this person, and trying to tactfully switch the focus to something else. No one can "make" you feel sad, or angry, or disappointed. That gives them the power. You can choose how to react. One woman responded to a rather mean statement by her daughter by saying assertively, "I'm leaving now. I am feeling sad and pretty disrespected by what you are saying. I love you but it isn't doing either of us any good carrying on this way. Please think about it." Things won't usually get better unless you address the problem. There are no guarantees that they will get better, but you can know that you have done what you can.

8. Avoid "stuck" people. If you know persons who get stuck on a subject whether it is their health, the health-care system, politics, or religion, let them know that you'd like to change the subject. If they can't, just leave.

9. Recognize passive-aggressive comments for what they are. For example, the person who answers your phone call with a comment like, "Well, a voice from the past" or "Hello stranger," let it roll off and chuckle to yourself.

10. Don't make people guess at what you are feeling. We are all capable of being in different places with our feelings even given very similar scenarios. For example, one moment you might like sitting with your partner in silence and a short time later you want some interaction. You could say, "Let's talk. I could use some diversion to get my mind off my aches and pains." Or he could be in a totally different place than you want him to be so it is up to you to let him know: "I feel frustrated when you talk about everything else in the world except what is going on with me. I need to talk about what is happening."

Discuss instances when you could be more assertive. What could you do differently?

LOCUS OF CONTROL

Locus of control is a construct that indicates the amount of control you expect to have in your life. Persons who want as much information as possible and expect a high degree of input in order to feel content with decisions have a high *internal* locus of control. Persons who do not desire much control and in fact experience a higher degree of anxiety if forced to make a decision exhibit an *external* locus of control. They want others to make decisions for them. After reading the following statements, circle the number that describes the degree to which you agree or disagree with each one:

1	2	3	4	5
Strongly agree		Neutral		Strongly disagree

1. I think that I have a lot of choice about who my friends are. 1 2 3 4 5
2. I expect to be involved in decisions concerning my own health. 1 2 3 4 5
3. In the past when I have been presented with a crisis, I have done pretty well with solving or adapting to it. 1 2 3 4 5
4. I have very strong opinions. 1 2 3 4 5
5. I trust my own decision. 1 2 3 4 5

Total Score _____

Scoring: High internal locus of control: 5–10

High external locus of control: 20–25

This gives you more information about yourself. Information that one would hope would be taken into consideration by your health-care team. Who is this person? How does she think? If a person arrives at the doctor's appointment with a list of questions and has thoroughly researched her symptoms, the doctor will probably get a clue. While it is better to be informed and have a collaborative relationship with your doctor, it's probably best not to be too extreme on either end of the scoring spectrum. There is no need to act helpless at the one extreme or, at the other end, to assume that you have more control over things than anyone has.

LIVE THE SERENITY PRAYER

There is much freedom in changing what can be changed. There is also great freedom in changing your attitude about things that you cannot change. You cannot change what other people do. You cannot change your genetics, the weather, natural disasters, floods, tornadoes, your predisposition to disease and virus. Many situations are unchangeable. It's important to accept this and move on. You can't change how you were parented, or even your own past parenting, but perhaps you can do something about your parenting or grandparenting now. Many a person uses his later life working on "getting it right" or "breaking a cycle" with their grandchildren.

You can only change yourself, your own thoughts and actions, your own attitude and willingness to change. You can be wistful over the bygone days and fantasize yourself still being an athlete. But you no longer are, so you are best off not squandering your time or energy on the past and getting busy enjoying the present. You can set new achievable goals and feel proud of what you can do. You can experience the liberating feeling of relief when you accept your powerlessness over being able to change anyone but yourself. Whenever a problem or dilemma arises, ask yourself these questions:

God grant me the serenity to accept the things I cannot change; the courage to change the things I can; and the wisdom to know the difference.
—Reinhold Niebuhr

1. "Is this something that can be changed?"
2. If yes, "Is this something someone else can change but is out of my hands?" It helps to name to yourself whose problem it is.
3. "Is this something I can do something about?"

Run Any Problem Through This Process

Problem	Can't change	Someone else can change	I can change

OPEN TO NEW OPTIONS—THE RULE OF SIX

When you are stuck on a thought and can think of only one not-so-satisfying reason for something happening to you, The Rule of Six is a tool for opening your mind to other ways of thinking. From Native American discipline, it requires that instead of coming up with the one best answer to the question or problem, we come up with at least six possible, or good, answers. We hold all six in our head and do not choose among them. It increases the probabilities for there being other possibilities. It gets you out of your subjectiveness and makes the whole scenario seem less fixed. Practice by applying the Rule of Six to one of these two situations:

1. You are in the hospital and the operation on your husband is lasting longer than you expected. You are stuck on being sure something terrible has happened. Think of six other less negative thoughts.
2. Your daughter hasn't called for quite a few days. You are sure she is mad at you. Write down six healthier ways of thinking, six other "maybes."

This process is bound to loosen your stuckness, help you think outside of the box. No matter how troubling the circumstance, you will stretch your brain and grow. You will think more positively. Whenever you adopt the attitude that you are going to learn from this, the circumstance is no longer meaningless.

PICK YOUR FRIENDS CAREFULLY

In friendship we get to know ourselves better. By sharing our inner thoughts and feelings we not only find the intimacy of letting ourselves be known to another but we see ourselves more clearly due to their questions. There is no better feeling than being known and loved. Seek out people who lift you up. Cut out or limit interaction with the toxic ones. Who are the people who find your strengths, inspire you toward healing, nourish you in some way, or just enjoy being with for any reason?

There is a difference between friends and buddies. Buddies are people you like to do something with … go bowling or to ballgames, or to play poker or bridge with. A friend is someone who knows how you think and feel, listens, and loves you through thick and thin. Women

> *I often think that people we have loved, and who have loved us, not only make us more human but they become part of us; and in some way we are a sum total of those who have loved us and those to whom we have given our love.*
> —*Author Unknown*

> *Oh! The comfort, the inexpressible comfort. of feeling safe with a person, having neither to weigh the thoughts or measure words, but to pour them all out, just as they are, chaff and grain together, knowing that a faithful hand will take and sift them, keep what is worth keeping, and then with the breath of kindness, blow the rest away.*
> —George Eliot

> *"A friend is someone who knows the song in your heart, and can sing it back to you when you have forgotten the words."—author unknown*

tend to have more friends; men have more buddies. You have probably noticed that women are usually having lunch with their friends; men who go out to lunch are usually having a business meeting or sharing some hobby or sport. A fair generalization for older men is that they find their intimacy through their wives. This is one of the reasons that they remarry more quickly after they are widowed. They are less likely to have male friends to help them through tough periods and depend on getting their intimacy and often their social life through their partners.

Find people with whom to share your journey. Seek out fellow travelers, perhaps someone of a similar faith tradition, a person or persons who can reinforce or give feedback about the path you are choosing, who will listen to your thoughts, feelings, and dreams. Just as it helps to have someone to exercise with, to walk with, to get you activated on those days "you don't feel like it," it helps to have someone or a support community to laugh with, to take this spiritual and attitudinal journey along with you. They lighten up your day. Some find that a guide, counselor, or spiritual director helps them stay on their path. In many senses, who we are is reflected by the friends we choose. Acknowledging that many a fine person has chosen to be our friend at some period of our lives lifts our spirits. Ponder who have been, and perhaps still are, some of the people you are proud to call your friends? (Be sure to tell them.)

> *Perhaps the secret of living well is not in having all the answers but in pursuing unanswerable questions in good company.*
> —Rachel Naomi Remen"

SELF-CARE

Taking care of yourself is important. Self-care involves knowing yourself, being aware of your feelings, and learning how to express them. Particular attention should be given to the feelings of grief, sadness, guilt, and anger because these are the ones that most frequently block persons from moving on with life. Self-care includes:

> Feeling your feelings
> Slowing down
> Managing your time
> Maintaining a healthy lifestyle
> Taking care of your body
> Learning how to maintain your balance.

> *Youth is a gift of Nature, but age is a work of art.*
> —Garson Kanin, **It Takes a Long Time to Become Young**

You are encouraged to create a toolkit for yourself full of ways to lift yourself up when you are need it … and we all need it at times. Ahead are suggestions about self-care that have worked well for others. They will give you a jump-start on your own set of tools for taking better care of yourself.

FEEL ALL YOUR FEELINGS

Welcome your feelings. They are simply barometers telling you what your gut feels about what you are thinking. They aren't good or bad. They are important indicators for helping you understand yourself better. Circle the feelings below that are typical for you:

> *The work you do on yourself is the gift you give to others*
> —Ram Dass

happy, content, bored, tired, frustrated, enthusiastic, achy, apathetic, rigid, patriotic, sensitive, lucky, confused, caring, introverted, extroverted, sentimental, stubborn, loving, sad, cheerful, mad, lonely, grouchy, cynical, nasty, depressed, productive, excited, invisible, well-off, satisfied, funny, regretful, free, patient, impatient, jealous, angry, other

Sometimes the reasons for your feelings are current and obvious; other times they are more complicated, perhaps the accumulation of a lifetime. The disease of depression, for example, often results from suppression of feelings, feelings that were stuffed for a variety of reasons. Perhaps you've developed a defense mechanism by now to insulate yourself from painful emotions, but these feelings are important signals that would allow you to change the thoughts behind them.

Pick one of your negative feelings. How do you usually express it? There are toxic situations and toxic people whom you are best off identifying and avoiding. What usually triggers this negative feeling? How can you avoid those triggers?

Conversely, there are situations and people that help you feel good. How can you get more of it?

What situations bring out the "me" I like? How can I get more of them? What people bring out the best in me?

Knowing what you are feeling is the first step to health. Journaling, writing down what you are feeling, is one way of clarifying; talking with someone you trust—a friend, family member, or professional—is another. Knowing and expressing feelings are two different things. Expressing feelings does a lot to lift a depressed mood whether it is a good cry, an assertive satisfying response, or a healthy argument. But there is an art to expressing feelings, definitely better and worse ways and times to do it. Let's discuss the difficult feelings of sadness and grief, anger, fear and anxiousness, and guilt in more detail, along with information and ideas on how to deal with them.

GRIEF/SADNESS

Sadness and grief aren't reserved for later life, but there are usually more losses during that time. (Depression will be discussed in the next chapter.) Sadness happens for many reasons—small reasons and huge reasons—loss through death, loss of health, loss of dreams, and sometimes for no apparent reason at all. Name the feeling when it comes. Write about what you think is going on with you, or talk about them with someone. Buried feelings will fester and pop up again in some form, usually in anger, depression, or illness. Fighting or denying your sadness just adds another layer. Knowing and accepting what you are feeling is being "in the moment," an important step toward healing. Grieving is part of the healing process. As unpleasant as it seems, grief is therapeutic and necessary, and you are better off going through the process than around it.

> *Suppress your feelings and your stomach and your heart keep score.*

Loss hurts. Burying your painful feelings or choosing to be numb takes a toll also. Denial may save you some pain temporarily and is an appropriate choice for some for a while, but the pain has to go somewhere. It has to be dealt with at some point. Suppressing feelings becomes a habit and the only way to break a habit is to reverse the process that formed it. Take slow, tiny steps toward being more open about your feelings. You may be fighting the laws of inertia and ingrained habit. Decide and declare to yourself that you want to feel better. Only a few people actually appear to vote on the side of staying miserable. Recognize feeling better as a choice. Feeling sad part of the time is part of being human. Later I'll provide many techniques for working yourself out of downtimes.

> *Grief turns out to be a place none of us know until we reach it. We anticipate (we know) that someone close to us could die, but we do not look beyond the few days or weeks that immediately follow such an imagined death. We misconstrue the nature of even those few days or weeks. We might expect if the death is sudden to feel shock. We do not expect this shock to be obliterative, dislocating to both body and mind. We might expect that we will be prostrate, inconsolable, crazy with loss. We do not expect to be literally crazy, cool customers who believe that their husband is about to return and need his shoes.*
> —Joan Didion[12]

You don't get through life without having incredibly sad things happen to you. Losses come in all kinds of packages—death, illness, divorce, rejection, financial bankruptcy, moving, losing a job, loss of dreams. Grief is your psychological, physiological, and sociological reaction to loss. You need a time-out from moving on with your life to deal with your loss. Everyone has his/her own style and rhythm. In her autobiographical recount, *The Year of Magical Thinking*, about the year after her husband's sudden death, Joan Didion talks of her experience.

This was her experience. Each of us grieves differently, and for every subsequent loss, we will probably do it differently from the time before.

You are who you are in part because of the people in your life. The closer you are to another, the more your own self and self-image are tied to them. When someone close to you dies, you lose not only that person but the part of you that is complexly intertwined with him or her. Part of you dies with the person, and you must redefine yourself without him/her. You cannot be who you were before. You will be a new person in some way. A widow, for example, takes on the work of "learning to be a single person."

Grief is the response to a wounding. It is a process. I will discuss it in more detail in Chapter Seven along with information on how to help another through it. It takes time and work to reclaim that part of your self that goes away. You have a scar and are forever changed. The wound, even when mostly healed, can reopen—although less frequently as time passes. Certain events or memories trigger re-openings throughout life. Additional suffering is caused by those who rigidly believe that there is a recommended order and a "proper" sequence of stages and reactions that should be followed and certain definitive feelings that must be expressed. No two people grieve the same way; there isn't a right or proper way to grieve. Give yourself a break. You don't need to feel guilty because you aren't doing it "right" on top of the sadness and confusion you are already feeling over the loss.

Some people are at risk for more complicated grieving. Risk factors for complicated grieving can include:

> Prior trauma
> History of psychological problems
> Inadequate social support
> Ongoing stressors
> Unfinished business with the deceased
> Extreme anger.

> *If it doesn't kill me, it makes me grow.*
> *—Nietzsche*

> *Those who don't deal, won't heal.*

Professional help might be required to work through the obstacles preventing them from moving on. Denial of sadness works for a while with some people. It sometimes serves as a buffer until they are more able to deal. The general rule remains that it simply isn't good to keep your sadness and fears bottled up. They hang around in your body and your unconscious, quietly taking a toll. Necessary steps toward healing are to recognize, label, and express your difficult feelings.

Let those feelings out through tears, wailing, writing, talking, remembering—whatever fits for you. As we get older, more losses occur and grieving happens again and again. We are often handed these multiple losses and each is grieved a little differently. We learn and relearn what best helps us through the grieving process.

Suicide is a loss in a class by itself. It is particularly hard for those remaining. Grieve the loss. Don't focus just on the how or why the person died. It is difficult to balance the many feelings around the loss—sadness, guilt, anger—and the persistent "whys" with realistic acknowledgment that it was his decision, his solution, whether or not you able to understand. Do not to waste your energy resisting and

> *Once you have experienced the seriousness of your loss, you will be able to experience the wonder of being alive.*
> —Robert Veninga[13]

> *It is funny how you can stand more than you thought and feel yourself inside get stronger, and taste the salt of your own wounds and the weight of things that have happened to you.*
> —Meridel LeSeuer[14]

analyzing his decision, allowing his decision or depression to become yours. In the midst of deep suffering lay the mysterious seeds of growth and change and renewal, often hard to recognize at the moment. These seeds lurk there waiting to blossom. Traumatic events usually cause you to ask deeper questions and lead you into looking at the world a bit differently. You perhaps think that this sort of thing just happens to other people, not you, or that you were doing everything right and now your sense of trust is badly damaged. You are humbled, you see with fresh eyes, and, you are forever changed. Gradually, grieving persons start to open to the world again, start learning new ways of living without the deceased. Often, with the new understanding of pain, they become more compassionate toward others. They grow in depth and fullness even though they would never have chosen that kind of learning.

Why me? At some point, philosophers, theologians, and nearly everyone else struggle with this question. You try to make sense out of the suffering you see and feel. The answer has to be arrived at individually. Each of us has a different history, a different spiritual and ethnic background, has read different books, and will travel our own path. You can read, discuss with others, listen and observe, but you can't impose meaning on another's experience. Grieving is an area where giving advice is to be especially avoided. How a person copes will be unique to them.

ANGER

Anger is an emotion that people often can't express well. It has many aliases and degrees of intensity. It is often described in other terms, such as frustration, apathy, hurt, sorrow, or disappointment. Early in your life, many of you probably got the message that "it's not nice to be angry." Feelings are not right or wrong; they just are. You have them and it is important for you to recognize and express them. One trait of a healthy person is the ability to express anger in a mature way. Anger in the form of discontent is the engine that drives many necessary changes. It appears best to bubble anger out as you become aware of it instead of suppressing it completely or storing the energy until it erupts in an inappropriately excessive way. The energy cycle of anger is as follows:

1. Because of unmet expectations, abuse, loss of respect for yourself or another, you become aware of your feelings of anger. You feel anxious, disappointed, uncomfortable, or powerless.
2. You feel an energy buildup.
3. Relief occurs only after the expression of this energy. There is no such thing as unexpressed anger. It goes somewhere. If not expressed appropriately, it reappears as one of the following:

DEPRESSION. Learning to express anger constructively is much better than becoming depressed, which usually flattens people, making them withdrawn and nonfunctional. To under-or over-express your anger isn't good. The under-expressers usually get sick. The ventilationists who let themselves explode (called the "pus theory") seem to just get angrier. They scream, vent, apologize, and then replay it. There is a tendency toward cyclical behavior with the over-expressers. Anger often gives you energy. It is not a "bad" feeling. It's a step up from being helpless. Many think that anger toward injustice has brought about more change in the world than love of justice.

PHYSICAL SYMPTOMS. When release of anger is inhibited, it manifests in tension headaches, stiff necks, high blood pressure, inability to have satisfying sex, low back pain, and the onset of many diseases. Explosive anger has festered to such a degree that the smallest incident can cause a reaction disproportionate to the triggering event. Explosions scare people away and inhibit the possibility of constructive communication.

> *Let your anger bubble out.*

PASSIVE-AGGRESSIVE BEHAVIOR. Anger leaks out in indirect and often unconscious ways. Passive-aggressiveness can take the form of cutting sarcasm, inappropriate humor, or hostile statements. Since the anger is expressed indirectly, it is often hard to discern. You find yourself thinking either acutely or vaguely, "That doesn't feel good." You just know that you have been hit and that it hurts. Another common example of passive-aggressiveness is when you receive a compliment that has a hook in it, such as:

"You look so nice; I didn't recognize you";

"Congratulations—I'm surprised you've done so well … must have been in the right place at the right time";

"Can't you take a joke?" The punch in the arm after a snide remark;

"It's so nice of you to visit me for a change."

What are some examples of passive-aggressive comments that bug you? What passive-aggressive comments have you made?

Appropriately expressing anger

You don't want to suppress your anger, nor do you want to let it accumulate until there is an explosion. It is best to bubble it out as you become aware of the feeling. If you are beyond the bubbling stage, a particularly satisfying technique for releasing anger is to engage in physical activity such as brisk walking, racquetball, jogging, dancing, aerobic exercising, chopping wood. Other safe, satisfying, and appropriate releases of built-up anger are screaming loudly in your car when you are alone, or lying on your bed kicking, flailing, wailing, or beating on a pillow. A quieter means of expressing anger is a good assertive response, as discussed earlier. Anger is an internal directive. It is as important to recognize and claim it, as you do when your body has a temperature; you know something is wrong. When you are angry, you are being given a message. Here are the steps for expressing anger:

1. Recognize the feeling. This takes practice. Mentally healthy people can have as much anger as the emotionally ill.
2. Identify the source of the anger. The intention is not to "get back" at another. Find a willing third party or professional upon whom to vent the energy.
3. Verbalize your anger in a healthy way: Describe what is bothering you. Be specific, such as, "You don't look at me when I talk to you."

   Express what you are feeling, using the "I" message. "I feel insignificant and all alone when you do that."

   Ask explicitly for a different, specific behavior, such as, "Please just look at me when I'm talking."

   Emphasize how a change would make it better. "I think that the atmosphere around here would improve for you, too."

Think of a time when you didn't handle your anger well. What could you have done differently?

There are better and worse ways to do anger. Remember every minute you waste being angry is a minute lost in the short time we have to enjoy life. You can stay mad at yourself for being an inadequate father or use this energy to become the kind of grandfather you want to be.

FEAR/WORRY

We are a fearful society. We all have worries and fears to some degree. What are yours?

Tell me about a particular time you were afraid?

Remember to recall the Serenity Prayer. Whenever you are gripped by fear, and you can't talk yourself out of letting it go, try following these steps:

1. Expect, allow, and accept that fear will arise. Don't fight it. If you slam on the brakes, trying to hold off the feeling, it will come at you even harder. Breathe. Do a relaxation exercise.
2. When it comes, stop, wait, and let it be. Face it; don't try to escape. Just let it happen … sit it out. See that your worst fear, whatever it is, doesn't happen.

3. Focus on and do manageable things in the present. Decide what will work for you, like breathing, counting, singing a song, repeating a helpful mantra. Visualize a safe place. You have a choice in how you respond to fear.

4. Rate the intensity of the fear on a scale of 1–10. Notice it go down.

5. Function with fear and pat yourself on the back for not retreating.

6. Expect, allow, and accept that it will come back. Go through the steps again.

Your fear will gradually be reduced. The fear and denial of death is probably our society's number one fear and it prevents us from living fully. If we become extremely cautious and worried in life, we miss out on some valuable living.

Worry becomes an unwieldy suit of armor: Instead of protecting us, it weighs us down and keeps us from taking in the joys and blessings our life has to offer. The dangers we most fear rarely happen, and the unanticipated ones just come. So why worry? You can let yourself be swept away by a tidal wave of worry or can see it for what it is: a series of mental images that wreak havoc in your mind and make your insides do crazy flip-flops. Learn to step back, look at the worry, see it for what it is. Soon it begins to have less control over you.

> *Worry does not empty tomorrow's sorrow; it empties today of its strength.*
> —*Corrie ten Boom*

> *My life is full of disasters that never happened.*
> —*Mark Twain*

GUILT

Guilt is pervasive. A little guilt can be helpful, forcing you to do something that will make you like yourself better. But the great majority of guilt is worthless. People feel guilty for doing too much, for doing too little, for what they have or haven't said or done, and for what they even think about saying or doing. Balancing guilty feelings is very difficult for some people.

SOCIETAL GUILT: Society has its own guilt-producing norms. For instance, it is rare for a family not to feel guilty about placing a parent in a nursing care home, even when it is the best possible solution. A more recent "new age" phenomenon is to feel guilty or bad if you even get sick, not to mention getting old and dying.

> *Guilt is the gift that keeps on giving.*
> —*Irma Bombeck*

Advertisers and the media inundate the public with messages that say if you eat right, exercise, and think right, you won't get old, sick, or die. This is obviously untrue, and it only wastes valuable energy to feel guilty on top of feeling sick. The odds of your dying eventually are quite impressive—one out of one

CHURCH-RELATED GUILT: Another source of guilt is the church. "No ills befall the righteous and the wicked are filled with trouble." (Proverbs 12:21) People believe they are being punished when bad things befall them. A little of this kind of guilt can keep some people on the straight and narrow, but once again, carried to the extreme, simply doesn't fit the facts. The painful death of a child, a plane crash, an earthquake randomly happens in this imperfect world. Another favorite guilt-producer is, "This is a test. God only tests those who can bear it." Keep in mind three factors: nature is morally blind; people make poor choices; death is natural.

FAMILY-INDUCED GUILT: Some family systems are accomplished at heaping on guilt. The following example is a typical guilt-producing statement followed by a good assertive response. Mother: "Elsie's daughter comes every day to visit her." Daughter: "I know you would like to have me come more often. I wish I could. I come when I can."

SELF-INDUCED GUILT: "I should be doing more with my life." "I should have called Mother." "I should…" Your own "shoulds" are perhaps your largest source of guilt. Some level of this self-induced guilt is important for getting things done or keeping things in balance, but too much makes you unreasonably hard on yourself and even dysfunctional. ("I was too hard on John. Why can't I be more patient.") A common guilt when dealing with Alzhiemer's is, "I know it's her disease, but her repetitiveness drives me nuts." This is called being human. Ultimately, you are your own worst and best critic. The ability to forgive yourself is a skill that can be learned.

STRESS

Stress is caused by anything that throws your body out of homeostasis, out of balance. Exciting things cause stress as well as difficult things. The trigger doesn't even have to be an actual happening. Just worrying about something that might happen activates stress, which then activates hormones—adrenaline and corticosteroids. You have some control over this. You can learn how to relax. You can find a process that works for you, that you can employ at a moment's notice. Helpful mantras or sayings help you balance. Breathe deeply. Taking three breaths can change your physiology. Candace Pert[15] identified the endorphins, the monocytes, that make us happy. You can learn how to think yourself into emitting these helpful hormones. Positive thinking and reframing can be lifesavers. Our response to an event is more important than the event itself. One woman who is raped sees it as a terrible experience in her life but moves on; another woman with a very similar experience gets totally derailed and unable to function. We do not have to be victims. We can always work on how to respond to stressful situations so your relaxation technique becomes a quick and primary reaction.

Being able to communicate your feelings to someone by writing or talking is vitally important to relieving stress. Stress, depression, and loneliness are clinically interrelated. Dr. James Lynch, author of *A Cry Unheard: New Insights into the Medical Consequences of Loneliness,* believes that exercises to improve our communicative health must be undertaken with the same seriousness and commitment as our aerobic exercising. He warns that the techno world, like face-booking and text messaging, are cutting down on our younger generation's communication skills. Because they only interact in the seclusion of their rooms on their computers and cell phones, they are losing the ability to be one-to-one people-persons and to interact in a group.

Emotions and personality have an effect upon the functioning and health of virtually every cell in the body; stress is usually a factor. You cannot really understand a disease in a vacuum, but rather only in the context of the many variables the person suffering from that disease has. Older people, if stressed, take longer to get back to homeostasis. If an older persons gets cold or hot, it takes longer to reestablish body temperature. We live in a highly stressful society. Mimi Guaneri[16] said that 75–90% of doctor visits are stress-related, and she underscored that it is not the situation but how one perceives it. If you are unable to get your stress under control, it can be toxic to your heart. The most impressive study published in 2004, called Interheart[17], examined stress of various kinds at home and at work, in 24,767 people, and found that stress raised heart attack risk 2.5 times, almost as much as smoking and diabetes.

The next two parts of this book are about learning how to slow down and how to relax. If you want the last part of your life to be as good as it can be, you will want to learn these aspects of taking care of yourself.

SLOW DOWN

Later life is the time when we can slow down, get out of the fast lane, and take time to pause and reflect. Many people simply don't know how to do this. Busyness continues to be the norm reflected by the number of retirees who report feeling guilty about having time on their hands. Some actually need to *unlearn* keeping busy in order to discover the art of staying in balance. Some believe that retirement has now forced them into idleness. They accept the societal standard that the best time of life is over and that it is now time to wither on the vine. They are in trouble. They are the ones who could be headed toward depression.

> *Slow down so you can wake up.*

> *Mindfulness practice is simple and completely feasible. Just by sitting and doing nothing, we are doing a tremendous amount.*
> —Sakyong Mipham Rinpoche

Sometimes it is helpful to think of this time of life as you look at vacations. What shall I do today? What activities would make me feel good about myself? What have I always wanted to do that now I can make time for? Maybe I can make up for some regrets I have, like not "being there" enough as a parent. Perhaps I can spend more time with my grandchildren. Maybe it is time to attend to friendships that I have let slide. Retirement is a time to reflect on the way you choose to spend your time. Busyness will be fitting for some, but knowing how to slow down and relax is necessary for mental and emotional health. You can't knit in a hurry, fish in a hurry, or listen to music in a hurry. Making love in a hurry isn't nearly as much fun. Generally speaking, you don't become wise on the run.

DO 'NOTHING' PROUDLY

Taking time to do seemingly nothing and appreciating that time is one of the most important things we can do for ourselves, and it's the best modeling we can do for those fragmented people around us. I love that my grandchildren know that when I am out sitting silently on the deck early in the morning overlooking the lake, they must also be absolutely quiet out of respect for me and whatever it is that I am doing there. I don't know exactly what they are thinking about what I'm doing. They may just think that it is weird, but I love that they sit there quietly and wonder. I overheard one of them say to another back in the woods, "Don't go to the deck. Grandma is sitting there appreciating that she is alive." I smile. Maybe that *is* what's going on.

What am I doing? Sometimes I am staring at the water. Staring is good when it is alert staring. Or I'm watching and listening to the birds, wondering how it would be to be gliding through the sky, feeling the updrafts and downdrafts. I'm absorbing the eerie and magical call of the loons. I'm wondering about the world of the fish under the surface of the water. I'm hearing the sounds of nature, noticing the sparkles on the water. I am paying total attention. I am practicing in nature how I would like to be full time. It is practicing being fully alert and present to every precious moment.

Whenever you are totally absorbed in what you are doing, whether it be knitting, crocheting, listening to another, working on a project, puttering, reading, walking, swimming, bird watching, cooking, eating, listening to beautiful music, gardening, you are living life fully in the moment. This may appear to be "nothing" but is actually the practice of "being." This is calming and stabilizing for your mind. In this state of non-doing, you are purely being who you are and feeling what you feel.

We are normally multi-tasking. When we are driving a car, we may be also talking to a passenger, or thinking about other things than our driving. If we practice being mindful, we are being present and alert. Mindfulness allows more coherence and lessens your stress by turning off outside stimuli. Whenever you are able to be fully in the present, whether it is eating slowly, and appreciating every nuance of what you're experiencing, or sitting quietly focusing on your breath. Read about mindfulness in the books of many teachers such as Jon Kabat-Zinn, Jack Kornfield, and Sharon Salzberg who have jointly been attributed with playing a significant role in bringing the practice to a new audience.

LEARN TO BE STILL AND RELAX

Take time every day to be quiet with yourself in a very focused way. If possible, make a healing place for yourself—a place where you won't be disturbed by noises from the outside, people, or telephones. Gather touchstones—comforting and empowering objects. These can be pictures of special people, places, or happenings, beautiful words or quotes meaningful to you. The touchstones might be favorite gifts, articles of clothing, or items that are symbolic in some way for you. Select mood prompters such as special books, music that delights your soul, candles, fragrances. You can choose to ask that others not enter this special place. It can be a part of your residence or a spot in nature.

We must find peace...

Many people report that retreating to nature is one of the easiest and most enjoyable ways to calm

Even the hurricane is quiet in the eye
Buried ever so deep in its heart is the
stillness found
A nucleus that is mysteriously calm.
Engulfed in the hurry, worry, hubbub of
our day
When everyone is flying aimlessly in all
directions
Try to find a silence of your own.
Discover your personal bit of inner peace
And cherish every minute.
—Tammy Felton[18] *(permission granted)*

themselves. Absorb the ways in which you can relate to the earth. You smell the freshness of the air, the musty richness of the soil, the sweetness of the flowers. You observe the changes of seasons and times of more light- ness, more darkness. When you are in true wilderness, you adjust your schedule to the rhythms of nature. You are not in control. You adapt. You adjust your patterns to the weather and the availability of light. You might say to yourself?

> *Let my mind become silent*
> *and my thoughts come to rest.*
> *I want to see*
> *all that is before me.*
> *In self-forgetfulness*
> *I become everything*
> *I can see everything.*
> *—Author unknown*

Create rituals to revere whatever it is in nature that you find most awesome. One woman told me that she liked to sit or lie down on the earth, cover herself with grass or moss or leaves, and absorb her connec- tion to the earth. Another prefers to clutch a special rock, a tight little bundle of energy that has sur- vived for centuries, appreciating that it signifies permanence and exudes solidness and strength. Some like to gaze at clouds with their ever-changing personalities.

RELAXATION EXERCISES

1. Sit quietly with yourself. A life-giving practice is one that focuses on your breathing. Breathe from your diaphragm. Breathe from your heart. I like to say on my inhalation "this moment" and on my exhalation "only moment" or substitute "holy moment" or "beautiful moment." Dedicate special time to this form of self-care. If you can give yourself one peaceful moment, it can't help but influence the next moment.

When you are sitting quietly with yourself, thoughts inevitably appear. Observe them … and then return to thinking about your breath and this particular moment. Thoughts just keep coming. Observe them and then practice returning to your breath. We all have pain and wor- ries; it is part of being human. But we can deal with moments. We can deal with this moment. We don't have to carry the worries, the planning about the future or the pains of the past into this very moment. Our goal is to recognize that we can move from whatever difficult thoughts and feelings we have, to peaceful moments. Being able to shift back to the moment anytime that you are feeling stressed is a transformative tool for your well-being. With practice, inten- tional breathing can become a way of being. Years ago, when I was working with individuals and families in severe stress, I learned intuitively that it helped me to pause before entering the room, take three deep breaths, and say to myself something like, "I do not have to fix any- thing. I only have to be present with them."

2. Be still and peaceful. You don't really have to have a special place. It is best to be able to calm yourself anywhere, in a traffic jam or in a dentist chair, by concentrating on your breath- ing and repeating relaxing phrases. Repeat "gentle" slowly—inhale "gen," exhale "tle." Walking is a wonderful way to feel peaceful. A favorite focusing phrase while walking is to simply repeat to yourself, "Still … ness, still … ness, still … ness" or "Peace … ful, peace … ful, peace … ful."

3. Find a spot in the sun, either outside or inside by a window. Stand on your tiptoes and stretch your arms as far as you can. Put your hands on your waist and twist, first to one side, then the next. Relax in a comfortable standing posture, torso erect, knees relaxed, and hands cupped in front of your hips. Focus on your breathing. Breathe in; draw the energy up from the earth toward the sky, lifting your arms, palms up, in an arc, straight in front of you. Breathe out; lower your arms to your side, bringing the energy from the heavens into your body. Repeat several times. Become the conduit between earth and sky. Feel the energy. Breathe in as you lift your arms, palms up, to the sky again. Embrace the air and the sun's rays. Know you are part of the universe. Breathe out, lowering your arms and drawing the sun's warmth to you; let it bathe your body.

How you choose to relax has to fit for you. Some guys go fishing. Some sit down, put their feet up, and have a beer. Some stretch out and listen to carefully chosen music.

What fits for you? How do you relax?

TIME MANAGEMENT

How do you spend your time?

	Not Enough	Enough	Too Much
Alone	❑	❑	❑
With people you care about	❑	❑	❑
With people you don't like	❑	❑	❑
On spiritual endeavors (praying, meditating, contemplating)	❑	❑	❑
Volunteering, helping others	❑	❑	❑
Working for pay	❑	❑	❑
Reading	❑	❑	❑
Watching television	❑	❑	❑
Listening to music/radio	❑	❑	❑
Going to church/synagogue	❑	❑	❑
Caregiving	❑	❑	❑
Shopping/errands	❑	❑	❑
Doing activities of daily living (preparing food, eating)	❑	❑	❑
Looking for things	❑	❑	❑
Walking/hiking	❑	❑	❑
Gardening	❑	❑	❑
Fishing/hunting	❑	❑	❑
Watching birds	❑	❑	❑
Traveling	❑	❑	❑
Exercising	❑	❑	❑
Other?	❑	❑	❑

What can you do to change the "not enough" and "too much" to "enough"? Other? What can you do to change the "not enough" and "too much" to "enough"?

Review for yourself what nourishes you. Some people report that it is walking in nature; others find that tending a garden, playing the piano, listening to music, caring for a friend, playing with grandchildren, puttering around the house. Whatever it is, you must take time for it. Plan more time into your schedule for it. Reinforce its importance to you by writing or talking out loud about it and how you find it uplifting.

THRIVING OR SURVIVING?

Robert Butler and Myrna Lewis in *Aging and Mental Health* describe good mental health in old age as the ability to thrive rather than just survive. You spend a certain percentage of your life doing important survival tasks, some pleasurable, others not. In order to live fully, plan time for truly thriving. Estimate how you spend your time and rearrange the tasks in the appropriate thriving or surviving category. Or perhaps this is a Doing/Being chart? What is pleasure for one isn't necessarily that for another (e.g., preparing meals). Monitor yourself for a week. Total up the number of hours, and divide by seven days to determine your average time spent thriving or surviving.

Time Log	*M*	*T*	*W*	*Th*	*F*	*Sa*	*S*	*Total Average*
Survival Tasks								
Eating, preparing meals								
Personal care								
Sleeping								
Shopping								
Errands								
Housework chores								
Looking for something								
Working								
Other								
Thriving								
Meditating, praying, centering								
Working for pleasure								
Volunteering								
Loving, being a friend								
Reading								
Participating in games, sports								
Traveling								
Hobbies								
Other								

Can you increase the number of hours dedicated to thriving?

CREATE YOUR IDEAL DAY

Using the previous charts as guides, pattern out an ideal day and think of how much time you would allocate to each.

# of minutes

How would you like to start your day?
What would you do to feel good about yourself?

Who would you like to see?
Where would you like to go?

How much time would you like to be alone?

What would be the right amount of exercising?
What kind of exercise would suit you? When?

How much time do you spend with activities of daily living?
(eating, bathing, cleaning, chores, doing errands)
How would you like to end the day?

Recognizing that this is just one day, expand this notion of an ideal day into generalizing about what a week, a month would look like. Decide what percentage of your time you would like to spend on various activities.

You have a lot to say about how the last third of your life will go. You can see it as a time of great transition and opportunity, a time to remove the filters and masks you may have put in place when you were younger, a time to heal wounds, a time to reap the benefits that you've worked so hard for, a time to enjoy hard-earned pleasures, and finally, a time to make choices that will help build meaning into your life. It can be a time when the spirit and meaning thrives. It can be a time of continued learning and new growth, the hallmarks of health at any age. You have choices to make about how you spend your time. There is increasing acknowledgment that the goal of finding meaning and making sense of your life is at least as awesome a project as any challenges or gifts that come with your earlier years. If you have been dreading this time of life, thinking of it as a time of loss and regression, it's time to reframe this belief. Do it now.

> *This is the best time of my life. I love being old. Why is it good to be old? Because I am more myself than I ever have been … I am happier, more balanced … and better able to use my powers.*
> —*May Sarton*[19] **At Seventy**

MAINTAIN A HEALTHY LIFESTYLE
Take Care of Your One and Only Body

This quote is especially poignant because Matthew is a paraplegic. But it applies to us all. Love and care for your body. It has carried you through a lot. You don't abandon old friends or expect them to be smooth and perfect. When things start to go wrong, don't jump to "It's all over now." Don't give up on yourself. Amazing things are being done for our bodies—heart bypasses, body part replacements, organ replacements. I, for one, am a titanium lady, practically bionic, having had two hips and one knee replaced. Be deeply grateful for what can be fixed and work lovingly with your body and attitude to deal in the best possible way with whatever is handed to you. It's a fact that as you age you lose flexibility, muscle mass, and strength, and this leads to different degrees of loss of mobility and independence. It is also a fact that regular 1) aerobic exercise, 2) balance and flexibility exercises, and 3) strength training can counter this inevitability. Even if you have physical limitations, there are safe ways to exercise. Jane Brody quotes Dr. Miriam E. Nelson[21], who is director of the John Hancock Center for Physical Activity and Nutrition at Tufts University in Boston, as saying, "with every increasing decade of age, people become less and less active. But the evidence shows that, with every increasing decade, exercise becomes more important in terms of quality of life, independence, and living a full life." It is never too late to start a good fitness program. I recently met a 102-year-old woman who started exercising at the age of 98 when she moved to a facility with a warm pool, a weight room, and helpful trainers to guide her. Her health has steadily improved! Studies are in agreement that "you use it or lose it" whether talking about physical exercise or stretching yourself mentally.

> *The mind and body I have are the only mind and body I have. They deserve my attention*
> —*Matthew Sanford*[20]

Eat healthy foods. Research is advising us to eat lots of fruits and vegetables, whole grain, high fiber foods, and to avoid saturated fats, decrease salt or sugar, moderate the amount of protein, and drink enough

> *Intentionally nourish yourself.*

water. There is agreement that taking a multi-vitamin and additional Omega-3's are good ideas. Studies and diets galore suggest what is best for you. My husband says, "if you are patient, they will come up with a study saying that what you, in particular, like to do or eat is good for you." At this writing, he's happy that coffee and dark chocolate are on the to-do list. Many like the study that says, "Three naps a week may help your heart." Specifically that report from the Harvard School of Public Health says that those who took at least a thirty-minute nap three times a week were 37% less likely to die from heart disease. It is advised to take a midday nap. The study doesn't mention the tried and true ways to help your heart—like maintaining a healthy weight, blood pressure, and cholesterol level, and not smoking.

For more information on food and nutrition go to:

- www.nutrition.gov
- USDA Food and Nutrition Service, www.fns.usda.gov
- MedlinePlus from National Library of Medicine, www.medlineplus.gov
- www.MyPyramid.gov (an interactive website that helps one learn about good exercise and food choices for yourself).

We need enough sleep. The amount varies from individual to individual. With our vision and balance a little more iffy, we need to be more careful about not falling. Get rid of throw rugs to trip over, put non-slip adhesive in the bathtub, buy and put nightlights around the house, and wear crampons when walking on the ice (for those of us in the north country). There are differences between mid-and late life.

The focus of this book is more on your inner fitness, the emotional and spiritual realms of your being, your attitude. But the importance of how you take care of your self physically cannot be separated from the rest. The tendency is not to notice or appreciate the wondrous fluidity and balance of your body until something doesn't work quite right. It's the something that is out of kilter, whether physical, mental, or emotional, that gets attention. We are getting smarter about looking at our whole self. Good health is a matter of a tranquil spirit as well as a fit body. More and more older adults want to participate in maintaining their health beyond just going to the doctor and are choosing to participate in various sorts of wellness and fitness programs. Whether you're healthy or not is determined by your genes, your economic situation, and an assortment of variables, but much is determined by your decisions and how you choose to think and live—as the studies discussed earlier in this chapter verify. People of all ages are reaching beyond conventional western medicine. They are exercising, watching their diet, and exploring complementary and alternative therapies. Older adults want to participate more in maintaining their health.

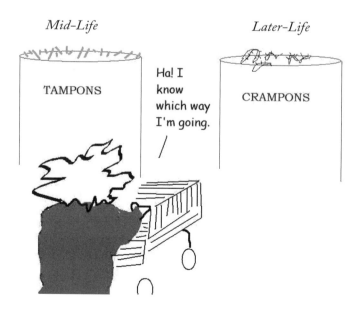

Mid-Life

TAMPONS

Ha! I know which way I'm going.

Later-Life

CRAMPONS

CHECK OUT YOUR OPTIONS.

Integrative Medicine is an approach to healing that combines treatments from conventional medicine with complementary approaches for which there is increasingly high-quality evidence of safety and effectiveness. These therapies are of interest to people who feel hesitant about drugs, especially those treating or preventing musculoskeletal conditions or other chronic aches and recurring pains. Complementary therapies are another way for older adults to address the powerlessness they feel when a doctor says, "There's nothing more I can do to help. You're getting older and these things happen!" Older people want to be active, to be part of their own healing. We know by now that what we think has a tremendous effect on our bodies, and that if we change what we think, our body changes.

Less than 20% of the world's population is being serviced by western allopathic doctors.[22] Western medicine has focused on treatment that "cures" and is deemed effective when a patient is restored to health. This way of thinking goes along with the dominate-and-control values characteristic of mid-life that were discussed in Chapter Two. Complementary therapies focus on "healing," which means restoring a wholeness of body, mind, emotions, and spirit.

Older adults are well aware that they will die before too long and want to live their remaining years in the healthiest way possible. To be "healed" is a spiritual concept. Complementary techniques offer the aging population a degree of personal caring and attention that our western doctors are only beginning to emulate. There is much to be respected and learned from both approaches. The hospice movement is leading the way in preparing us to think more wholistically about the end of life. Medical schools are beginning to offer more courses on listening, communicating, and integrative techniques.

Western medicine is high tech and emphasizes acute care, focusing on diagnosis, treatment, and cure. Millions of elderly have chronic illness and are dealing with the gradual physical diminishments that come with late life. They don't want to rely solely on western medicines options of surgery or medications. They know you don't cure old age. Complementary care options look more at the whole person. These practitioners take more time to listen to their clients, providing more choices and additional tools to help their clients participate in their own physical and emotional well-being. This kind of mind-body-spirit connection and healing involves far more than curing.

Older adults are actively involved with chiropractors, acupuncturists, nutritionists, massage therapists, meditators, energy workers, moving meditation specialists who teach yoga, TaiChi, Qigong, and the many exercise programs available now in the YMCA and YWCA's and other fitness centers. Healing involves improving your lifestyle to make your quality of life better. While our first choice remains being cured of a disease and returned to a life with high quality, the reality for the majority of us living a long time is that our physical body takes more of our time and focus. Older adults are turning to complementary therapies when conventional medicine no longer has any answers for them or appears ineffective. An increasing number of physicians make referrals to these therapies, but many others remain close-minded and not knowledgeable about the options and successes of these approaches to health. Complementary medicine is often rejected because the efficacy of the treatments has not been demonstrated through double-blind randomized controlled trials. Patients are interested and are drawn to these alternative therapies when the word gets out that they work. This seems to be proof enough of the efficacy of the treatment. It is as important to monitor these therapies and to check out the reputation of the practitioners, as it is to pick a regular doctor. The trend toward use of these complementary therapies is exploding and is evidenced across the country.

In my city of Minneapolis, for instance, there are several notable examples:

1. Pathways is a health resource center for healing that has been in existence since 1988 providing programs designed to support a creative healing response to illness. Pathways affirms that healing occurs at physical, emotional, and spiritual levels. Persons who are ailing (families, friends, and caregivers) are encouraged to explore new possibilities. The group and one-on-one sessions run the gamut, from meditation, Qigong, energy therapies, emotional support, imagery, to classes like Renewing Life, Choices, and Imaging Immortality. The impressive thing is that Pathways is a volunteer-sustained, non-profit resource center, offering services free-of-charge by over 120 providers who volunteer two to sixteen hours per month. I'm proud to have been one of them for the last thirteen years.

2. The Penny George Institute for Health and Healing at Abbott Northwestern Hospital in Minneapolis, both for in-patients and at an outpatient clinic. It blends the best of conventional medicine with healing philosophies and a variety of healing therapies. These therapies, often drawn from other medical traditions, emphasize caring for the whole person and focus on healing as much as curing. The therapies include acupuncture, aromatherapy, biofeedback, energy healing, guided imagery, healing touch, nutritional consultation, massage, reflexology, herbal consultation, therapeutic yoga, healing coaches, and spiritual guidance. An eight-week course called Resilience Training includes being checked out by both a nutritionist and an exercise physiologist, and provides suggestions for tools to change a clients consciousness by thinking differently.

3. The University of Minnesota's Department of Spirituality and Healing offers a graduate minor in complementary therapies and healing practices, a post-baccalaureate certificate program and health coaching track, study-abroad, numerous continuing education programs and online learning. The Center provides health-care professionals, students, and the greater community access to the latest approaches in complementary and alternative health-care education. The Department of Spirituality and Healing has been a great community asset in sponsoring conferences and bringing in notable speakers.

The world is getting smaller thanks to technology. We are becoming more aware of the beliefs and medical practices of traditional cultural groups that have been practicing for centuries. There is Ayurvedic medicine, a branch of traditional Indian Medicine, which emphasizes the principle of biologic individuality. Native American spirituality was and is still practiced by our country's first inhabitants. Traditional Chinese Medicine (TCM) looks at underlying causes of imbalance and patterns of disharmony. Many, many healing approaches fall into the category of complementary or alternative therapies[23].

Meditative practices include:

a. Transcendental meditation is where you sit comfortably, close eyes, breathe naturally, and repeat to yourself a mantra, word, or phrase enabling you to sink into a state of deep absorption, free of your worries. Studies suggest that this practice reduces stress and lowers blood pressure.

b. Mindfulness meditation involves sitting comfortably and focusing on your breathing, allowing the thoughts that inevitably come to your mind to pass through as you return your attention on your breathing. Much emphasis is on what is happening moment to moment. There's evidence that this practice helps with chronic pain and depression and retrains your thinking process.

c. TaiChi is a moving meditation that incorporates slow continuous movements that help balance the energy of the body.

d. Yoga emphasizes breathing techniques and specific postures (-asanas). There are many schools and approaches, some more physical than others, but the goal is total absorption with the process and release from your day-to-day thoughts.

Energy medicine practices include Reiki, therapeutic touch, Qigong, homeopathy, and acupuncture.

Body structure and function practices (The philosophy that improving the structure and functioning of your body will improve health and treat disease) include:

a. The body workers—massage, Rolfing, Feldenkrais, Trager, Alexander Technique

b. Chiropractic medicine—works on the misalignment of bones

c. Osteopathy—focuses on musculoskeletal components of the body, the interrelationship of structure and function using soft-tissue techniques and cranial sacral manipulation.[23]

Expanding your idea of the many ways of taking care of yourself, your whole being, is one of the several areas of choice that can help you on your journey to finishing well. Which of the above practices have you tried? Which are of interest to you?

LIFE IS A BALANCING ACT

A recurring theme in taking caring of yourself and developing a beneficial attitude is learning the fine art of staying in balance. Finding the balancing point between the following tensions and questions is a major developmental task of older adults. There are no easy answers.

Want to do something useful, but	want to enjoy my freedom.
How can I contribute without	being tied down?
Want to exercise, but	what is enough? Too much?

Want to appear capable and independent, but	maybe it's time to get a little help?
Want to keep doing all that I have been, but	is it time to let go of some things?
Feel like slowing down, but	maybe it's better for me to keep pushing?
Needing to "do" to feel good, so	is just "being" really enough?
Want to be careful, yet independent, so	does using a cane make me dependent? or more independent?
Want to have control, so	is "letting go" losing or gaining control?
Want people around, but	would like more solitude?
Want to stay in bed, but	what's best for my body?
Want my views respected, so	should I stick to my guns or keep quiet when I'm pretty dependent on their help?
Want to keep driving my car, but	is it responsible with my failing eyesight and slower reaction time?
Want to feel all my feelings, but	when am I wallowing? What is too much?
Like "doing nothing proudly," but	when am I doing nothing too proudly?
Can't do some things for myself very easily, but	how do I know what I should keep trying to do, if even a bit more slowly? When should I hand things over?
Want to be helpful to my ailing spouse, but	am I hovering … doing too much?
If I "accept" his/her terminal prognosis,	does it mean that I am giving up hope?
I want to remain in my house even if I am getting more more forgetful, but	how do I know when safety is more important than my autonomy?

Balancing one's life is a delicate business and important to think about. We respond differently depending on our particular set of circumstances. Every situation carries its own variables and each one carries its own subjective weight. There's an endless number of examples that have us hovering between the extremes. What do you find you are trying to balance right now? Which of the above are you pondering?

The balancing act between complementary and opposing forces is a fluid and dynamic on-going task of old age. What's too much? What's enough? Constantly walking this tightrope between these tensions takes artfulness and patience learned through the range and depth of your experiences. Every one of the tensions listed has variables that play into a decision. For example, think of the variety of issues that might be involved in the autonomy vs. safety issue:

1. How intensely does a man in failing health treasure his privacy, his ability to do things his way? Does he understand the risks? Some people choose to risk; others don't.

2. What is this woman's boredom level? Will she be perfectly content to do less because of her physical limitations, or will she want to try doing some things that may involve risk, because she values stimulation more than safety? Perhaps she is seeking a controlled life, one with little variation but also little chance of embarrassment or disappointment. Or maybe she values spontaneity and excitement and could care less about what other people might think?

3. Does this person live in an apartment? Would leaving the burners on cause danger to others?

4. Driving is important to this person, but is his driving a risk to other people's lives?

These are just a few of the myriad of complex situations that have to be individually evaluated. You need to be perfectly honest with yourself. What can you still do? What can you no longer do? What's important to you? It is often a balancing act between becoming passive and overprotecting yourself, thus surrendering more physical capacity, overdoing and pushing yourself to do more than your body can handle. What is just the right amount of activity?

> *The crucial task of age is finding your balancing point.*

> *Jack Benny balanced his guilt after receiving an award by saying, "I don't deserve this award but I have arthritis and I don't deserve that either."*

Almost everything involves finding your balancing point, the serious matters and the not so serious.

Think about the areas in which you might want to move more toward the center. Do you live every day as if it's your last, or do you save your money on the chance you'll live twenty more years? Do you work too hard, or do you slow down to smell the roses so full time that you don't get anything done? What's too much? What's not enough? We are always teetering one way or the other:

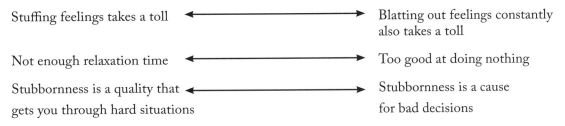

Stuffing feelings takes a toll	⟷	Blatting out feelings constantly also takes a toll
Not enough relaxation time	⟷	Too good at doing nothing
Stubbornness is a quality that gets you through hard situations	⟷	Stubbornness is a cause for bad decisions

DEVELOP YOUR OWN TOOLKIT

This is your very own personalized balancing kit. It's best to keep this kit in a separate journal or scrapbook. You need this kit because it is hard to think of the positives when you are bummed out. When you are feeling good about yourself, get busy filling up this journal with things that will snap you back into shape when you aren't feeling too well. If you aren't a writer, pick someone to help you. Write down stories from your life that you find uplifting. You won't remember them when you are down, so get them on paper. Make it a humor journal, too, recording funny things that have happened or jokes that give you a kick. Every time you hear or recall a story that entertains you, write it down. Nothing can whip you out of the doldrums like a good laugh, and no one knows better than you what lightens you up.

If you completed Chapter One of this book, you probably rediscovered memories or, if you reflected on what gives meaning to your life in Chapter Three, you can use some of those insights. Recall your peak moments. Always keep in mind something you would like to do. We all need things to look forward to … at any age. Recall how you have coped with and survived rough times, demonstrating a strength and courage that may have surprised you, or a tenacity that kept you plugging along. Keep a running collection of quotes, poems, or phrases that make sense to you and could help you get back on track. Name the things you have done in life of which you are proud. Describe how your children have turned out, the friends you have had, particular accomplishments, bounce-backs from hard times, and good choices you have made.

What was your most exciting time? Describe it. When you are feeling gloomy, treat yourself as you would an ailing friend in a time of trauma—seek out comfort food, rest, surround yourself with warmth, whether that comes in the form of chosen people, your favorite music, or a book. Make a list of these favorites, and add to it any time you have a new idea. Add pictures, letters, and cards you have received.

The more aware you are of the beauty in your life, the more beautiful your life will feel.

Focus on those things you are thankful for, and make an ongoing gratitude list. A good practice is to think every night, as you drift off to sleep, of three things that happened that day for which you are grateful. This not only helps you exit the day in a fine mood, but, if it becomes a habit, keeps you looking for your three things for your nightly check-in. It's also good practice to have something on your agenda to look forward to that you can focus on.

If you have favorite prayers or meditations either put them in your toolkit journal or have them handy. Your tool kit will be powerful because you create it and you know what works for you. Ask someone to help you put it together. It is a delightful project.

> **Titles for parts of your toolkit could be:**
> Gratitude journal
> Humor journal
> Favorites:
> > Things to do that give me pleasure
> > Sayings
> > Music

Food

Games

Places to go

People I have loved and why

Inspiration:

Prayers

Meditations

Spiritual words to ponder

Poems

Things in my life I treasure

Affirming statements

The following are some written statements that have helped some group participants to see clearly:

I gave an assignment to a group to make some "Today, I …" statements. Here are a few:

- Today, I don't have to carry burdens alone. I can ask for help from (Jesus, Buddha, Mary, my higher power, my doctor, an organization, health service, a friend).
- Today, I am going to put positive thoughts in my mind. I will focus on all the possibilities instead of what I can't do.
- Today, I will be a good listener.
- Today, I will treat myself exactly how I want to be treated.
- Today, I will use my energy in the most fulfilling way possible.
- Today, I will find things to do that will make me like myself.
- Today is a new beginning. I will live it well.
- Today, I will let Joe know that I respect him and why I do. I tried his idea and it worked!
- Today, I am going to tell my friend Delores how much I like being with her, how comfortable she makes me feel.
- Today, I'm going to focus on being thankful for what I can still do instead of being preoccupied with what doesn't work right.
- Today, I can brighten up my day by thinking of ways to brighten up someone else's day.
- Today, I will focus on today, not worry about the future.
- Today, I will be fully present with whomever I am with.
- Today, I will call one friend to let her know I am thinking of her.
- Similarly I ask people to list some "May I" statements that work for them. This is a simple form of prayer or meditation. It is recommended that you make up your own, ones that fit for you.
- May I accept myself as I am.

> *I know how to take care of myself. I will take time to reflect on the good things in my life every morning, listen to my favorite music, allow my body to relax every afternoon, and make sure that I will do at least one thing every day that gives me pleasure.*
> —*Jane*
>
> *I know myself. I know that I only have so much energy and, like money in a savings account, I have to be careful how much I withdraw and use. I have to decide each day how to best invest my precious energy.*
> —*Mary Anne*
>
> *I'm going to make this getting old look good. I won't fake it. I will let younger people see the difficulties also, but I am going to model the best possible take on this time of life.*
> —*Sue*

- May I have fresh eyes to see the beauty around me and see life as an adventure.
- May I know that my happiness and unhappiness depend largely on my actions and inactions, not on forces outside myself.
- May I befriend suffering and let it deepen my wisdom and compassion.
- May I appreciate and focus on what I have versus what I don't have.
- May I practice peace and loving and use my voice and actions for good.
- May I tend to the earth reverently and do my part to leave it a better place.
- May I relax in the presence of what is … whatever it is.
- May I take time every day to be still with myself and focus on how I am blessed.
- May I do what I must do with dignity and a positive attitude.
- May I keep my heart and mind open.
- May I remember the ways I have coped with hard times and acknowledge that I am strong.
- May I choose the best option available to me.
- May I rest in the knowledge that I can handle whatever comes.
- May I continually work on my attitude knowing that I can choose how I think.
- May I be gentle with myself.
- May I acknowledge that surprises happen; how I respond is my choice.
- May I move beyond the feelings of inadequacy, shame, and self-doubt that I have learned so well and learn to trust that I can now let light into my life.

Borrow any of these or make up your own list. What ones appeal to you?

CONCLUSION

"How do I make my life as good as it can be? " We have much to say about how our lives work out, even taking into account the many surprises that happen. Even those of us who have resisted enculturation find that we have swallowed our parents or our society's script for how we are to live life. Most of us have an idea or an expectation of what life will be like. Some of us will be able to stick fairly close to the "plan," but many of us will hit bumps in the road of various magnitudes, get or make opportunities for ourselves inconceivable to our imagination. Only through learning from our experiences and adjusting to what life brings will our limiting illusory beliefs be revealed. Then we can sort these things out for ourselves, finally becoming our own person. This is *our* life and *our* spiritual journey.

The older we get, the more we see that many events and experiences cannot be controlled, and, they are not given to easy handling by scientific knowledge or professional expertise. The art of living is handling the uncalculated by developing a way of being that best helps us go with the flow, no matter what kind of hand we are dealt. We can plan, learn about, and choose among the many options available, check out what seems to work best for others who have already made the journey, work on our attitudes, and practice the art of taking care of ourselves emotionally, spiritually, and physically.

> *You live that you may learn love.*
> *You love that you may learn to live.*
> *No other lesson is required.*
> —*author unknown*

We can figure out what makes life meaningful for us, what nourishes and sustains us. We can create a toolkit for ourselves that can help us stay in balance. We can become good stewards for ourselves.

We are a work in progress until we die. We can choose to discard some of life's conditioning and adapt new ways-of-being. Many of the bumps in the road can eventually be viewed at a distance and serve as signs for seeing more clearly. This section of the book provided a roadmap for helping us make the final chapters of our life as good as they can be.

> *Self-care in never a selfish act.*
> *—Parker Palmer* [24]

Chapter 5

What Ways-of-Being
Lead to Being Wiser?

"Real isn't how you are made," said the Skin Horse.
"It's a thing that happens to you."
"Does it hurt?" asked the Rabbit.
"Sometimes," said the Skin Horse, for he was always truthful.
"When you are Real, you don't mind being hurt. It doesn't often happen to people who break easily, or have sharp edges, or who have to be carefully kept. Generally, by the time you are Real, most of your hair has been loved off, and your eyes drop out, and you get loose in the joints and very shabby. But these things don't matter at all, because once you are Real, you can't be ugly, except to people who don't understand."
—Margery Williams',
The Velveteen Rabbit

Certain ways-of-being appear repetitively in older adults who seem to be thriving in old age. These people seem to be authentic, comfortable with paradox, flexible, hopeful, humble, able to befriend mystery, have a sense of humor, and recognize grace when it happens. These are often the wise ones.

BE AUTHENTIC

It is important to be yourself, to be real.

We don't have to wait until we get in bad shape to be real. We can be real now. Our lives often take us by surprise. We are more unscripted than we ever dreamed. Our illusory beliefs are revealed through experience, and then, we can finally become real, our own person, feeling an intimate communion with who we are and how we fit into the whole picture. When we become consistent with ourselves, the person the outer world sees is pretty much the same person we see. Becoming real is part of our spiritual journey. It is about accepting who we are, the warts and all.

There's not a perfect one amongst us. We may envy people who seem perfect but we probably don't feel close to them. We feel closest to people who know us inside and out, pluses and minuses, and still love us. We have a better-self and a smaller-self. I like it when friends share some of their small-self realness with me; they are being very human and honest, which is preferable to being false and nice. Not one of us is always cheerful and put-together. We love who we love because of their flaws as well as their finer qualities. The trick is accepting ourselves as we are and working toward being our better-self more of the time. You have fears, insecurities, weaknesses and strengths. People want to see the real you.

With whom have you been able to be real? Who have you allowed to really know you?

BE COMFORTABLE WITH PARADOX

Many become more comfortable with paradox. We are better able to embrace holding two apparently contradictory ideas, facts, beliefs, or feelings at the same time. In so doing, we open ourselves up to better experience the richness of life and its many nuances. Instead of seeing everything in dualities, dividing things into two piles to choose between … light/dark, male/female, spirit/ matter, good/bad, black/white, right/wrong … we are often able to see the complexity of the situation.

"Being" vs. "doing" is often presented dualistically as though a decision has to be made between one or the other. Anyone who loves what they are doing and feels fulfilled by it is doing and being at the same time. There's a spectrum. Some "doing" has no "being" in it, but is perhaps necessary, like having an okay job because it pays the bills. Other "doing" is loaded with "being" at the same time. Being is a relational term. Old people may no longer be able to "do" some activities but have a vital inner life. They can be more compassionate because they know life can be tough. They can see that a man may be a lousy husband but a good father or vice versa.

> *Life has changed me greatly, it has improved me greatly, but it also left me practically the same. I cannot spell, I am over critical, egocentric and vulnerable. I cannot be simple. In my effort to be clear I become complicated. I know my faults so well that I pay them small heed. They are stronger than I am. They are me.*
> —Florida Scott-Maxwell,
> ***The Measure of My Days***[2]

> *When we are able to "let go," we are more in control. When we accept ourselves as we are, we can change.*

Later life is a time of reconciliation of opposites, a time to hold the contradiction of living with pain and sorrow and at the same time you can be enjoying beauty and treasuring what you still have. We recognize the double feelings, sadness at our body's loss of ability to do some things it used to be able to do, and thankfulness for not having to do some of the things you used to have to do. We know the feeling of pride in the accomplishments of a daughter, and sadness that this will take her to a new job far away geographically. Double feelings become familiar to us. Our hearts can be very full, cracked open with a great range of feelings.

When we experience wrenching grief, we can also recognize the glory of this grief, having had the privilege of having loved so intensely. Our tears track this confusion, bursting forth in times of sadness and stress, leaking out when we feel great pride, surprising us when we are overwhelmed by some work of beauty, like witnessing the miracle of the birth of a baby. We learn to live with the full range of feelings and with the ambiguity as well. We get better with this the longer we live. I remember my recognition of this phenomena, the awesomeness of trying to understand this mixture of feelings that I was having early in my career. I had just left a hospital, after spending time with an old man I had grown to love who was dying. His "I love you" sat in my heart, along with such sadness. Such fullness. Such grace.

Double feelings abound in all aspects of our lives:

Sadness while feeling thankful

Frustration with church though it remains important to you

Frustration with actions taken by your country but loving it fiercely

Hating war but wanting to support the troops

Anger, fear, and love for a child you're worried about

Wanting your children around but knowing the importance of letting them go.

Think of examples in your life where you hold paradoxical beliefs or feelings:

BEFRIEND MYSTERY

Mystery, by definition, cannot be known or understood. The older we get the more we see that many events and experiences are not given to easy handling by scientific knowledge, that we live with questions and more questions. Atrocities and suffering, as well as the precious and pleasurable, fall under the umbrella of mystery. The "will to live" is mystery. It can't be measured and yet is recognized as more important often than anything measurable. It is difficult to live gracefully in this unruly world. It takes resilience and the ability to be creative with whatever is handed to us. The surprises often turn into opportunities for great leaps forward, even transformation.

To many, the concept of mystery will always be considered somewhat un-American. It comes too close to saying "I don't know," which indicates, in this culture, a state of inadequacy. Our society values control and knowledge when in reality life often sweeps over us and gives us many surprises. This tension between not knowing and wanting to have some answers makes life challenging at any age.

Richard Bresnahan, a master potter at St. John's University in Collegeville, Minnesota, gave me an amazing metaphor for life. While we were admiring a beautiful work of art, he said to me, "You know, one third of this vase is the result of the quality of the clay from which it is made, one-third is the vision, the design, and the craft of the artist, and one-third is the mystery of the fire." St. John's has the largest wood-burning kiln in the United States, and when the carefully crafted works of art are placed in the kiln during its once-a-year firing, the artist is allowing the fire to have its way with the treasured item. Maybe this fits for the lives of humans. One-third of how we turn out has to do with our DNA, our experiences, and how we are raised. One third is the

> *You must not understand life; only then will it become a feast. And let each day happen to you like a child who comes along and lets herself be showered with blossoms. To gather them up to save never enters the mind of a child. She lets them go from out of her hair and holds with open outstretched hands her dear young years to whatever will come next.*
> —*Rainier Maria Rilke*

vision we have for our lives, how well we take care of ourselves, our attitude and everything else I talk about in this book. And the other third is mystery. We can reduce the effect of negative mysterious happenings by planning and by working with our feelings, our attitude, and those things we can change. Then we have to lean back and marvel at the delightful side of mystery. Because of years of experience and being buffeted by life, it appears that older people are often better able to befriend mystery and the accompanying unknowns. People who notice the wonders of nature like a pine tree growing mysteriously out of a crack in a granite wall, who listen in awe to their brand of preferred music, who stand in astonishment while viewing a rainbow or northern lights are into living fully.

BE HUMBLE

Sometimes I think life is like a giant strip tease act. Every time you start to feel like you know something for certain, watch out, another piece goes. There is some lesson lurking just around the corner that will humble you a bit. The cliché "The older you get, the less you know" carries great truth. Perhaps even better is "The more you know that you know less than you thought you knew, the more you know." Often we become more humble as we age, more self-forgiving and able to smile at our unknowing. It becomes obvious there is much we don't know and will never know.

> *I wanted a perfect ending. Now I've learned, the hard way, that some poems don't rhyme, and some stories don't have a clear beginning, middle, and end. Life is about not knowing, living to change, taking the moment and making the best of it, without knowing what's going to happen next. Delicious ambiguity.*
> —*Gilda Radner, written shortly before she died of ovarian cancer*

> *The most beautiful thing we can experience is the mysterious. It is the source of all true art and science. He to whom this emotion is a stranger, who can no longer pause to wonder and stand rapt in awe, is as good as dead: his eyes are closed.... To know that what is impenetrable to us really exists, manifesting itself as the highest wisdom and the most radiant beauty which our dull faculties can comprehend only in their most primitive forms—this knowledge, this feeling, is at the center of true religiousness.*
> —*Albert Einstein,* **My Credo** *(originally in German)*

The older you get, the more you witness. You realize that the situations you encounter, while novel to you happen to other people all the time. You are not all that unique. Other people have relationship problems. Other people have had cancer. Other people have financial problems. Other people are hurting. This is very humbling on the one hand and very connecting on the other. It's called being human.

We understand that our viewpoint is not the only one and that there are many levels of understanding. When we were younger we thought we knew all sorts of things and that our parents were clueless. For most of us this perception gradually changes. In fact it changes to a degree that the more we know and see the less we are sure about. This uncertainty, this unknowing becomes a mark of wisdom. We seem to come with a sort of macho adulation of invulnerability, wanting to control any situation that comes along. This notion dissipates either slowly or abruptly with experience. You start to appreciate vulnerability as a strength—a hard earned strength. We become more able to tolerate ambiguity, to be without answers.

The physical diminishments that often come with old age school us in the art of humility and self-acceptance. They force us to surrender pride and to accept our human limitations. We learn to appreciate how our body works—or doesn't work—in ways that we formerly didn't have to think about, things we took for granted. Because we can't rely on our former attainments and on our physical strength, we must search more deeply within ourselves for a fund of inner strength and wisdom. We become more aware of our vulnerability as a nation when we witnessed the Twin Towers go down on 9/11. We become more aware of our vulnerability as individuals when we get a scary diagnosis. This vulnerability makes us feel small but at the same time immediately forces us to see the bigger picture and our humble place in it. When people report that their cancer has been a gift, it is because they are seeing with new eyes. Surprises and hard times force growth, test our courage, and often give us depth and compassion.

I remember how impressed I was when a much-respected doctor told an audience about a ninety-two-year-old patient of his who came in every six months for a physical. She claimed to be doing well, so he checked her out and renewed her three prescriptions, which appeared to be doing their job. When she died, she had someone send him a shoebox full of all of the unfilled prescriptions, not a one of which had ever been acted on. He was big enough to be able to laugh at himself, admit it was humbling, and recognize a good wake-up call.

Life has been one humbling event after another for me. I was a professional gerontologist and psychologist and my shtick, for awhile, was leading caregiver groups for people caring for an aging spouse or parent. I knew quite a lot about the complexities of caregiving, listened to multitudes of stories, recognized the importance of talking and being listened to, taught tools of self-care, referred participants to the many services available to help caregivers with this wearing and important work. It wasn't until my mother with Alzheimer's disease came to live with my family, and until my sister went through a harrowing time living and dying with Lou Gehrig's disease, that I really "got" at a deeper level what the strain and drain of caregiving amounted to.

Then I formed a company, called Journeywell, with two good friends who had been part of the original hospice movement in our city. We were quite knowledgeable about dying and grieving. We talked and lectured and I think were of service to many, but only after both of them died (one in a car accident and the other of AIDS), did I get the in-depth nuances of grief that a person can't

> *After I am dead, I would rather have one ask why Cato has no monument than why he has one.*
> —Cato the Elder

Life Humbles You

by Nyles Gunderson, Age 99

When you're young, you don't realize what you're up against. You think all those grown-ups sure have compromised. They definitely don't know how to live right. You swear there's no way you'll ever be like that. No way. Then it starts. You run into some bad luck. Even good luck can get you stuck in a certain direction. The years go by. You find things out. Some of your best-laid plans go bust. Pretty soon, there comes a day when some young guy with a chip on his shoulder gives you that look. He's swearing to himself never to be like you. You see it in his eyes. That's how it goes. He won't understand until his time comes.
—from What's Worth Knowing by ©
Wendy Lustbader[3]

get any other way. Humility and deepening simply happen as we accumulate experience. We discover that we know less than we may have thought. This humbling does not come easily, but it becomes less of a major shock as the humbling happens time and again. There are major league humblings and then little humblings. My husband has come to realize that the squirrels in our backyard are smarter than he is. He can only hope to increase their cleverness to new levels by continuing to try to outfox their amazing abilities to get at his bird feeders.

What experiences have been humbling for you? What did you learn from them?

Through experience we often move from a black and white knowing to a comfortable place of gray, of not knowing much of anything for sure. When you hear older adults facetiously saying, "Man, I wish I knew as much as I did when I was forty!" it's actually a hint of wisdom peaking through, acknowledging that there was a period in this strangely evolving life when we really thought we knew a considerable amount for sure. We want to "know" and we want to be in "control," both worthy wants, but life has its way with us. The trick is to continue to learn, to continue to plan, to be hopeful and positive, but at the same time, to fasten our lap-strap because at any moment we will be humbled by one of life's jolting surprises. We have witnessed parents who seem to have done a good job raising their kids experience heart-wrenching disappointments with their adult children. We have witnessed seemingly lousy parenting result in some interesting, contributing young adults. We have witnessed friends who have "done everything right" as far as their attitude, eating and exercising habits go, who die of cancer and cranky old codgers who seem to live forever. Capital "T" Truth gets muddled.

Have you had or witnessed disappointments like this? What lessons were in this for you?

BE FLEXIBLE

A key ingredient for remaining vital and healthy is to remain flexible. It is important to go with the flow or as May Sarton put it, learn how to glide.

People at any age exhibit a stubborn resistance to change. They say things like:

> You can't make me.
>
> I don't have to.
>
> This is just the way I am.
>
> It's too late to change now.
>
> I can handle it myself.
>
> If it gets worse, I'll do something.

I am far better able to cope at seventy than at fifty. I think that is partly because I have learned to glide instead of to force myself at moments of tension.
—May Sarton[4], *At Seventy*

> *You have got to remain flexible, both physically and mentally, if you don't want to get bent out of shape.*
> —Fran Bell, ninety-two-year-old mentor

It's hard to do anything with this type of person except to continually point out to them that it's their choice and, if they ever change their mind and choose to do something differently, that you'll be around. Some people get quite comfortable with their unhealthy situation. We can keep opening the door for them, but we cannot make them go through. I knew a couple who had been married for 50+ years, had a Virginia Wolfish, often-violent, relationship. They had learned how to live with this volatile and potentially dangerous situation, until the woman developed heavily symptomatic Parkinson's Disease and was unable to keep up her side of the "sick" arrangement. Finally change happened.

There is always a choice. You hope for better or worse options. Let's stay out of ruts and routines that don't serve us. When we come into a situation with our own fixed agenda, it blocks us from seeing the person and the subtleties in front of us clearly. Remember your tools, the Rule of Six, and the Serenity Prayer exercises discussed earlier. Living well with uncertainty is an art. Very few things are certain or solid so going with the flow makes things easier and takes less energy. Let's grow and change with each new learning. Even though we want some control in our lives no matter what our age, by the time we have reached old age we have discovered that we don't have the amount of control we may have thought we had in mid-life. We're adjusting a wee bit better. There is preciousness to living your life in your own rhythm, following your own instincts. Eat when you are hungry, sleep when you are sleepy, get up when you feel rested, do a great many things that can't be described as anything in particular, set no goals.

CULTIVATE A SENSE OF HUMOR

Maintaining a sense of humor is a good attitude enhancer. I was having lunch with a quick-witted old friend, and we were engaged in conversation with our young waitress, who inquired at some point of my friend, "Have you lived your whole life in Minnesota?" She replied, "Not yet!"

I entered the lobby of a hi-rise and saw several folks I knew. In response to my question, "What are you all doing?" one guy answered, "Just sitting around forgetting together!" More recently, I approached a bunch of women and asked a similar question, and one said "Oh, it doesn't look like we are doing anything, but actually we're practicing our Kegel exercises." They all burst out in a mighty guffaw. Many older adults have a knack for laughing at their situation. It's

I think every day above the grass is a good one.

much like blacks telling black jokes and Jews telling Jewish jokes; it's okay to joke amongst your own. Some quips from famous humorists:

"I'm at an age where my back goes out more than I do." (Phylis Diller)

"Except for an occasional heart attack, I feel as young as I ever did." (Robert Benchley)

"At my age, it's nice to be anywhere." (George Burns)

"I get a standing ovation for just standing." (George Burns)

Being able to laugh at ourselves and at life makes life far more enjoyable. This ability to lighten up comes naturally for some of us. It happens to others after they've been roughed up by life a bit; they learn the hard way that they simply don't have enough energy to "sweat the small stuff" and that it feels better to let go of some of the intensity and start being gentler with ourselves. Look for the humor and the silliness in what you hear, see, and read.

I appreciate research on unnecessary or far out subjects. One that piqued my interest was titled, *"Elderly armpits can lift your spirits."* It seems that hormones detected by smell can alter one's mood and the armpit smell of older ladies is mood-enhancing. The Philadelphia study[5] at the Monell Chemical Senses Center divided thirty participants into age categories and a gauze strip was strapped to their pits to absorb any odor. Then 300 students sampled the smells at random having taken before-and-after questionnaires designed to test their moods. Students who smelled the samples from older ladies responded significantly more positively while young men's smells had a depressive effect. Someone probably earned a Ph.D. on this study.

Probably someone earned a Ph.D. on this one!

Study Shows People Feel Better When Loved!

BE HOPEFUL

There's a lot of talk about renewable energy supplies running out. Hope is energy. Without it, a person gives up. Unlike oil, hope can be renewed by an act so simple as being heard and attended to by another. Hope is a renewable energy source and we all need it. Hope can move us out of helplessness to feeling alive. Just a hint that something can be better is hope. When people are given no hope by doctors, or told that their aches "are just what happens to older bodies," people started flocking to chiropractors and alternative non-western

Hope is a state of mind, not of the world…
It is an orientation of the spirit,
an orientation of the heart;
it transcends the world that is immediately experienced,
and is anchored somewhere beyond its horizons…
Hope, in this deep and powerful sense, is not the same as joy that things are going well,
or willingness to invest in enterprises that are
obviously heading for…success, but rather, an ability to work for something
because it is good, not just because it stands a chance to succeed.
—Vaclav Havel[6], former President of Czechoslovakia

> *Although the world is full of suffering,*
> *it is also full of the overcoming of it.*
> —Helen Keller

specialties such as acupuncture, herbalism, healing touch, and nutritionists, all of which gave hope, a sense of participation, and often positive results.

Illness reveals the many faces of hope. First there is hope for recovery. Some people retain hope for recovery in the face of all odds and fight their illness until death. Others feel hope for recovery dwindle and switch to other goals—like hoping to live long enough to witness a birthday, a graduation, a birth … or to accomplish something specific. Hope may change direction, like wanting to finish unfinished business, or to die with dignity. Hope evolves with the circumstance and is always changing, changing, changing. Some have no fear of death, look forward to it with curiosity, with excitement at the mystery of it all. Others look forward to meeting their loved ones, but they are still hoping for a death without much suffering. It is the duty of their loved ones to support whatever they are hoping for. Such people are directing the dying drama.

Without hope, a person cannot activate his/her inner resources to do all that can make the best out of the situation. Remember, hope is a renewable resource and we all need it. There are always things to do or ways to think, whether it is medical or not. Meditation techniques can help reduce stress that will enhance one's quality of life. Continual reassurance and support during this trying time is vital. Beyond that time, "hope" can be turned away from our living and allowed to illuminate our passing.

> *When the Grandmothers speak, the world will be healed*
> *So weave a new world, dear Grandmas*
> *Love's your needle, truth your thread*
> *Embroider our souls with watchfulness*
> *Stitch in hope for the journey ahead*
> *You walk in the garden with the Reaper of Death*
> *The black seeds of change, you sow with your breath*
> *Blow on them gently before you pass by*
> *Teach us to live, teach us to die.*
> *When the grandmothers speak, the world will be healed.*
> *So lift up your voice, there's no other choice*
> *Lift up your voice and heal.*
> —Circle of Grandmothers

RECOGNIZE GRACE WHEN IT HAPPENS

Living with grace refers to those moments when we are the recipient of unexpected, unmerited good things and become more aware of the love and abundance that surrounds us. Through this awareness, we know we are loved and valued. Moments of grace change us, disrupting our thought patterns, and bring the possibility of turning fear into love and scary situations into peacefulness. We can open the way to grace through prayer or meditations, or an attitude of appreciation and gratefulness. Often we learn about grace through very ordinary people and experiences. Grace just happens. It is important to look for it, recognize it, and bask in it. It is seen by many as God's love freely given, not earned or merited.

Old age can be a grace-filled time. Old age can be a time of fulfillment (as well as a time of challenge) and a time for harvesting the goodness of life.

Can you name some of times when you have experienced the gift of grace?

EMBRACE WISDOM

All of these ways-of-being described here—authenticity, comfort with paradox, befriending mystery, humility, flexibility, sense of humor, being hopeful and grace filled—are components of wisdom. The wise have a solid sense of self. They have learned from experience. It is hard-earned. It's not about book knowledge. Intellectual growth is not synonymous, yet not incompatible, with wisdom. Wisdom presents itself as extraordinary common sense. Some people seem to be born with more wisdom than others or have experiences in early life that nurture it. Being older is not a precondition of wisdom. Since older people have had more experiences, however, they have a better chance of being wise.

Who do you know that you consider wise? Why do you attribute wisdom to him/her?

Watch out for those who declare they are wise. Those who declare they "know" are automatically suspect; they certainly haven't been humbled. We all know these kinds of people who flaunt this autocratic pseudo wisdom. People who are truly wise don't need to flaunt it. Their wisdom sneaks up on you. At some point it dawns on you that the person to whom you are listening is truly wise.

Chapter 6

What's My Responsibility?

Decisions need to be made. To make the very best ones, it is helpful, if not crucial, that we communicate how we think and feel about subjects discussed in this chapter. You look carefully at what quality-of-life means to you. You are given information, scenarios to ponder, and then suggestions to help sort out how you feel about the many complexities of health-care decision-making, including what you need to know when creating a thoughtful advanced directive. You look at the many housing and services that are available, and the questions you might want to ask when you are contemplating a change.

WHAT MAKES QUALITY OF LIFE?

Attaining a high quality-of-life is the shining grail for all of us. We will all have our own ideas about what this means. When asked what a high quality-of-life would be like, people use words like "having a feeling of well-being or happiness, a sense of personal satisfaction, being healthy, continuing to be able to love and be loved, to care about people and things, and to engage in favorite activities." They want to continue to learn and grow, feel like they are contributing in some way, function as optimally as possible, not be a nuisance or burden to others, and be at peace with their particular manifestation of God (Jesus, Buddha).

Perceptions of what quality means to you change with the introduction of new events, new opportunities and interests, and losses of varying magnitudes. The notion of what quality-of-life means is not static nor is it predictable. People interpret very similar situations quite differently. I see older adults adjust, adjust, and adjust. What appears to be a lowering of standards to an outsider is the modeling of an awe-inspiring ability we humans have to adjust to new circumstances. Part of life's mystery is not knowing what our adjustment quotient is—until we are tested. Just as our definition of what hope is changes as we move along, so does our opinion of what quality-of-life means.

> *The essence of struggle is neither endurance nor denial. It is the decision to become new rather then to simply become older. It is the opportunity to grow either smaller or larger in the process.*
> —Joan Chittister [1]

How would I describe what quality-of-life means to me right now?

We don't know how we will die, at least until close to the end, but pause for a moment and think about how you think you would define quality of life at that time. Here are a few examples of what some people have written in their living wills:

"If I cannot engage in activities that make life worthwhile, if I am no longer aware of what's going on, or able to feel love for those I love, I wouldn't have the quality of life to justify my being here."

"If my body, which has been hearty and pushed to an extreme, loses much of its ability to function but my mind, my imagination, and my heart still function, I will be able to define what quality means to me at that time. Now I am a person who needs to keep learning and growing and caring for other humans in order to feel good. As long as I can do this my life will have quality."

"If I am unable to communicate any longer about what I want, I trust that my daughter can make choices for me."

Keep in mind that we are always changing so that it is important to keep asking what quality-of-life means to us and communicate those thoughts to the people who need to know.

QUIZ—WHAT BRINGS QUALITY TO MY LIFE?

Relationship with:	Have Enough?	Want More?	Want Less?
God (Jesus, Higher Power, Inner Wisdom)	❑	❑	❑
Someone who listens to my:	❑	❑	❑
Stories	❑	❑	❑
Feelings	❑	❑	❑
Someone with whom to laugh	❑	❑	❑
Someone with whom to feel safe	❑	❑	❑
Someone who gives:	❑	❑	❑
Warmth	❑	❑	❑
Touch	❑	❑	❑
Companionship	❑	❑	❑
Sexual pleasure	❑	❑	❑
Intellectual stimulation	❑	❑	❑
Others for whom to care	❑	❑	❑
Freedom to:	❑	❑	❑
Make decisions for myself	❑	❑	❑

Relationship with:	Have Enough?	Want More?	Want Less?
Be alone, have privacy	❑	❑	❑
Travel	❑	❑	❑
Get out in nature	❑	❑	❑
Engage in pleasurable activities	❑	❑	❑
Work for social change	❑	❑	❑
Engage in intellectual discussions	❑	❑	❑
Be of service to others	❑	❑	❑

What might you change to generate more quality in your life?

HOW DO FAMILIES START TALKING ABOUT DELICATE ISSUES?

Self-initiated

Be direct. A elderly mother says to her son…

"I worry about suddenly dying or getting very sick, burdening you with all sorts of confusion and decisions. It would feel better sharing with you what I value and clarify everything I can now."

Something like this needs to be said in a straightforward, matter-of-fact way. Ask for time. Tell the persons you wish to inform what you want to discuss and why. Ask them for a block of their time and set a date so they know you are serious. This process can be an opportunity for important modeling. You can make discussion about death and dying a comfortable subject in your home. I distinctly remember when my dad astonished me by saying, "I made a will today and I'm going to talk to you all about it after dinner." I was about fourteen and the mere thought of my dad dying was incomprehensible. I sat silently and aghast at the beginning of the discussion, but gradually lightened up because he was not at all morbid. Quite the contrary, he was obviously delighted with his decisions. It dawned on me, for perhaps the first time, that death is a reality for us all and need not be a taboo subject. It was one of my first lessons on how large a forbidden subject looms until it is aired and opened up for discussion.

Other-initiated

If you are an adult child, a spouse, or a concerned other and want to initiate discussion about health-care issues, several approaches can be taken. Directly express your concern. "I get worried sometimes that I won't know how you would feel or what you would want done if certain things happened. I'd want to do what you would wish, but I need to know what those wishes are. Would you help me out?" Discuss what if's. "What if, down the road, you can't manage in this house any more? What would you like done? What services might help you stay here? Have you considered any particular housing option?"

Indirect Approach

Some older people flatly refuse any direct approach to this discussion broached by a spouse or family. It's time to be creative. One son brought up stories of people he and his parents knew that helped clarify their thinking about the delicate subjects—George and Elizabeth have moved into that new high-rise for seniors downtown. What have you heard about that place?

Which of these approaches fits your family dynamics?

HEALTH-CARE PLANNING

Information Gathering

The next step on our pilgrimage to having the quality-of-life we want is to gather information and reflect on particular health-care issues that could surface at some time. We look at our own personal health and our experiences with the health-care system. With the information provided about controversial late-life issues like resuscitation, artificial food and hydration, euthanasia, and assisted suicide, we will be more qualified to fill out advanced directives. Our beliefs may be absolute and certain or may reflect our confusion and uncertainty. The discussion is important for us and our surrogate decision-maker (named in our advanced directive) for clarification and making responsible decisions congruent with our wishes. At some period in your life, you will probably have to make some hard decisions about health-care and living arrangements. This segment of the book asks questions and paints scenarios to help you contemplate how you think and feel about specific issues. This kind of reflection can be difficult. Please persevere because it is exactly these delicate areas that need to be pondered and discussed.

Reflect on the Following

You have a chronic illness and have been growing more dependent on your child or spouse for care for years. You want to remain at home, but your caregiver is getting worn out. What do you think you would do? Do you think that your caregiver should have as much to say as you do, or even more, about your care plan?

Do you think decisions about the type of funeral or whether or not to be cremated should be up to the surviving family or to the previously stated wishes of the deceased?

Your loved one has advanced Alzheimer's and needs penicillin to alleviate pneumonia. You are the designated decision-maker according to the advanced directive. Would you ask that penicillin be given or avoid the treatment and let nature take its course, provided he or she can be kept comfortable?

Your loved one has advanced Alzheimer's and needs a hip replacement operation in order to be mobile and more comfortable. You never discussed this possibility with him or her. Would you ask that it be done or avoid the operation and let nature take its course?

By consensus of the American Medical Society and American Academy of Neurology, people in a persistent vegetative state (PVS) feel no pain and have no awareness. Some people are troubled by allowing such people to be taken off life-support devices. If you were in a state of permanent unconsciousness (PVS), would you want to be maintained by artificial measures?

There are examples of complicated ethical dilemmas in your newspapers or magazines. It is important to get in the habit of discussing these situations and letting your views be known to whomever may make decisions for you someday, if you are no longer able.

The Right to Die

The world of religion and philosophy was shocked when Henry P. Van Dusen and his wife ended their lives by their own hands. Dr. Van Dusen had been president of Union Theological Seminary; for more than a quarter-century he had been one of the luminous names in Protestant theology. He enjoyed world status as a spiritual leader. News of the self-inflicted death of the Van Dusens, therefore, was profoundly disturbing to all those who attach a moral stigma to suicide and regard it as a violation of God's laws. Dr. Van Dusen had anticipated this reaction. He and his wife left behind a letter that may have historic significance. It was very brief, but the essential point it made is now being widely discussed by theologians and could represent the beginning of a reconsideration of traditional religious attitudes toward self-inflicted death. The letter raised a moral issue: does an individual have the obligation to go on living even when the beauty and meaning and power of life are gone?

Henry and Elizabeth Van Dusen had lived full lives. In recent years, they had become increasingly ill, requiring almost continual medical care. Their infirmities were worsening, and they realized they would soon become completely dependent for even the most elementary needs and functions. Under these circumstances little dignity would have been left in life. They didn't like the idea of taking up space in a world with too many mouths and too little food. They believed it was a misuse of medical science to keep them technically alive. They therefore believed they had the right to decide when to die. In making that decision, they weren't turning against life as the highest value; what they were turning against was the notion that there were no circumstances under which life should be discontinued.

The general reaction to suicide may change as people come to understand that it may be a denial, not an assertion, of moral or religious ethics to allow life to be extended without regard to decency or pride. What moral or religious purpose is celebrated by the annihilation of the human spirit in the triumphant act of keeping the body alive? Why are so many people more readily appalled by an unnatural form of dying than by an unnatural form of living?

"Nowadays," the Van Dusens wrote in their last letter, "it is difficult to die. We feel that this way we are taking will become more usual and acceptable as the years pass. Of course, the thought of our children and our grandchildren makes us sad, but we still feel that this is the best way and the right way to go. We are both increasingly weak and unwell…. We are not afraid to die." Henry Van Dusen was admired and respected in life. He can be admired and respected in death. "Suicide," said Goethe, "is an incident in human life which, however much disputed and discussed, demands the sympathy of every man, and in every age must be dealt with anew…. Death is not the greatest loss in life. The greatest loss is what dies inside us while we live. The unbearable tragedy is to live without dignity or sensitivity."—quoted by Norman Cousins[2], *Saturday Review*, June 1975 (reprinted with permission).

What do you think about this?

Warren Wolfe[3] wrote the following article in the *Minneapolis-St. Paul Star Tribune*, on May 29, 1991:

Man would refuse ruling to take wife off respirator

A Minneapolis man said Wednesday that he would refuse to obey if a judge appoints him as his wife's conservator and then orders him to remove her from a life-sustaining respirator. "I don't think I'd go with that, as a matter of conscience," Oliver Wanglie testified at a hearing in Hennepin County District Court. The hearing is to determine whether he or an independent conservator should be appointed to decide whether to remove Helga Wanglie's respirator. She has been in a persistent vegetative state for more than a year. Both Wanglies are 87. Officials at Hennepin County Medical Center, where Helga Wanglie is hospitalized, want to remove the respirator, saying there is no hope of recovery. Oliver Wanglie opposes the move. "We're living in hope and faith that a miracle will happen so she can recover," he said. "I will follow her best interests, [but] I do not want to remove ventilation and snuff out her life," Wanglie replied. He said his decision is based on religious beliefs held by the Wanglies and on her instructions to him earlier that all means should be used to prolong her life. Helga Wanglie has been attached to a mechanical breathing device for 17 months, longer than any other comatose patient her doctors know about," said Dr. Steven Miles, a medical ethicist and gerontologist at the hospital who also has treated her. Her family and doctors agree that she has been in a vegetative state since last May, when she suffered a heart attack and blood flow to her brain stopped for an unknown amount of time. She had been on a respirator before that at Hennepin County because of pneumonia that developed after she fell and broke her hip. Her care, which hospital officials say has cost $800,000, is covered by private insurance. Other insureds are paying for her care in having to pay higher premiums. The two medical doctors testified yesterday that keeping Wanglie on a respirator is "inappropriate medicine" because her condition is irreversible and the machine will do nothing to cure her or improve her quality of life. Without it, Miles said, she likely will die. He said the irreversible brain damage has destroyed her ability to feel pain or to be aware of her surroundings. (Reprinted with permission)

What do you think about this?

The hope is that these scenarios and questions will have helped you clarify how you feel about these difficult subjects. Most of us hope we won't ever be in these situations, and probably won't be. Congratulate yourself for taking the time. This sort of reflection provides a sound basis for journeying well.

My Health

My current state of health is…

What bothers me the most about my health is…

Am I satisfied with my medical care? If not, how could I make it better?

Am I usually honest with myself about my health?

Am I honest and straight-forward with others when I talk about my health?

Do I pay enough attention to my health?

Do I dwell on my health too much?

What kind of a patient will I be when I get really sick?

       Stoic?

       Wimpy?

       Resilient?

       Assertive?

What are my good health habits?

What are my bad health habits?

Before proceeding, it might be helpful for you to review Appendix E—a glossary of health-care, legal and ethical terms—Appendix F—Resuscitation and Artificial Food and Hydration.

Now that we have given some thought to our health and looked over the definition of terms in the appendices, it is time to look in more depth at some of the puzzling and complicated issues of late life. Be gentle. These are important but delicate subjects.

Technology has forced reconsideration of the definition of death. In the past, when our heart stopped beating and we stopped breathing, we were pronounced dead. Now it's harder to be dead. Patients can be placed on heart-lung machines when they are unable to breathe or pump blood on their own; thus they are very much alive. Life-sustaining devices are capable of maintaining heartbeat and respiration in patients who have suffered irreversible loss of brain function. There are consequences to the decisions we make. Neurological criteria have been added to the definition of death because of life-sustaining technology. Would our grandparents ever have believed that there would be a day when there would be no consensus about what it means to be dead?

When machines can keep us organically alive beyond the body's natural abilities, it is important to think about these issues. How you personally define death and quality of life are the two questions at the crux of many decisions we may be asked to make. Reflect on the following questions:

What specific mental and social functions do I feel are essential to being human?

Does being human include the capacity to remember, to reason, to have sensory awareness, to be conscious?

What is consciousness? Does life for me have to do with maintaining my identity, my sense of psychological continuity and connectedness?

My bet is that most of us feel staggered by questions such as these. It's important to appreciate their complexity. Our belief system plays an integral part in the decisions we make. Two specific issues, resuscitation, and artificial feeding and hydration, are discussed in more detail in Appendix F. It is important for us to know how we feel about these two subjects, and to let the appropriate people know—enabling a clear clinical pathway in case either situation should arise.

MANAGING DEATH

In the last few days of life, many people who have been sick for a period of time choose not to eat. This used to be considered a "natural death" but in recent years intravenous feedings and nasogastric tube feeding and gastrostomies have become much-used options. Still voluntary refusal of nutrition and hydration is a common method used by the terminally ill to hasten death today. It results in a peaceful death in an average of about fifteen days. Patients can be maintained for decades on artificial feeding, kidney dialysis, and mechanical ventilators. Some think this sounds like a fate worse than death; others choose to live as long as possible.

Advanced industrial democracies are in a stage of societal development in which their members are less liable to die of acute illnesses but of delayed degenerative diseases characterized by late onset and

> *With technology and social values constantly changing, medicine and morality cannot be fixed in stone.*

slow decline. According to M. P. Battin[4], this situation applies to 70%–80% percent of the population and presents altogether new dilemmas and a shift of emphasis on quality of life questions.

With all this talk about choices at the end of life, it is important to note that most health-care decisions throughout life are clear decisions. Most medical care does not require any ethical decision-making because the decisions do not need debate when using sound medical knowledge. For instance, respirators are routinely used as temporary, normal recovery devices after some operations. This choice is not debatable because there is consensus that it is sound medical practice and a transient part of treatment. Patients usually return to normal lives.

There is consensus that therapy would be worthwhile if it helps you recover or maintain an acceptable quality-of-life. If the treatment would hurt you and only prolong your dying, you would have to make a judgment based on your value system. People are more often saying "No" to the assumption that because something can be done, it should be done. Research is clarifying which medical treatments are useful and which ones are useless in various situations. End-of-life decision-making is becoming more rational and open (Hoefler).[5]

Physician-assisted suicide, self-deliverance, and voluntary death are hot topics and have moved to the forefront as our society has increased its ability to fight death. Physician-assisted suicide is an act in which a doctor gives a patient the means and specific instructions by which to take his or her own life. There remains a small percent of instances in which incurably ill patients suffer intolerably before death, despite the hospice movement and comprehensive efforts to provide pain relief and comfort.

Consider the following patients: a man with ALS (Lou Gehrig's disease) who has been a quadriplegic for years and no longer wants to linger captive in his body is dependent and praying for death; a woman with oral cancer who has a gaping, foul-smelling wound, who can no longer eat, and no longer wants to live. Both would rather die than live and feel that there should be "aid in dying."

What do you think about this?

Oregon and Washington are presently the only states where a dying patient can openly and legally receive life-ending medication from a doctor and self-administer it. The chief benefit of decriminalizing the practice is easing of fear of the dying process in particular cases. Instead of increasing the incidence of suicide, Oregon data shows that regulating aid in dying reduces its frequency to about 25% of the covert practice that now exists in states where it remains illegal.[6]

The basic argument in favor of assisted suicide's legality runs as follows: Competent individuals have the right to refuse treatment, including life-sustaining treatment, with full knowledge and acceptance that death will ensue. In respecting these wishes, physicians may commit an intentional act—such as removal of a respirator—that results in a patient's death. Patients may receive medication intended to relieve pain even though the unavoidable, known, and accepted consequence is the hastening of death. Given this state of the law, the argument goes, there is no logical reason why a competent, terminally ill patient, fully informed of the facts and consequences of such a decision, may not ask a physician to commit the purposeful act of providing medication intended to end the patient's life, when that patient decides that life has become an unendurable existence. Scofield[7] argues that, beyond satisfying the patient's right of self-determination, this act promotes beneficence because it ends a patient's pain and suffering. According to this line of thinking, assisted suicide is the next step in the legal evolution of autonomy and respect for an individual's choice.

Scofield[7] also explains the opposition to this thinking: "the nature of the act, intent, and chain of causation involved in assisted suicide differs significantly. Death is not accidental, natural, or even the result of unintended iatrogenic (physician or drug caused) complications; it is chemically induced….Writing out a prescription with the intent that it be used to end life is not like entering a DNR order. Even the nature of the patient's request is different. One asks for interventions to cease, the other that medicine directly intervene to make death occur. One risks, the other seeks, death." This is a complicated issue; there are ardent supporters and opponents in the debate over legalizing physician-assisted suicide.

What are your thoughts about physician-assisted suicide?

The national organization, Compassion and Choices (http://compassionandchoices.org) provides information and educational forums on self-deliverance, voluntary dying and all aspects of the dying-with-dignity issue. When do you think enough is enough as far as life support measures are concerned? These are weighty difficult decisions. Letting a person die, even if is distinctly "right" in the sense that it is respecting his choice, is tremendously difficult. The heart that wants to touch a warm body tussles with the rational mind while trying to decide what is best. The question for many of us is, "What is the most loving thing to do?" It helps immeasurably to have talked about these feelings beforehand.

ADVANCED DIRECTIVES

During the 1970s and 1980s, an outcry rose from people fearful that their lives might be extended far beyond quality years or their ability to think. They feared for themselves and they feared for their families. They demanded a mechanism to save them legally from what they considered unwanted life extension. By 1993, all states and the District of Columbia had responded to this demand by legalizing one or two forms of advance directives—the Living Will and the Durable Power of Attorney for Health Care (DPAHC). These are legal documents that allow competent individuals to retain some control over health-care decisions in the event they are no longer able to do so in the future.

We can let our wishes be know several ways:

1. Fill out one of these official forms. State health departments and local hospitals will probably have approved advanced directive forms. You can get a form on the Internet by looking up advanced directives and getting the form recommended for your state.

2. Simply write your wishes down and sign them.

3. There is a Five Wishes document legal in forty states as of 2007 and is preferred by many because of its holistic approach. Five Wishes lets your family and doctors know:

- Which person you want to make health-care decisions for you when you can't
- The kind of medical treatment you want or don't want
- How comfortable you want to be
- How you want people to treat you
- What you want your loved ones to know.

Laws about advanced directives vary state by state. It is safest to comply with your state standards. In 1990, Congress enacted the Patient Self-Determination Act (PSDA), which requires hospitals, health maintenance organizations, home health-care providers, and nursing facilities to advise patients of their rights to make health-care decisions in advance by using advance directives. The PSDA opens the expectation of choice, but, since it does not require a process of exploration of the patient's values, facilities merely ask, "Do you have an advance directive?" These will be discussed in more detail in this chapter and you are encouraged, if you haven't already done it, to fill out the easily accessible forms available from the hospital, your doctor, or over the Internet. Careful thought, reflection, and communication of your feelings about these matters are integral to the process.

Why not avoid this gloomy subject?

"I don't need to think about this. I'm just going to die the 'good old way.'"

"It won't happen to me."

"This is morbid. Who wants to think about dying?"

"Who cares? It'll be someone else's problem."

"I'll do it next year. I'm feeling fine."

"I'm afraid to sign one of those things. No one will take care of me then."

"I trust my doctor to know."

"I trust my children/spouse to do the right thing for me if something should happen and I couldn't decide for myself."

"No one would pay any attention to it anyway."

"I can't possibly anticipate how I'm are going to die. Trying to do so will only confuse things."

Sound familiar?

There are new questions. Technology can keep us alive. It is now our decision whether and in what circumstances mechanical interventions should be used or withdrawn. Obviously we cannot know precisely what our dying circumstances will be. But we can let our general views be known to our doctor and to those to whom it is important and alleviate the pressure they will have if they don't know. We need information, definitions of terms, and time to think and discuss these weighty decisions.

> *The time of death—once a matter of fate—is now a matter of human choice. Nearly every death involves a decision whether to take some medical procedure that could prolong the process of dying.*
> —Supreme Court Justice Brennan in the Nancy Cruzan case

The Terri Schiavo case brought the necessity of having an advanced directive, at any age, to a head. If her husband Michael had had her Living Will in writing, there never would have been a case. Terri had been diagnosed as being in a persistent vegetative state for several years when in 1998 he requested that her feeding tube be removed. Her parents opposed this, arguing she was conscious and alive in their eyes. Courts determined that Terri would not wish to continue life-prolonging measures. The battle stretched on for seven years and included involvement by politicians and advocacy groups, courts, the governments of Florida, and the U.S. Supreme Court before it was over in 2005. Families disagree on basic issues. This protracted battle could have been avoided.

Spare your family members the anguish of not knowing how you would feel about these matters. Being open to discussing these issues is a responsible and loving gesture for your survivors. Making them guess what you prefer is what leads families into difficult, divisive times that could have been avoided by thoughtful self-investigation and preplanning. If you have complete faith in your physician's decision-making and for this reason decline to make out an advance directive, let this decision be known to your family. But recognize that in this world of specialists, sometimes your family doctor isn't handy at the right time so communication of your thinking is still important. Doctors do not want to get involved in sticky family dynamics and prefer to speak to one decision-maker. It is advisable to choose a single proxy and an alternate, although they can confer with others, who might best articulate your views. Since this can be a delicate matter, explain to your family the necessity of having one decision-maker and whom you have designated as your surrogate so that they will not be surprised later.

For a spouse or parent reluctant to discuss these matters, these are suggestions for approaches that some have used:

1. "I get concerned sometimes about what could happen, and need an idea of how you are thinking if I or someone else had to make decisions for you."
2. "I have filled out an advanced directive for myself and think it is important in case something should happen and I couldn't make decisions for myself. Can I help you do one?"
3. "I know that you like to have as much control as you can over situations, like I do, so I think we ought to make out advanced directives."
4. "My friend Jack's mom had a stroke and couldn't communicate. The doctor asked Jack some questions about his mom's wishes, and he couldn't answer because they had never talked about the subject. This made me think that I'd hate to be in that position. So let's do it."

The Living Will is a written statement signed by you and witnesses that gives guidance to your family and doctor about your health-care wishes in preparation for a time when you might not be able to make decisions yourself. You can state whether you want to undergo particular life-prolonging medical procedures when your condition is considered irreversible and terminal. It is important to note that in many states, a Living Will only goes into affect when you are in a terminal condition. The Durable Power of Attorney for Health Care, discussed in the next section, is activated if you are in a non-terminal or terminal condition but unable to make or communicate your health-care wishes.

Many states have legislated guidelines for advance directives. While specific provisions vary from state to state, they all generally authorize a "competent adult" to execute a declaration in advance, stating his or her intent about health-care preferences. A proxy decision-maker can also be named in many states' Living Will forms. This designated proxy will make medical decisions on your behalf if you become unable to make them yourself. A Living Will document provides a vehicle to ensure that those decisions are made in accordance with your preferences. Questions:

How is it determined whether one is competent to make his or her decisions?

Usually your attending doctor, a psychologist, or a neurologist determines your capacity to make health-care decisions. With dementia, there is a progressive loss of decision-making ability that makes assessment complicated. Assessment often involves "ruling out" any possibility of other causal factors, such as tumors, infection, or possible drug reactions, creating the cognitive impairment.

Is a special Living Will form required in your state?

Yes. Every state and the District of Columbia have some form of advance directive.

What if I spend half of my time in one state and half in another?

To be safe, write two Living Wills. Get forms for both states.

What do I do with the Living Will after it is executed?

Give copies to your doctor, proxy, family, clergy, lawyer, and anyone else closely associated with you and discuss them. Put the original in an accessible place—not your safe deposit box. Check to see that it is in the official care-plan if you are in a hospital or nursing home. Update it when there is new information.

Can I change my Living Will once it has been signed and witnessed?

Yes. A Living Will can be revoked at any time. It is advisable to renew it on a regular basis. Situations change; your living situation, health, or even a relationship may change, warranting an update of your Living Will.

Should you discuss your Living Will with anyone?

You are not legally required to do so, but it is strongly encouraged. A Living Will serves as an excellent discussion catalyst for subjects not reflected upon in many households.

What about the "extra protection" of a proxy appointment?

If at all possible, you should also name a person you trust and who knows you well enough to make medical decisions in accordance with your wishes if the time comes when you cannot make them for yourself. The proxy appointment is the most important part of the Living Will because it allows you to designate someone to implement on-the-spot decisions as you wish them to be made. It enables you to have someone "stand in your shoes" to discuss treatment alternatives when you cannot speak for yourself.

What types of treatment should you think about?

The procedures that should definitely be included are your general thoughts about cardiac resuscitation (DNR order) and artificial feeding and hydration.

How specific should you be?

There is great danger in over-medicalizing or over-specification in advance

Get out that Living Will; I've got some new thoughts.

Hosp. Bed 3A124

directives. Since you cannot know the details about how you will eventually die until close to the end, discussing specific interventions without clarity about the context of those actions obscures the issue and lessens the chances of your wishes being respected. It is better that your trusted surrogate and your doctor understand your general views and then be able to apply them to decisions that have to be made.

For advance directives to be most effective and workable, focus on the process. Statements such as "Never let me die" or "Never put me on a respirator or feeding tube" can effectively negate your wishes because the statements are too extreme to be considered medically sound and physicians can override them. Once it becomes more obvious near the end of your life what will be involved such as dialysis, antibiotics that cannot realistically improve your chances of recovery, respirator, chemotherapy, you could update your document and these procedures could be specified.

Should I include organ donation information?

Yes, this can be included. Skin tissue and corneas of older people are valuable. Organs of younger people, especially if they die suddenly like in an accident are terribly needed. If you desire to have your body donated to research, this needs to be stated.

What if my doctor doesn't agree with my wishes and choices?

Your wishes should prevail unless they are out of the bounds of reasonable medical practice. If, after thoughtful discussion, your doctor doesn't agree with your preferences for treatment, he or she is obligated to make a reasonable effort to transfer you.

What if my family or friends disagree with my treatment choices?

Here, too, your wishes should prevail. But your family will be less likely to disagree if they can discuss your preferences with you and get a clear idea of your reasoning. Pick a spokesperson (proxy) who will carry out your wishes. If you suspect that there will be objections by someone in particular, note that in writing. If you are terribly worried about family upheaval, you can request conservatorship.

If I refuse life-sustaining treatment, will I still be taken care of?

Yes. Living Will laws usually state that comfort care should be provided, which includes medication for pain, nursing and hygienic care, and treatment administered for the purpose of keeping you as comfortable and free from pain as possible.

The Durable Power of Attorney for Health Care (DPAHC) is a legal document written for the purpose of designating another person (the agent) to make health-related decisions on your behalf if, in the judgment of the attending physician, you are unable to do so yourself. This document is comparable to the proxy designation of a Living Will and is preferable to the Living Will if your state does not provide the opportunity for proxy designation. Remember that unlike the Living Will, the DPAHC enables the designated agent to make decisions if the principal is temporarily or permanently unable to make decisions. Check to see if your state has a statute that authorizes this document. Some states have a Durable Power of Attorney that applies only to property matters.

Make sure it is clear what you want to accomplish with a DPAHC. This could include accessing medical information and records, employing and discharging medical personnel, refusing or consenting to specific procedures, requesting pain relief, or arranging for care and lodging in a hospital, nursing home, or hospice. Go over this part of the book with your agent. Just as with the Living Will, think about what you could tell someone that would help him or her make decisions in your best interest, recognizing that it is not possible to predict all circumstances that might occur.

Who knows how you think about these subjects better than anyone else?

The person you choose as your surrogate decision-maker in you DPAHC or Living Will needs to be willing to do so. Not everyone wants to assume the potential ethical and emotional burdens that can be involved. Keep in mind that the person you designate will have a great deal of power over your health-care if you become incapacitated.

Should I have both a Living Will and a Will and a DPAHC?

It is important to designate an agent or proxy decision-maker. If you can do that in one document in your state, that is enough.

What if I change my mind?

You can revoke the advanced directive by:

1. destroying it (and any copies),
2. creating a written, dated statement to supersede the original,
3. verbally announcing to two witnesses (who don't need to be present at the same time) that you no longer want the original to be in effect,
4. write a new one and date it.

Look in Appendix E and F for more information.

Once you have taken care of filling out your advanced directive and given it to the appropriate people, you can move on to enjoying the peace of mind that comes from knowing that you have done what you can to plan for future unknowns. This whole matter can be carried out in one sitting if opinions of your family members aren't in huge conflict. I brought copies of advanced directives from my state and the two other states where my family live to a family gathering that included everyone. We went over many of the questions together declaring our feelings about the different scenarios and filling out the documents together. It is important for all views to be out front and especially important to be clear whom you designate as your proxy decision-maker. You and your chosen decision-maker may want more in-depth conversations later. The discussion was fascinating, and the business was accomplished. We ended up per usual having fun with it, deteriorating into making up epitaphs for our tombstones. I shared the infamous one "I told you I was sick" and my friend's request "Please stuff some Snicker bars down here" to "I'm sorry if I snore."

It is important for adults of any age to have an advanced directive. Most all Supreme Court decisions have related to young people who haven't had them and were still in the stage of life where it hadn't been discussed.

Most of the decision-making in later life isn't nearly so dramatic as the health-care issues just discussed, but there are plenty of them and they need careful consideration. Where should I live? What services are available? What do I want to do with my time? Am I still a safe driver? Below are scenarios and questions for you to contemplate:

When you are old, single, and feeling less able, would you prefer to:

a. Live alone in your own home or apartment, recognizing the risks and freedoms?

b. Live with family, if that's an option?

c. Live in your own apartment/condo with people of all ages?

d. Live in a continuum of care complex for seniors only (with amenities available such as transportation, optional meals, activities)?

e. It depends.

"It depends" is an understandable and thoughtful response to many questions. The only way to ascertain what "it depends" means is to uncover as much information as possible about the variables involved in the situation, to ask questions, and to discuss the nuances. The discussion around specific "what if" dilemmas is a good way to generate the information needed. When you know and have expressed your feelings and biases about health-care, living arrangements, and personal preferences, the fog begins to clear.

Some people spend considerable time worrying about their old age. Others don't. Even the non-worriers wonder at times, "If something happens to me, what will happen to him or her?" or "I'm shoveling the snow and mowing the grass now, but I suppose some day I won't be able to. What then?" Most of us want in to be in charge of making our own arrangements, but unfortunately a combination of procrastination and denial too often prevails. While things are going well, we put off planning. The best planning occurs when we have time and aren't in crisis. What worries you?

Perhaps you love tinkering around your home doing chores. Perhaps you love your neighborhood and knowing people when you go shopping at the grocery store. Perhaps you no longer feel up to the maintenance your house requires and you're finding that you get out less and less, and are seeing fewer people. There is quite a large group of older adults who continue living in their lifetime houses, who have a deeply embedded belief, that "they want to stay in their house no-matter-what," and they "certainly don't want to ever go to a nursing home." This belief persists no matter how socially isolated and, in some cases, miserably lonely they are. They do not know the options out there, or are deaf to learning about them. I know many examples of persons who have adamantly resisted getting out of their beloved homes who have ultimately loved the socialization, comfort, and safety of an assisted living set-up. The aunt of one of my friends declared that she would never speak to her when she was moved against her will to assisted living. Then a short five days later her aunt called, saying cheerily, "Dearie, would you get me some ear rings. I'm meeting so many people here. I'd like to get more dressed up." It is crucially important to get familiar with the options available, the services that can help you stay in your home, the kinds of housing available in your area, and the ever important factor of cost.

If you should require considerable assistance in activities of daily living (feeding, toileting, bathing, and dressing), would you prefer:

    a. Remaining in your own home with:
      1. Family assistance
      2. Professional home-care service
    b. Moving to an apartment with:
      1. Family assistance
      2. Professional home-care service
    c. Moving in with a family member who would then become your caregiver
    d. Moving to a facility that provides a continuum of care.

If you get a serious diagnosis will you share the news with others? Who would you tell? In what order?

Roy is eighty-five years old and lives with his daughter who works out of the home five days a week. He is extremely frail and needs help with many things such as walking, bathing, and meal preparation. Roy has episodes of confusion, but his physician has not officially diagnosed dementia. On the days that his daughter works, she leaves her father alone in the locked house for about four hours until the home-health aide arrives; the aide then stays with Roy until the daughter returns. The daughter has refused more home-health aide service because she says she can't afford it. Her father says that he doesn't mind staying home alone. To date, he has not been injured while staying alone.

What do you think about this? Consider the different viewpoints.

Jane has an eighty-eight-year-old friend, Alice, about whom she's worried. She really cares about Alice and doesn't know what to do. Alice has a lot of spirit and has taught Jane much about being tough and persevering. Alice is hard-headed about some things, but Jane admires how she plugs along. Lately, Alice has grown weak and dizzy. Last week, Jane noticed a gash on Alice's forehead and Alice confided that she had fallen. She refuses to go to doctors and, above all, doesn't want her daughter, Shirley, to know how weak she is. Alice tells Shirley all sorts of untruths over the phone about how well she is. Jane is caught in a confidentiality muddle. Alice asks her, with a twinkle in her eye but with obvious conviction, "not to let the cat out of the bag" and tell Shirley about her recent difficulties. Alice says that she "doesn't want anyone to worry." Jane is beginning to feel irresponsible because she thinks that she is the only one Alice trusts, but that something ought to be done. Do you think Jane should tell Shirley how Alice is really doing? What other options might there be?

You promised your parent (or spouse) that you would never put him/her in a nursing home, but, after years of caregiving to the best of your ability, you think that you must do so. Would you break your promise? Discuss.

*A good generalization is to avoid saying "never." You can't know all the variables down the road. You can only honestly say, "You will always do what seems best for your loved one given the circumstances."

Your father is eighty-five years old. You are worried about his driving. Even though he tries to be cautious, his vision is failing. He ricochets off curbs and has particular trouble with his nighttime driving because of the glare. You love him and know that he will be hurt and defensive if you bring up the subject. Would you:

    a. Do nothing and pray for a minor accident in which no one would be hurt, so that the police or Department of Motor Vehicles would become involved, and you would not be forced to take action?

    b. Carefully bring up the subject, stating your concern, then back off, hoping he would take some action?

    c. Give information about the services available like senior center shuttles, metro mobility, public transportation, and taxi services to help him see the options other than driving that are available in the community?

    d. State your concerns and insist on some action?

Your father continues to drive. You and others make excuses to avoid riding with him for your own safety. You worry about the safety of others. Would you:

    a. Still do nothing?

    b. Bring up the subject again and request that he see his physician for an assessment of his visual acuity and a judgment about his potential driving competence?

    c. Remove an important part from the motor so that it mysteriously won't start?

    d. Hide the keys?

    e. Tell him you are going to notify the Department of Motor Vehicles requesting an intervention, a vision test, and a written/road test?

    f. Notify the Department of Motor Vehicles but not tell your father?

The question about whether or not to keep driving is a very delicate issue in most families. What do you think should be done? Do you think if someone ignores or is unaware of his decreasing ability to drive safely, it is the moral responsibility of the family to act in some way? If you were having trouble with the glare at night while driving, what do you think you would do? If you began to have "close calls" and felt that your driving reactions were slipping, what would you do?

Whether to continue to drive or give up your license and accompanying freedom is a huge decision and causes major disruptions in families. It is often easiest if a family doctor, lawyer, or other outside-the-family party initiates action … when safety to the driver and others becomes a concern.

The privilege of driving is always contingent on competency. You can report an unsafe driver, with, confidentiality, to the Department of Motor Vehicles. The DMV then requests that he retake his driver's written and road test. When this happens, he often becomes more realistic about his situation, or he takes the tests and proves to all concerned that he is still an able driver. Have you talked about this sensitive issue? States vary in how they handle this. You must do research to discern the best possible approach.

HOUSING OPTIONS AND SERVICES

Another area of information gathering that is necessary for responsible planning is to review the numerous housing options that are available for older adults and the increasing number of services that are making it easier for persons to remain in their own homes. Bringing services into your home helps relieve stress for the caregiver and can greatly enhances overall quality of life.

What Services Are Available?

Some of the services are listed below and described more fully *in Appendix G* along with information on how to get in touch those available in your area:

- Emergency response systems
- Friendly visiting/Stephen ministers
- Meals on Wheels
- Home health-care agencies
- Homemakers/aides
- Chore service helpers
- Transportation services
- Delivery services-dry cleaners, food markets, pharmacies etc.
- Escort services
- Library service to the homebound
- Adult day care
- Legal assistance
- Mental health services
- Respite care for caregivers
- Telephone reassurance or communicare
- Hospices
- "Golden Age" banking services
- Case management
- Congregate dining
- Weatherization and fuel assistance.

The National Eldercare Locator Line, 800-677-1116, will link you with the service providers in your area. Have the zip code of the area you want to know about handy.

We are seeing housing options increase as our numbers do. Some of them are listed below and explained more thoroughly in Appendix H. What these housing options are technically called is continually changing. Not all of them will be obtainable in your area, but if you inquire, you might be surprised how many are.

HOUSING OPTIONS

- Accessory apartments
- Share-a-home
- Reverse mortgage/home equity
- Condominiums and affordable houses
- Cooperatives
- ECHO (Elder Cottage Housing Opportunity)
     granny apartments
- Senior citizen apartment communities
- Rental housing
- Adult care homes—foster homes
- Life care communities or continuum of
     care retirement communities (CCRCs)
- Assisted Living
- Care centers (nursing homes)
- Eldercare membership communities

> *Knowledge is power.*

Knowing your options empowers you. Even if you don't choose to move, knowing that there are options available is comforting.

QUESTIONS FOR CLARIFICATION

When deciding whether it is time to make a move, some of the questions people with whom I have worked ask themselves:

- Do I want to live near family?
- Do I want to live with people of all ages or with my age group?
- Am I doing this because I want to or because my spouse or others want me to?
- If I got more household help, could I stay in my home?
- Is my present living situation getting to be more than I can handle?
- How much will I miss puttering around doing the things I love to do?
- Do I want to live in a different climate?
- Will I feel safer?
- Will it be better or worse for general comfort level?
- Will it provide a meal or meals?
- Will I have more opportunities for socialization? Learning?
- Will I be able to get more or less physical exercise?
- How much am I going to miss my friends and groups I am in?
- Will there be room for my family or friends from out-of-town to stay with me?
- Can I take a pet along?
- Will there be fewer step? Wheelchair access?
- What is the reputation of the place I am considering moving to?

- Is there anyone living there who I can talk to about how well they like it there?
- Should I move while I am still able to get out and make new friends?

If I need someone to care for me now in order to keep living in my present living situation, and that person should die, what would I do?

What are your questions?

Perhaps it would be helpful for you to put a weight on how important these variables are to you when trying to decide if it's time to make a move. Answer yes or no to the first two columns and then weight these responses: very important -V, somewhat important -S, not important- N.

Variables	Where I live now	Where I may live	How important
Will it be a safer neighborhood?			
Will the climate be better?			
Will I be near:			
Public transportation?			
Family?			
Friends?			
New people? Potential friendships?			
Opportunities for learning?			
Stores?			
My place of worship?			
Place to exercise?			
Walking? Biking paths?			
What amenities will be available?			
Meal(s)?			
Accessible transportation?			
Socialization activities?			
Steps? Elevators?			
Built in safety (e.g., handrails, shower access)			
Help with activities of daily living?			
Will I have less upkeep?			
Can I have a pet?			
Will there be a mix of ages?			
Will I need to get a new:			
Doctor?			
Dentist?			
Driver's license?			
Will I have a higher quality of life?			
Add your own variables to this list.			

What is really important to you?

This exercise is a good conversation catalyst. Think about it and have your partner, if you have one, go through it also. What seems exciting about moving? One variable may be the biggie (such as loneliness, better climate, don't want to leave friends, want to live near family, etc.). This one variable may outweigh the rest and clarify whether or not this is the time to make a move and what the motivation truly is. Making a decision isn't always all that rational. I remember when my husband requested that I make a list of the pros and cons of having another child. I made a long list of cons on one side of the page (can't afford to, shouldn't bring another being into this troubled and overpopulated world, not enough room in the house, etc.) and on the other side, the pro side of the page, I put three words, "I want to." We did.

If you are considering moving, the first thing to do is figure out how much it costs to live where you do now and then compare it to the proposed cost of living at the place you are considering.

Can I afford to move?

	Where I live now	*Where I may live*	*Cost*
Mortgage/fees per month			
Electricity/gas			
Telephone/cable			
Health			
Long-term care			
Car			
Taxes			
Maintenance/repairs			
Outside—repairs, raking, shoveling, painting, gardening help			
Inside—repairs, laundry, plumbing, cleaning help			
Garbage/trash pick-up			
Entertainment			

Total each column and compare costs. Will it cost more or less?

An example of an effort for keeping elderly people in their own homes is the membership-based Beacon Hill Village concept that is serving as an innovative nonprofit prototype of a community effort to keep local residents in their homes in their own community. By partnering with proven providers of services, Beacon Hill Village is able to offer its members access to social and cultural activities, exercise opportunities, and home maintenance services, as well as medical care and assisted living at home. There are many neighborhood groups springing up patterning themselves after this Beacon Hill approach. Often older adults begin to "think smaller." They are through raising a family and don't need as much space. They realize that they don't want to continue doing as much upkeep or have so much expense and start looking at various options. The numbers of housing options are mushrooming as demand grows. There appears to be a trend toward living intergenerationally with people of all ages in intentional communities, co-housing, cooperatives, or staying in their own communities in a smaller home instead of segregating themselves with others of their age group. Many retirees are busily volunteering in their communities advocating for the kind of neighborhood they want and the kind of older adult amenities that appeal to their age group—like accessible transportation, sidewalks, and walking paths with benches. Bye-bye to shuffleboard and bingo. Fitness and wellness classes are becoming commonplace. Some facilities have swimming pools and full-service fitness centers. You can see old people playing with the Wii machines! The young-old and the healthy old-old are hiking, biking, swimming, lifting weights, doing yoga, Pilates, and TaiChi.

Chapter 7

Finishing Well

"Finishing" your life is a subject that many people don't like to think about, much less rehearse. This is unfortunate because, like any other time of life, there are better and worse ways to live your last years—including your dying time. The emphasis in this chapter is on how to best *live* during this time. Having lived a longer time than you have left to live, you have a sharpened perception of mortality and the preciousness of life.

CAREGIVING

At its best, caregiving is giving and receiving at the same time and can be thought of as a spiritual practice as well as a necessary and practical one. Most of us will spend a period of out lives caregiving … as a parent of young children, perhaps during a time of unexpected hardship in your family or to a friend, or in late life as a spouse, or as an adult child of an aging parent. The numbers of family caregivers are exploding with one out of every four households involved in some way, many trying to dodge the costs of long-term care professional help. Gail Sheehy[1] reports there is "an unpaid army of 44.5 million" people in our country caring for ailing adults. Acute care, which is high-tech, low-touch, in hospitals is well funded. Chronic illness, which is low-tech, high-touch care, is woefully under-covered. Family members, most of whom are unpaid and non-reimbursable, do 75%–80% of all caregiving. Very few people can afford to pay professional caregivers at home, and in order to have the government pay through Medicaid, you have to deplete most of your assets.

Caregiving can bring out the highest expression of who we are … an opportunity for kindness, compassion, and service to another. It is a difficult time. No matter how hard you try to make it possible for the person you love to die with grace and dignity, there are always many things that can't be controlled. And all the while you are experiencing loss. Loss is loss and can't be prettified. Important lessons are learned during these unrequested periods of time. We are forced to let go of some of our comfortable

> You know … there are only eight inches between a halo and a noose.
> —caregiver group participant

patterns and reestablish some more fitting ways of taking care of ourselves while caring for another. The goal of family caregiving is to maintain the dignity and well-being of the person cared-for in the best possible atmosphere. Balancing that with managing to take care of yourself is challenging and stressful.

There are fears of what's to come, competing demands on the caregivers' time, and a myriad of feelings … anxiety, sadness, anger, guilt … often draining one of energy. Some caregiving is done reluctantly. I led caregiver groups for years and in any given group there was a wide range of ways people regarded their role. Many were accepting, enjoying the group as a respite time that allowed them to get out of the house, share their feelings, get support and ideas about coping techniques and resources from the other group members. For the most part, this group of the relatively content found considerable meaning and satisfaction in their caregiving roles. Others couldn't wait for this period of their lives to be over and needed much listening, support, and suggestions for getting through this time.

The stories of caregivers cover an amazing spectrum. One woman I recall had an abusive, philandering husband. She had been contemplating divorcing him before his life-threatening illness, but had decided to stay as his caregiver for financial reasons and out of a sense of responsibility. Adult children, who had been abused as children, were now being called upon to care for their once abusive ailing parent. Adult children whose parent had major alcoholism problems, sometimes recovering, sometimes not, were faced with the call to help. These adult children, who may have, through years of therapy, reached a truce with their parent found themselves renegotiating their relationship. Truces seem to work when both parties are independent, and then change when the parent becomes dependent and needy. An elderly couple who had a volatile, Virginia Wolf-ish relationship for years, came out of this not-to-be-admired balance, when the wife became so disabled with Parkinson's Disease, that even hitting him with a cane would no longer do the job. I have seen dementia make the cared-for into such a different person that the caregiver no longer feels safe. And then there were the many caregivers in loving relationships who had to save themselves when the care burden became too much for them to handle physically or emotionally.

Every situation has to be listened to, scrutinized, and weighed. In a caregiver group there are the "ain't it awful's" caregivers sitting right next to the "fulfilled and content." Caregiving has thousands of permutations. It was during a tension-filled situation that a small voice uttered the priceless words of wisdom quoted above, "You know there's only eight inches between a halo and a noose." Quite a silence followed the speaker's statement as we contemplated its truth.

It's hard to generalize about caregiving. Caregivers have different personalities as do the cared-for. For some, caregiving seems like a natural evolvement and satisfies ones need for intimacy, purpose, sense of usefulness, and loyalty at this time of life. Those who are comfortable feel that they are doing something worthwhile … that they are making a difference to this person and to the family. Caregiving situations are constantly in flux and the help that is needed has to be reevaluated regularly. Is caregiving in your home the best option for you and the cared-for? Check out the services available in your area in Appendix F, on the Internet, and at the library. Talk with friends and family, find out what resources exist in your community, put the cared-for's name on the list of a preferred care center way ahead of time, check the availability of respite support help, talk to a financial planner about protecting your assets, and above all, keep communicating as the situation continues to change.

Take care of yourself. Remember that you can't be a good caregiver unless you take care of yourself. Some days this can seem impossible. Even if you have never been a very assertive person, it is now time to start. Ask for help so that you can have time away to do things that give you pleasure and keep you in shape for this big job. Create a toolkit for yourself that will help you balance your life when the going gets tough—meditations, favorite music, prayers, a list of people to call, techniques that help you center. Find healthy releases such as outings with friends and exercise. Communicate your needs to the cared-for, family, and friends, perhaps a leader in your place of worship, which often has an outreach service. Get as much help as you can from local resources saving yourself for the things only you can do.

Your job as a caregiver for a person who is nearing the end of his life is to "be there,"do what you can, and, at the same time, be preparing the cared-for and yourself to let go. Great satisfaction for lay caregivers comes from the notion that they are "doing what can be done" for the person they love. If this is a long drawn-out venture, it is important to continue communicating your feelings and needs as honestly as you can to someone so that you don't feel alone during this trying time. Caregiving is a natural and mysterious process that most of us will probably go through. As draining and difficult as it often is, it can also be a rich and fulfilling time for both the caregiver and the cared-for.

Caregiving is a journey full of unknowns, often with more downs than ups, often involving much sacrifice and deep learning. Ideally it is a journey with a loved one with the goal of making this time as comfortable and respectful as possible for him/her. It is an emotional and physical stretch for most. Honesty is usually, but not always, the best policy in caregiving. Openness with your feelings, under the umbrella of honesty, can sometimes be cruel. For your own survival, it is important to be honest with someone about your true feelings, if you are the major caregiver, but who that someone is has to be carefully selected.

If you as the caregiver are exhausted, or enormously depressed, or martyred, it is imperative that you talk about your feelings with either a professional, compassionate friend, or family member … or join a support group. This is to suggest that perhaps the care-receiver, who also probably has his/her hands full, may not be the best choice. Exploding with an honest "I just want this to be all over. I can't do it anymore" or a more subtle withdrawal from being able to be present with the care-receiver are signals that you need to talk, need help, need a new plan. How honest to be with the person who may be the person closest to your heart becomes a balancing act. It is a time when the caregiver needs to be listened to and heard, and helped to figure out the best way for proceeding through this difficult time, perhaps by making a change, or getting additional help. The emotional, physical, and spiritual status of the caregiver requires constant reevaluation. If you are a caregiver, what would be most helpful to make your important work easier?

Caregiving will probably be part of our natural cycle, a period in our life that calls for great inner strength and can reward us with a core of self-respect and "knowing" that no other experience in our life can provide. Many older adults have reevaluated their mid-life values and understand that the gentler values of being kind and caring give them the meaning and purpose that they are seeking in this time of deep inner work. Nothing puts these values to the test more than caregiving. It does not have to be done alone. There are many community resources available to help in providing transportation, respite help, meals on wheels, adult day care, hospice care, and financial expertise. (Check Appendix G for list of services possibly available.)

The period of caregiving can be a healing time for families, or the strain can cause family implosions. It is a time when self-care for the caregiver is imperative. Clear communication is enormously helpful and gentle assertiveness on both the caregiver and care-receiver's part is key. Caregiving is a dynamic time. It calls for much learning. Caregiving comes more naturally for some than others. Flexibility is also a key. You get settled happily on a care plan and something changes. A new plan has to be developed.

Why do it? The answer is different for everyone. Caregiving is nothing that anyone ever orders. It is thrust upon some and creeps up on others as your loved one loses his ability to do things for himself. Who wouldn't prefer that everyone be healthy and able and not have to go through a period of need? But it happens. It calls for a flexibility that requires being able to roll with the punches and accept this new state of affairs as what is. Most of us will be caregivers and cared-for at some point. The art of living life successfully is playing whatever hand you are given the best you can. The role of caregiving is often dictated for financial reasons and the emergency need to cope with an undesirable situation—some being far more difficult and complex than others.

Caring is not only about what we "do," but also about how we choose to "be." It can mean being in the background. Often when with a person who is close to death, we don't have anything to offer but our own feeling of helplessness. That feeling helps us truly connect because we are just there—all that we are and are not. What is … is. We don't want our loved ones to be sick, nor would we have chosen to spend our time doing whatever it is we now find ourselves doing. But we have found by now that we are not as "in charge" of our precious lives as we once thought we were. Things happen and we cope. We really have only two choices—to cope or not to cope—and most of us choose to do so. Sometimes it is very hard to keep our heart open and to keep balanced in the face of the difficulties that simply happen. Caregivers often use "the Braille method"—feeling their way along from moment to moment in uncharted territory. A professional can't just say to a lay person, "This is how to do it." There are too many variables and too many unknowns for any cookie-cutter answers.

Caring at its best lets the cared-for know somehow that you are on the side of their deepest and best hope for themselves. Many report that caring for another helps them see that they are a link with all that has gone before and will come later. I got in touch with that primordial feeling when I was putting Vicks vapor rub on my granddaughter's chest. At that moment, I had a sense that, besides being a grandmother, I was my mother, and I was myself as a child. It felt comfortable, complex, and eternal.

If you are a caregiver, recall times when what you are doing has felt just right, moments when you said to yourself, "Yes—this is why I do this!"

And then there are the many times you may say to yourself, "How can I get out of this? When will this end?" If you are a caregiver now, what do you find the most difficult to handle?

Caregiving is not a basket of fruit. Emotional reserves become exhausted. Caregivers often report feeling isolated and dulled to the rest of the world. They become demoralized, feeling that it is just too big a job, often feeling worse than the person who they are supposedly helping. They feel under-appreciated, have interpersonal conflicts with doctors and the health-care community, faulty communication with family, and a staggering paperwork overload. To impress members of caregiver groups that I have facilitated about the pervasiveness of guilt, I started meetings by asking the members to share what they felt guilty about that week. The question never brought silence. Caregivers feel guilty about an amazing array of things … doing too much or too little for the care receiver or for themselves. That process lightened things up and helped them see the encompassing nature of this feeling.

> *I feel bad that I don't feel worse.*
> *—one group participant's guilt report*

There are positive and negative ways to be a caregiver:

Positive	Negative
Listen carefully	Give advice, scold, argue, patronize
Empower-offer support, but encourage independence	Do it all, invite dependency
Validate the strengths of the cared-for to perform	Assume helplessness in cared-for
Be patient, caring, empathetic, encouraging, respectful	Be smothering, infantilizing, impatient
Encourage discussion of feelings	Discount or ignore feelings, stick to doing tasks
Encourage life review, reminisce	Take care of physical needs only
Ask what care receiver wants	Assume you know
Take care of yourself, role model	Be a martyr or a saint
Be assertive	Be a door mat

There is an art to caregiving:

- an art to having people believe you care
- an art to listening

- an art to helping people feel safe and important
- an art to having people know you can be trusted, so when you say "what do you need from me?" they believe you mean it.

Caregiving is holy work and it is hard work. It is a gift you give another who is experiencing a hard time letting him know that he is not alone with it. If seen as a privilege, it can give down deep satisfaction like few other endeavors. You have to continually work on your mindset. It's easy to be derailed. It is easy to let yourself go and not take care of yourself. Be sure to program special time for yourself so you always can be looking forward to something. Reread the many tips for self-care in Chapter Four. There is an art to balancing caregiving for another and taking care of yourself. Even when your care-receiver cannot be healed, he/she can be valued and comforted. There is an art to being present for another.

WHAT DOES 'BEING PRESENT' TO ANOTHER MEAN?

Often we are told that the most important thing we can do for another is to follow our intuition and just "be present" for the other. What does this mean? Intuition has been defined as "knowing from within." Intuition is recognized as being vital on the one hand, but discounted and mistrusted by our society's preference for the scientifically provable. It is about trusting your hunches and feelings, and opening your heart to others that you are able to be present. Do you trust your intuition? Give some examples of times when you've witnessed your intuition at work.

Presence means "being with," a holistic concept involving body, mind, and spirit. This concept of being present challenges our health-care system's tendency to deal only with the body—using drugs, machines, and technology to keep it working. Often professional and lay caregivers get so caught up with the "doing" tasks of caring and the rush-rush atmosphere that they lose focus on the equally important "being" there. There is an art to "hanging out" just "being" in a situation. It means you have no goal, no destination, but just an awareness of the moment. We are acculturated to try to do whatever we are doing "right" so it is hard to just "be there" often feeling helpless and vulnerable. It's hard to learn to *allow* versus pushing for things to happen. Henri Nouwen[2] said, "Healing is the humble but also demanding task of creating and offering a friendly empty space where strangers can reflect on their pain and suffering without fear, and find the confidence that makes them look for new ways right in the center of their confusion."

Think of times when you have felt totally attended to. Describe them.

Who do you think of when you think of a person who is particularly good at "being present"?

My business partners, two nurses, and I set about exploring these concepts of intuition and being present. We created a video, "Being Present: Opening the Door to Intuition" to help caregivers—both lay and professional—reflect on why they are doing their rich and important work, what they are receiving from it, and how to demystify the concept of intuition. Intuition requires being present, which has four intertwined components:

1. Intention: purpose
2. Centering: ability to focus
3. Mutuality: relationship to the other
4. Connectedness: relationship to all

INTENTION means stating the purpose for what you're doing. There are two questions to ask:

1. What am I "doing" here? This is the task intention and is usually easy to answer. "I'm keeping everything cleaned up, making appointments, orchestrating the regimen of pill-taking, getting the meals...."
2. What is my purpose for "being" here? This is the deeper caring intention. It is important not to get lost in the task intention and forget the caring intention. The hope is to be able to integrate them. The general rule of caregiving is that you respond to the level most in need at the time. Some of the time the tasks to be done take priority and are what is most important. Other more subtle times it is your caring purpose which is to "be with" the cared-for, to let him/her know you care, to reduce stress, to create a healing/loving atmosphere, to listen, to lighten things up when it's most needed. If you are being drained by the tasks, it is time to get other helpers in to do them so that you can save yourself for the "being" part of caring. Ask yourself, "Is my caring intention being overridden by my doing tasks?" They hopefully can be kept in balance.

My business partner Frank told of an encounter that illustrates how important it is to attend to and appreciate simple things. As a hospice nurse, he was caring for a ninety-two-year-old woman with ovarian cancer. When he brought her breakfast tray, he asked if he could open the shades and let in some sun. She said "yes." She immediately said, "Isn't the sky a beautiful blue?" At first he responded with a feeble "Yeah" and continued hurrying about his tasks. When she exclaimed again about the beautiful shade of blue, he stopped and gave her his attention. She went on to marvel at the beautiful crimson color of the cranberry juice. Since she had cataracts, Frank held the juice up to the sun for her and agreed that it was a stunning color. He then brought the flowers she had received over to her bed for her to examine more closely. She sparkled and seemed so alive. The whole encounter of "being there" took only a minute and Frank wouldn't have thought any more about it, but she died that night. It struck him then that her last words to him were about the beauty in the world and, had he not paused, he would have missed what, in retrospect, was a powerful interchange. Do not miss your chances to share such moments of magnificent simplicity. The sky can be so blue, the cranberry juice so crimson, the flowers so beautiful. Life becomes so elementary, and simple things take on major significance at the end of life.

CENTERING is the second important component of being present. It is about focusing on how best to quiet and take care of yourself. How you choose to center yourself has to fit for you. Recommended techniques are:

1. Relaxed deep breathing Sit down and take some deep breaths. Then start repeating to yourself, on the in-breath, "this moment," and on the out-breath, "only moment." Repeat this over and over and feel yourself calm down. This can become a transformative tool for well-being … and you can do it anywhere.

2. Imagine yourself in a favorite healing spot. Recall the feelings. Visualize surrounding yourself with protective white light during difficult interactions.

3. Repeat calming statements.

    "I am enough" "I don't need to fix anything … I only need to be here … and care"

    "God (Jesus, Mary, Buddha) is with me. I am not alone." "I must be gentle"—with myself and with the care-receiver.

4. Center yourself using what works. Roots to the center are multiple. For some it's singing, listening to music, praying, meditating, reading, gardening, knitting, walking, or swimming

What works to help you center?

MUTUALITY is the third component and addresses the relational aspect of "being present." As caregivers, we're operating under the umbrella of interdependence and behaving in such a manner that the cared-for senses that "we are in this together," "we are a team and learning together."

Being present frees you of the weightiness of the burden of having to "do" something. When you are simply "being" from within, there is a lightness, a spaciousness, a freedom from thinking you should or can control things. You are open to whatever might happen. Your inner knowing takes over and you know what to do and how to be. It is not about serving the weak and broken. It is about serving the wholeness in each other and wholeness in life. It's about taking your turn in the cycle of life. You have no idea how you will behave when you are faced with serious illness or death until it happens to you. Your cared-for is one of your teachers. Learn from him/her, perhaps how to be … or one way you don't want to be.

Our responsibility is to care with compassion for them for their journey. Compassionate action is not done for others. It is done with others for ourselves. Mutuality means putting your ego aside. You are not a fixer or a healer. Being present is a selfless act. It is about being compassionate through your attending, and caring for another human being. We can't eliminate suffering, but we can bring truth and kindness to hard situations, create a loving environment, and seek out information that can help make better choices. Being present is hanging out with another. It is being part and parcel of the situation. Hanging out allows you to go deeper within yourself, being conscious of what's going on but at the same time not being lost in it. In this space, even in the most difficult of circumstances, you can float in the love and humanity of it all.

When I can hear you—what you be—
what lives most deeply in you—
when your hearing speeds
the beating of life for me—
then the meeting is a song,
and harmony invades our silences
and all the language that we know
is love.   In fact,
                     loving is
                     a language
                     of the ear—
not so much the words you use,
not the thoughts I share,
                     but
                     how urgently
                     we tune ourselves
                     to the meaning
                     of each others.
—Janet Peterson[3], ***A Book of Yes***

We have learned from witnessing and experiencing the frailties of our human condition much about the art of humility and how alike we all are. When we are caregiving, there is a power differential. One of us is healthy, lucid, and has more energy than the other. But in the great cycle of interdependence, we are conscious that we will all take our turn. There is a deeply embedded sense of interrelatedness—the helping of one for another because "we are in this together." This person I'm caring for might be me in a few years. Who I am and who she is, is who we all are. You are serving the wholeness of this person. We live in a world of interrelatedness and interdependency. We take turns. Perhaps the greatest gift we have to give is letting the care-receiver know that he/she is not alone in this and that we don't view giving and receiving as two discreet separate acts, but as one. We have only a dim idea how we will behave when we are faced with our own dying. The person we are caring for is our teacher. We may learn how to be or how not to be. Our responsibility is to love them with compassion for their journey.

Rachel Naomi Remen talks about the difference between service as a form of connection with life, and service that is a veiled form of judgment, a statement that someone is broken and needs to be fixed. With a "fixing" mentality, there is an inequality of power that can easily become a moral distance and it's harder to be present and serve if you have this distance between you. We serve well when we are profoundly connected. If you are a caregiver, it is important to ask yourself: How do I see myself in relationship with the other? How is she/he like me?

Mutuality lets the other know somehow that you are on the side of their deepest and best hope for themselves.

This works both ways. The caregiver has to be taking care of herself also. When this feeling of mutuality exists, the relationship is a two-way street; you are both giving and receiving. What is needed so that the integrity of each of us is equally respected?

CONNECTEDNESS flows out of mutuality.

If mutuality is about you and me, connectedness, the third component of being present, is our relationship with all things. We get this sense of "us-ness," of feeling connected to the much bigger picture in other ways … perhaps when we are listening to beautiful music, hearing a touching piece of poetry, experiencing the wind, observing spiders work their magic. We are better able in late life to have a perspective of the whole. We see all the changes that have occurred, the things that happened we couldn't have planned for or expected We realize everyone has had their own journey with their own surprises.

> *The deepest act of love is to help a person love herself.*

We realize the multi-facetedness of all beings, the magnificence and mysteriousness of human existence, and that this later time of life can be a peak, a climax—not an anti-climax.

Think back to the part of the book where we reflected on our peak moments, those moments when we stand in awe of nature or a work of art. They may be moments when you felt fully known, accepted, and loved by another, or moments of giving and receiving love simultaneously. They are timeless immortal moments when we may feel like a small blip in the big scheme of things, but still very much a part of it. This feeling of being part of an awesome cycle is often with you when you are a caregiver or care-receiver … the grandest of gifts.

> *Being present is a privilege.*

When have you felt this connectedness? Can you describe the feeling?

Being present is caring to the ultimate. It begins when you make the choice to open your heart.

HOW DO I WANT TO BE TREATED?

There is a variation of the Golden Rule, "Do unto others as you would have them do unto you." that applies especially well to caregiving.

This calls for good respectful communication. It is a two-way street. Both parties deserve respect. You are in partnership with the other. In order for the Platinum Rule to be followed, the cared-for have to let themselves be known—their stories and their idiosyncrasies—much more than what is on a medical chart. I am reminded of a story a wonderful author and writing teacher, Sandra Benitez, related to me. She told me of a documentary film that observed Pablo Picasso over a period of several hours as he worked on a painting. "We see him work first in pencil, his broad strokes. Then we see the erasures and the additions. After this, Picasso starts laying on each color, one by one. At first, it looks as if Picasso

> *The Platinum rule—"Treat others as they want to be treated."*

is painting a chicken: there is the comb, the beak, the feathers, the chicken feet. But then, he adds more color, and the painting begins to change into something else. All the while, the figure of the chicken is beneath all that is painted on top. In the end, the painting looks like a mask, a cat-mask, but the painter knows the chicken is still on the canvas. Picasso says he paints so that he can "see the truth at the bottom of the well." There is "a chicken" under all of us. No matter what we see or other people see, there is so much more. Older people want to be known and respected for who they are now, and the chicken that lies hidden. This is why sharing stories becomes so important.

Older people want to be known. Remember they were not always old. We might be surprised at some of the amazing things they did when they were younger. We need to know this to treat the whole person now that their bodies won't let them do things they used to love doing. Rakhma Homes in the Minneapolis/St. Paul area are residences that house ten to twelve elderly people who live family-style. They regularly have life-review sessions focused on one of the residents at a time, where the others can get to know who this person is. Sometimes the resident and the family gather pictures and put together elaborate slide shows honoring the individual. Although most of the time it is best to live in the present, sometimes the present doesn't seem so pleasant. Even that has to be kept in balance. As Henry said in the earlier cartoon, "It's okay to live in the moment, unless the moment sucks." When your life is in disarray it is helpful to focus on fond memories and appreciating the yesterdays, remembering the experiences and the people you have loved. Most people love to be asked to share the richness of their life experiences and especially cherish having a good listener. It cannot be emphasized enough the importance of being validated. (See Appendix A: The Art of Listening.)

Our society has a sad way of viewing the very old or sick in terms of whatever ailment or symptom they have. In the hospital you're liable to become identified as "the broken hip in Room 215," "the failing liver in 218," or "the Problem in Room 233." You don't want to be defined solely in terms of your "functional deficits." When other people start defining you that way, your self-esteem is likely to plummet. Besides, what is perceived to be a behavior problem in an older adult could actually be that person's strength. Child psychologists have long recognized that the child in a dysfunctional family who "acts out" is often the healthiest one in the family—the one who is trying to break out of a sick system. A stubborn or "problem" elder may be the one who has the courage to defy the system. It might just be the system that has the functional deficit.

One dear friend called me on the phone from the hospital and said pretty desperately, "Help me with my sanity. Remind me I'm human. I just saw that the sign on my door and it says, 'Warning, radioactive material inside.' That 'material' is me!" (She had had some radium inserted as part of her therapy) And, she continued, "I fell down and smacked my face and they *glued* my cut." She wanted reassurance, and a listening ear. Seemingly gone was the person who has a high appreciation for music and fine food, who loves people, and loves fun. This is sad and, unfortunately, not atypical.

Imagine that you are quite old and less able to get around. How would you like to be treated?

It's safe to say that people, at any age, want to have something to look forward to, and always, always want to be treated with kindness, dignity, and respect. In addition to this generalization, however, there are the nuances that reflect an individual's particular personality. Now that you have given some thought to how you would like to be treated, go a step further. Let people know. Then the platinum rule can be applied. In order to be treated the way you want to be treated, it is your responsibility, or that of someone close to you who can speak for you, to let the right people know in an assertive way what your desires are. There are no guarantees but, if you let folks know what you want, your chances are greatly improved for success. It's true about the "squeaky wheel."

The first thing to find out in a hospital or care center is how a person wants to be addressed … first name … or more formal name … Mrs. Smith, Mr. Johnson, Dr. Jones. Older adults usually do not want to be called "Honey" or "Sweetie." They want to be called what they want to be called. If you want the atmosphere to be respectful and loving, you're best off modeling this. If you want to be treated well, your best chance is to treat those around you well. This is just common sense. I have been doing five-day retreats for women in the north woods of Minnesota for twenty-three summers and the sure-fire, what-can't-help-but-work instruction that I give my co-leader is "love these women out of their shoes for these five days." You can't lose if that's the atmosphere out of which you operate. If you create a safe and loving atmosphere of mutuality in a care center, recognizing that you are learning from and with each other, a healing spirit develops.

In a care center, it's helpful for everyone to have her own personalized toolkit, which was discussed in Chapter Four. The words used in quality facilities are "Patient Centered Care." The idea is to design care to what's important to the resident—their needs, values, and priorities. In addition to needing to be kept physically comfortable the professional caregivers are expected to give emotional support and have an integrated understanding of a person's world. Who is she? Who is hidden in there?

A Whobody Chart, is an idea that will help design a shared care plan based on bottom-up power, through the resident's perspective, rather than the usual top-down approach which doesn't work nearly as well. One adult day center I visited described its focus as respect for everyone involved … starting with the residents, then the staff, and finally everyone who entered the center. Program planning had to be enjoyable for everyone, insuring that staff was involved with participants rather than doing something for them. Doing for is patronizing; doing with the resident's input is respectful

In better care centers, care conferences are coordinated with the doctors' physical care plan and the rest of the resident's emotional and spiritual needs. Electronic records from the primary doctor and specialists are, or before long will be, available for the resident and families to see. Care conferences are a time to update the residents concerns, to answer questions, to find out how she is doing, to relook at the Whobody Chart, and to figure how to make things as good as they can be. If there is a problem, formulate a plan for resolving it, and check it out at the next care conference to determine how the new plan is working. That way the resident knows she is being heard.

WHOBODY CHART

- How do I want to be addressed?
- Who makes up my support system? Who do I want around?
- What's important to know about me?

- What are some of my favorite stories?
- What am I interested in learning?
- What subjects do I like to talk about?
- What are my habits?
- What gives me pleasure?
- How can I be of service to others?
- What did I do for work?
- What am I proud of?
- Who are the people you have loved?
- What are my favorite foods?
- Music?
- Writers?
- Poets?
- What else should be added?

> *I hope that the hand that helps me when
> I am truly frail knows who I am.*

Everybody's Whobody Chart should be individualized and during family care conferences be updated, when it becomes obvious that something should be added or subtracted. The toolkit described in Chapter Four is another approach to letting oneself be known.

COMMUNICATE WHAT YOU WANT

All too often, health-care professionals or family members assume they know what you want, when that assumption might be entirely wrong. Your assertive self is responsible for letting people know what you are thinking. If you eventually reside in a care center, which twenty percent of Americans will do after the age of eighty, let your wants be known. Most of your values will remain the same even if your circumstances change. If breathing fresh air and getting outside to watch the birds and squirrels is important to you, think about this now so you can plan and let people know. If you usually prefer to be alone, or with a chosen few, let that preference be known. A health-care professional's job involves following a care plan. Your job is to let people in charge know what you value, what being treated in a dignified manner means to you. Ask that this be written into your care plan and respected.

If you have strong feelings about certain things, it is important to let people know. Unless we tell people what we want, we can't expect to get it. We don't necessarily always get what we want even when we ask, but our chances are greatly improved if we communicate clearly. So often older adults with whom I work believe they are misunderstood. On further inquiry, I discover that they are misunderstood for good reason. One common example of this is, when their adult children ask their parent how they are doing, they reply, "Just fine." Perhaps they answer this way because they value not complaining, or because, at that very moment they are feeling okay, but the response erases the validity of their complaint that their kids don't care. The kids don't have the straight scoop! The inability to communicate is often the primary problem. We can be fine most of the time and still need help some of the time. We simply can't expect others to know what we need if we don't explicitly tell them what help we need. Learning how to ask for what we want and learning to "receive well" may be one of our hardest life lessons and one of the most important behaviors to model.

Think carefully about your communication with those people close to you. How can you make it better?

_____

_____

Following are some specific thoughts that some older adults have shared about how they want to be treated. Some apply to persons in senior living residences and care centers. Some apply to anyone. What ones fit for you?

1. "I want to be included in whatever is going on or being discussed. Whether it's about me or about something difficult going on with someone I love, I don't want to be overprotected and treated like a China doll. I'm not dead yet. I want to be treated like I am alive until my last breath."

    Would you like to be included in all discussions, or would you rather not have to deal with anything other than what is already on your plate?

    _____

    _____

    _____

    _____

2. "I'd like a certain atmosphere created in my room to keep my spirits up. I want pictures of people I love or have loved in sight. I want some of my favorite objects and albums of favorite memories."

    What do you want in your room to make if as perfect as it can be?

    _____

    _____

    _____

    _____

3. "I want my crazy rhythms to be respected." Examples: "If I want to stay up late finishing my book, watching Charlie Rose on TV, or playing spider solitaire, don't snap off the light. That's me." "I need to have a cup of coffee first thing in the morning … before I talk." "I love my TV show between 4–5 PM. Please don't let anyone disturb me."

    What habits or rhythms are important to you that you would like to have respected?

    _____

    _____

    _____

    _____

4. "I want to be able to let my needs be known and to have choices." Examples: "I dislike pain. I have a high pain tolerance so if I complain, take me seriously." "I would like to have a say in who is coming to visit, when, and for how long."

"I want to know and care about the people who care for me. I do not believe in the 'remain detached' model that so many health-care professionals have been taught." "I like my alone time." "I hate to sing." "I like to joke with people."

What do you want people to know about you?

Don't assume how people want to be treated. Ask them. They like choices. I was asked by a daughter to visit her eighty-six-year-old mother in the care center where she lived because she was "getting difficult." She no longer wanted to go to her son or daughter's houses and refused recently "to go on a ride to look at scenery," in fact, was reported to have said, "I hate scenery." I went to the center and found a witty dynamo of a woman who was, indeed, angry with her adult children because she didn't feel listened to or respected. She was told that, "We are going on a ride to look at the pretty scenery" versus being asked. She loved her friends at the care center and, because she was relatively healthy and alert, had made herself very useful to her friends—helping them with a variety of tasks. She was choosing them over scenery.

Laughter is healing. A favorite memory of mine was visiting a client in a nursing home who I especially loved and had seen often years before when she was still in the community. Now I was hearing that Eleanor was pretty depressed and mad that she just kept on living and was using up all of her savings. She had wanted to pass some money on to her daughter, was blind, and probably getting close to dying. I went to the facility, asked for her room number, and then was surprised to not find her there. I asked the nurse where Eleanor was, and the nurse said that she had escorted her to the lounge. I went to the lounge and there was Eleanor … smoking. I told her who I was, gave her a big hug, and said, "Gee, I didn't know you smoked!" She said in her droll way, "I just took it up. They say it kills you!" I burst out laughing … and she did … and we had a delightful time, much to the astonishment of the staff and other residents. She died three days later, reportedly still in a better frame of mind … and I still smile.

5. "Ask me what I want to talk about, and I will tell you." Examples: Perhaps I will want to have someone listen to me and help me sort out what I am thinking and feeling. Perhaps I want to be distracted from what's going on with me. If I am in bad shape, I may just want to be dislodged from the trajectory of thinking about dying or being sick. I want to talk about baseball. Perhaps I want talk about what's going on with you. Perhaps not. I change. Ask me.

6. "Ask me how I want to be treated physically." Don't assume. Examples: "I like touch. I like hugs and foot rubs." "It's hard for me to get up out of chair. The best way to help me get up is…" "I don't want anything done for me that I can do myself. If you want to offer help, say so and give me the prerogative of saying yes or no.

_____

_____

_____

7. "I want to keep on learning. I want to exercise my brain, have book discussions, and talks about interesting subjects. I want to know what is going on in the world and be able to discuss it. I don't want to be talked down to. I want to learn in partnership with you."

What subjects are you interested in pursuing?

_____

_____

_____

_____

8. "Some things have changed for me. I want you to know about them and be respectful." Examples:

"I would like to meet in an environment where distractions are filtered out." (Turn off the TV.)

In a class, "Could you present the lesson we are to share at a moderate pace and loud enough to be heard? If you speak too fast or too quietly, your bubbling about what we are going to do together may sound like babbling to me."

"Give me time to process salient information, please." Silence and quiet can provide valuable thinking and processing time."

"As we move from one location to another, please avoid hurrying me along. "(Slow your rapid walking pace to match my slower steps.)

"When it is possible, give me a written review of the tasks I'm supposed to do." (a phone number to call, a name and address for a contact)

"It's easier for me if you emphasize the tasks requiring verbal skills."

"Make sure that my tasks in the learning process are meaningful and relevant, not busy work, please."

Which of these applies to you? What would you add?

9. "If I get very sick, I don't want to be blamed for it. Well meaning people seem to want to theorize on just why I got sick. Theorizing, unless I ask for it, doesn't help me. It may help them in some way but it doesn't help me. It is no time to be told I may have done something wrong. I probably will question myself to some degree, but I don't need others to speculate. The "why?" has become secondary to how to best respond to the situation now that that it's here. Maybe I will want more information Maybe I will want advice but I will ask for it if I do."

10. "There are lots of gifts that would be fun to receive." Examples:

"The gift or your presence. I love visits."

"Pretty stationary or cards to send to people and someone to write my words for me."

"An offer to rewrite my address book in large readable printing."

"Interesting books to read."

"My eyes aren't so good. I'd love to have someone read to me."

"Promises to drive me to appointments and for pleasure outings."

Those who are living independently in the community say: "I love getting certificates for snow shoveling, leaf raking, lawn mowing, house cleaning, laundry help."

What gifts would please you?

Treat others as they want to be treated. Communicate. Ask them.

2. GRIEVING LOSSES

HOW TO HELP ANOTHER WHO IS GRIEVING

You can't assuage someone's terrible grief and pain. Consolation is an art. Your job is to be there, to listen, and to walk with him/her through the process without denying or overriding it. Let them feel it. When someone much loved dies, pain is part of the legacy to the ones left behind. Looking at it from this angle, there is a certain glory in grief. It is an indicator of how much you have loved. It is sad someone dies and no one grieves.

> *I saw grief drinking a cup of sorrow*
> *and called out,*
> *"It tastes sweet, does it not?"*
> *"You've caught me," grief answered*
> *"and you've ruined my business.*
> *How can I sell sorrow,*
> *when you know it's a blessing?"*
> *—Rumi*

> *Grief expressed is grief diminished.*

It is important to go through the often agonizing but purifying process of grieving. We will all do it differently. There is no "right way" to grieve. Some people do not show their emotions publicly. It's really okay if you don't cry at all. It doesn't mean that you are an unloving, uncaring person. It is true that a person often feels better when he/she cries and lets some of the tension out, but it doesn't mean that they are better persons than those who don't. Tears relieve pressure and serve as a balm for your wounds.

The grieving person might exhibit some form of confusion early in the grieving process. In my experience, more people seek professional help after a major loss because they fear they are crazy than because they are sad. These moments of seeming craziness come, gradually diminish, and finally leave. Often people who are grieving have accepted the notion that there is a right way to grieve or a certain length of time that is legitimate for them to feel terrible. This isn't true. There are generalizations that are often applicable, but we will do our grieving our own way. We may have vivid flashes of the image of the person who has died and worry about our sanity. We may hallucinate about seeing the deceased in a crowd or on television, or may hear the person calling to us in the night. There is a similarity between this confusion and the searching behavior of a young child separated from a parent in a crowd. The child wanders about, not quite believing it, looking around, calling out, hoping that it's not true.

Often there is anger. It's usually directed at doctors, at the person who died, at others, or at themselves. Guilt often comes in the form of, "If I had only...." Sadness may be exhibited many ways—gray emptiness, meaninglessness, and even suicidal thoughts. There is as great a spectrum of variation in the expression of grief as there are people. If it has been a long dying process, there has often been anticipatory grief going on for a long time, and these people might bounce back relatively quickly. Others take a long time.

There is no one best way to help a grieving individual. What might help varies from individual to individual. Answer the two questions that I asked 317 members of peer counseling, caregiver, and grief groups I facilitated:

1. What helped you the most after you suffered a major loss?

2. What didn't help at all?

The individuality of the responses expressed led me to the conclusion that there are only a few generalizations that are safe to make. The most important criteria for helping another are to be sensitive to what the grieving person is thinking and feeling, and to be aware of your particular relationship with him/her. These will be your best clues to how to nourish healing and be present. Sometimes people responded with the same answers to the opposite questions. For example, in response to the first question "What helped?" many people reported that they loved hugs, but to "What didn't help?" there were occasional responses like "If this gives one more person the right to hug me, I'll scream!" It's important to know your person and be aware that what you might like may not fit for the other. Another category of interesting responses to "What didn't help?" were those who disliked being told they were "so strong" or "like the Rock of Gibraltar" realizing that their façade, which they both wanted and didn't, was so successful that they inadvertently were isolating themselves. The few generalizations that may be made to help people who are greiving are the following:

Do's:

- Let the person know you care.
- Listen. An open heart is often more important than words. A simple "I'm sorry," a touch, or hug (if appropriate) is worth a hundred words.
- Let the grieving person talk if he/she wants. Ask if he needs up-time or down-time.

- Perhaps there is a need for diversion.
- Reminisce. "I'll never forget…" "Remember the time…" "I wish that I had known him better; tell me about him."
- Give the bereaved information about the process of grieving. People are frightened by their feelings, their sense of feeling "out of control." They need reassurance that there are many facets and stages to the grieving process and they are not abnormal or crazy. It is a hard and painful journey.
- Make specific helpful gestures. Say "Let's have lunch on Wednesday," or "I will call some friends and tell the news, if you'd like," or "I'll handle the dinner after the funeral, if you'd like."
- Let the grieving person choose what she wants to do. Let her be the boss. Stick with her.
- Long after the loss has occurred, reach out to her. She generally will have little energy or initiative to do so for some time. Refrain from feelings of rejection if early attempts fail. Reach out again.
- Send snail-mail cards with personal notes.

Don'ts:

- Discount or minimize another's grief by comments such as "I know exactly how you feel," "It's a blessing," "Join the club," "I know someone who has it worse!"
- Avoid vulture-like comments like "If you're thinking of selling your house, I'd be interested!"
- Don't give advice unless you are asked. People are mixed up enough at this time without having to wade through conflicting advice. "Slow down," "Get busy," "Live with your daughter," "Don't live with your daughter," "Cry, it's good for you," "Don't cry; it doesn't help," "Take a tranquilizer; it helped me." All examples of things probably best left unsaid unless advice is specifically requested.
- Avoid any directives or "shoulds."
- Don't offer non-specific promises such as "Call me anytime," or "let's go to lunch sometime." Be specific with an offer. The person probably has little energy to follow through and could be very disappointed.

Being there and validating whatever the other is feeling are the main two ingredients for being helpful. Opening the door for the grieving person to talk can be helpful. By asking questions like, "What seems to be hardest for you? What do you miss the most?" you may open the door to some sharing. It is their call. Regret and guilt may be part of the grieving process, something the grieving person wishes he had or hadn't done or said. Being able to talk to someone or write about one's feelings are excellent ways to process.

Grief is a whole body response to loss … more than just the emotional response. Initially after a death, the grief stricken is viscerally exhausted, cognitively out of sync, and often spiritually challenged. Mourning is the outward expression of grieving. It's important to mourn. Funerals and rituals are a help to the process. Grieving is not about "getting over" the loss but adjusting to it, restoring yourself, and moving on. You know you are healing when you are infused with the feeling of love that you had for him/her and start to focus on some of the fun and good times, instead of just feeling overwhelmed with the raw sting of the loss. Real love does transcend death. You can no longer touch this person but you have not lost the essence of the relationship. You mourn the lack of the physical presence but the communion you had is there. Your focus, if you are a widow, shifts to "how to live as a single person." You know you are healing when you start truly caring again about other interests and other people. This is called the "caring paradox"—the only way you can heal from loss, as a result of caring and loving, is by more caring.

> *The essence of struggle is neither endurance nor denial.*
> *It is a decision to become new*
> *rather then to simply become older.*
> *It is the opportunity to grow*
> *either smaller or larger in the process.*
> —*author unknown*

Why me? At some point philosophers, theologians, and nearly everyone else struggles with this question. You try to make sense out of the suffering you see and feel. The answer has to be arrived at individually. We all have different histories, different spiritual and ethnic backgrounds, have read different books, and will travel our own path. We can listen, and observe, but can't impose meaning on another's experience. Grieving is an area where giving advice is to be especially avoided. How a person copes at this time is his own unique process.

> *If it doesn't kill me, it makes me grow.*
> —*Nietzsche*

Meditation for someone who is grieving (to be read by a friend) This person could be grieving the searing pain of a recent loss, the accumulated personal losses of a lifetime, or a pervasive, global pain about the injustices in the world.

Find a comfortable spot to relax. Take some deep breaths. Notice that part of your body where you hold tension and heaviness. Put your thumbs on the aching spots … perhaps your neck and shoulders. Massage the tender spots. Place your hands there and rub gently. Feel your feelings. Don't analyze anything—just feel the feelings. Locate another spot on your body that accumulates pain and massage the hurt there. Breathe and feel. Breathe and feel. Press your sensitive area and massage it gently. Appreciate your pain. It is a result of caring and loving. Let the feelings come. Know that they are signs of your aliveness, your ability to care and love. Feel love for yourself. Release the pain. Feel it go. Know that this is good. The only path to healing is this letting go. Breathe in the freshness … breathe out the pain. Breathe in the freshness … breathe out the pain. Appreciate your grief as the path to your own healing. Release your hands from your sensitive spot. Release the pressure. Know that this is good. Take another long deep breath. Gradually return, knowing you are further along your path.

HOW IS THE PROCESS OF GRIEVING DIFFERENT FOR OLDER PERSONS THAN IT IS WHEN YOUNGER?

Don't assume that grieving or dying is going to be easier because one is older. There are different variables playing into grief and bereavement in every scenario. At no time in one's life is it harder to predict one's reaction to a major loss.

- Sometimes it is a victory. It is welcomed. "Time to move on."
- Sometimes it is the final indignity. Watching a painful death, especially someone who you've spent 50–60 years with, takes with it a total loss of meaning, your role, and your desire to go on living.
- Sometimes grieving elderly choose to withdraw, to be alone, and do some very personal inner work.
- Sometimes the bereaved are alone, not by choice, and are painfully lonely.

William Worden's[4] four basic tasks of mourning:
1. Task one: Accept reality of the loss.
2. Task two: Work through the pain.
3. Task three: Adjust to the environment in which the deceased is missing.
4. Task four: Emotionally relocate the deceased and move on, invest energy in new relationships.

Older people do grieve and think about dying differently than younger people. Using William Worden's[4] tasks as a framework, you can appreciate some of differences.

Task one: Accept reality of the loss

It is different for elderly because there is often a certain readiness, whether conscious or not, a predictability, an expectation that this is the time of life that you die. Eighty percent of people who die are over sixty years of age. In 1900, sixty-two percent of families could expect a death of a child; now only four percent experience this. Now the expectation is to die in your eighties or nineties; any death before that is thought to be premature. At that age, older adults are very aware of their finiteness, the temporariness of bodies, and are less cocky about how much control they have over things in general. They have had a lifetime of easing into the reality of endings. They have observed at the very least their change in hair color or amount of hair, new aches, other shifts and sags, and a lowering of energy levels. Younger people still have the illusion of control mightily embedded in them so the shock of feeling helpless may be more terrifying and daunting.

The predictability of dying leads then to less protest, less denial then deaths at an earlier age, less of "why me?" Some of the diminishments that come with late life are already in progress. Getting old, the process itself, brings with it enough trauma and challenge that death loses some of its ferocity. There have been a steady stream of adjustments and acceptances. There's been a subtle or open anticipation of death approaching for a long time by both the dying and the caregivers … more time to get ready and to finish unfinished business.

Task two: Work through the pain

Major differences in how one grieves in this stage revolve around the unacceptability for persons in the old-old age bracket to really express their feelings. There is often much negation of feeling. There are still persons in this age group who believe that "crying doesn't help anything," "not complaining is a virtue," "displaying any expression of feeling is a sign of weakness," and they certainly don't want to "fall apart" … out of consideration for others. There is a belief that it is unpleasant for others to witness emotional pain. This difference is changing. The young-old are more into expressing their feelings. Denial of feelings get some through the rough times without the discomfort of openness, but this denial takes energy and takes a toll on the body. Working with and working through pain and suffering is far more healing in the long run.

Depression amongst the old-old is grossly under-diagnosed by the widow, family, and doctors. Because there is still a great stigma attached to being mentally ill in this age group, depressed older persons feel more comfortable complaining of physical aches and pains. This discomfort, along with lack of information and ageism, is why depression is so often under-diagnosed. If a forty-year-old man doesn't feel like eating, doesn't feel like getting off the couch, and just watches TV all the time, the family would wonder and check it out. If the man is eighty and behaves the same way, the family thinks this is the way it is when you get old and, doesn't pursue seeking help.

> *Young widows weep:*
> *old widows get sick.*

People are depressed when they appear lifeless and have no interests. It can manifest in a myriad of ways. Some people can function and others cannot. It is the most holistic of illnesses. It can affect your sleep, your eating habits, your GI tract, your hormones, and body chemistry … and most definitely your relationships. You feel spiritually disconnected. Depression in the elderly is often harder to diagnose because it masquerades as physical symptoms, memory problems, and confusion. Depression is a complex syndrome, a combination of biological factors, an interplay of illnesses and the accompanying treatments, the strengths and weaknesses of the individual, and his/her belief system. This under-diagnosis is especially tragic because depression *is* treatable at any age. Sixty-eighty percent can be helped.

Working through the pain may be more difficult in later life because you may be dealing with multiple losses. There is often concern over their health and big decisions to make. They have by the simple fact of longevity and the number of years that they have spent in relationship with the deceased, a higher degree of interdependence. The symptoms of this multiple grieving process manifest themselves by a certain unpredictability of reaction. You are apt to see stoicism to the major loss and complete compulsiveness to seemingly inconsequential events. Because they are much closer to the end of their own lives, their loss has less of an aura of impermanence to it than happens to their younger counterparts, who know at some level that they may pull out of this, regroup, and start anew. Early recognition of depression is helpful because its progress can be derailed by learning techniques to relieve stress, adopting an exercise regimen, and developing your own personalized toolkit for helping improve your attitude.

Some portion of this age group welcomes death. Because of the expectation and timeliness of death, you hear comments like:

- "I'm so happy that he could finally move on."
- "I wouldn't want her to live on and be so very sick."
- "He lived a full life."
- "Wasn't he lucky to just die in his sleep."

We have seen a radical change in the last decade or two because of the many new ways of saving lives. The refrain of the elderly not infrequently seems to have switched from "Doctor, please save me" to "doctor, please let me die." People are far more interested in "quality of life" than extending the number of their years in a qualityless existence. The average American says he would like to live to age eighty-five. Only 5% would like to live to be 100 and only if they could be guaranteed some quality. An advantage of being old and grieving would seem to be that you are not on fast track of younger generations so theoretically have the time to grieve. There is a flip side to this. Having too much time on your hands can literally be a "killer." Loneliness, no way to divert your attention, lack of touch, and no one with whom to talk through your feelings is more prevalent in this age group.

Task three: Adjust to the environment in which the deceased is missing

It is harder for old people to adjust because there are fewer options at that age. It is often harder to find someone to share and witness the process of grieving in an empathetic way. It is harder to work all the way through the grieving process before being hit by something else. It is harder to redefine yourself. Many studies say older men often have a rougher time adjusting because they are less talented in survival tasks such as feeding themselves and planning social outings. Men often receive more help, and it is true that they often remarry. It is often harder to adjust when you are older because decisions need to be made and you probably have less energy to pull yourself out of the abyss.

Task four: Emotionally relocate the deceased and move on, invest energy in new relationships

This is a much, much harder task to do when you are very old yourself. There is less opportunity, time, energy, or often desire to do so. It is harder for older people to think in terms of starting anything … relationships, projects. Whereas younger persons may often desire new relationships, the norm, in my experience, is that older

> *I always think of the story of the sick little boy in the hospital who pressed the button to get help and was asked over the speaker system by a voice, "What do you want?" to which his small voice replied, "A face. Could I see a face?"*

people have less interest and expectation for this. There is no timeline on how long it will take someone to get through these tasks of mourning. Your mind and body will indicate when you are moving on. You know you are recovering when you begin noticing things that make you glad you are here to experience them. Moments of joy sneak up on you. The need to write or talk about the loss cannot be overemphasized. There is a high risk for depression and loneliness.

3. LONELINESS

We know what loneliness feels like. It comes and goes with different degrees of feeling sad, lonely, and hollow. You may be missing someone, or just feeling empty and wanting human contact. It is a very human emotion that visits most of us for various lengths of time no matter what our age.

Being lonely is different than being alone, being by oneself. You can be lonely when alone, or exuberant about being alone. Being alone by choice is treasured solitude for many. You can feel lonely in a crowd if you aren't feeling any particular closeness, and connection. Prolonged loneliness is probably depression. Think about the times that you feel lonely? Do you know what triggers these times?

What makes those times of loneliness go away? What could you do to get you out of these periods more quickly?

MINNIE

God,
my hands are old.
I've never said that out loud before
but they are.
I was so proud of them once.
They were soft like the velvet smoothness
of a firm, ripe peach.
Now the softness is more like worn-out
sheets or withered leaves.
When did these slender graceful hands
become gnarled, shrunken claws?
When, God?
They lie here in my lap,
naked reminders of this worn-out
body that has served me too well!
How long has it been since someone
touched me?
Twenty years?
Twenty years I've been a widow.
Respected. Smiled at.
But never touched.
Never held so close that loneliness
was blotted out.
I remember how my mother used to hold me.
God.
When I was hurt in spirit or flesh.
She would gather me close,
stroke my silky hair
and caress my back with
her warm hands.
O God, I'm so lonely!

I remember the first boy who ever kissed me.
We were both so new at that!
The taste of young lips and popcorn,
the feeling inside of mysteries yet to come.
I remember Hank and the babies.
How else can I remember them but together?
Out of the fumbling, awkward attempts
of new lovers came the babies.
And as they grew, so did our love.
And, God, Hank didn't seem to mind
if my body thickened and faded a little.
He still loved it. And touched it.
And we didn't mind if
we were no longer beautiful!
And the children hugged me a lot.
O God, I'm lonely.
God, why didn't we raise the kids
to be silly and affectionate
as well as dignified and proper?
You see, they do their duty.
They drive up in their cars;
they come to my room to pay their respects.
They chatter brightly, and reminisce.
But they don't touch me.
They call me "Mom" or "Mother"
or "Grandma."
Never Minnie.
So did my friends.
Hank called me Minnie, too.
But now they're gone.
And so is Minnie.
Only Grandma is here.
And God! She's lonely
—Donna Swanson[5]
(Used by permission of publisher)

So sad. And there are many Minnie's. It is an example of how we don't want to be. We are fearful of this happening to us. What's wrong with a system that doesn't recognize and do something about such loneliness? She feels totally disconnected, isolated, and hopeless.

What do you think would help Minnie's situation?

In workshops, the responses are varied. Some think she needs a cat or a dog. Most agree Minnie needs someone to talk to, needs to tell her children what she is thinking and feeling. They may have no idea that she craves being touched. It's her responsibility to let them know what she wants. Often such a thick wall has been created over time in family dynamics that it is easier for an outsider to get someone like Minnie to open up. She needs someone to be interested in her story. She needs a Whobody Chart, someone to help her create a toolkit for herself. She might need just one person to truly care.

4. COURAGE

Who are the most courageous of all? Many of the frail elderly exhibit more courage on a daily basis than any other population. Their deeds certainly don't get the headlines that the younger, healthy, adventurous sorts do who challenge mountains and do marathons. Their deeds may appear humble, but if the measure includes degree of difficulty, they are major victories. Many frail elderly persons model how to face limitations and increasing dependence on others with a grace and dignity that needs to be appreciated.

It takes courage for the chronically ill to keep plugging along knowing there is no cure for what ails them, that this is no temporary trial but a long trip downhill, an inevitable decline.

- It takes courage for the painfully arthritic just to get out of bed in the morning when they seriously doubt if their wobbly legs will hold them up.
- It takes courage for the dignified elderly to venture out to eat when they fear spilling and embarrassing themselves and others.
- It takes courage to continue crocheting afghans with your shaky hands when you know that the finished product won't be what it used to be.
- It takes courage to simply look in the mirror and see an old face and say, "Hey, not so bad. I like the way I look, wrinkles and all," when society seems to be saying, "Be ashamed of those wrinkles; keep looking young," as if there is something unnatural or wrong about aging.
- It takes courage to be responsible and give up your driver's license and all that freedom when you know your eyesight and reactions are no longer good enough.
- It takes courage to find the balance between letting people know how you feel and what you need and reaching out of the narrow world of aches and pains, and be genuinely interested in the feelings and activities of others.
- It takes courage for caregivers of the chronically ill to "stick with it" when their energy is being drained, and, despite all their efforts, their loved one is getting worse.
- It takes courage to swallow your pride and ask for help. We all know people who exhibit this kind of courage. This is a kind of courage-by-default that most of us hope we'll never have to know. We like to think we will live a healthy, relatively carefree, full life and then die suddenly and painlessly in our favorite chair. A few do. It is a fact that we are living longer, healthier lives. This improvement and the technological triumphs that increase longevity have only postponed having to look at the calloused attitude toward those who are no longer as able and are aware that their days are numbered.

- It takes courage to be hard hit by the losses that life brings and be able to bounce back modeling great appreciation for small kindnesses, and a heightened sensibility to the beauty of an otherwise ordinary event.
- It takes courage to face your encroaching limitations. Old people are forcing younger people to look at the illusory nature of always thinking that there is a "cure" for whatever ails you. They know that their bodies probably won't get better and definitely not younger.

Wake up America. Very old people are quietly waiting for society to respect one's full life cycle, to stop worshiping the young, the unblemished bodies, and to recognize them as fellow humans, repositories of fascinating stories, who are leading the way. They are our roots, and our future.

5. UNFINISHED BUSINESS

Ask yourself these questions:

What do I have to do for myself to have peace of mind? Do I have things to clarify, to straighten up to make things easier for my loved ones?

What have I always wished I had asked my parents (or anyone) and never did? Can I do something now to relieve this frustration?

Do I feel complete with my life as it stands? If not, what is left for me to do?

Are there things that happened to me that I haven't forgiven or I just can't forgive? Are there things I did that others haven't forgiven me for?

> *Even if you have made some terrible mistakes in life, you can choose to do something to redeem yourself. Falling down is one thing: refusing to try and get up is another.*

Are there things I haven't done or places I haven't seen that I can possibly still do?

Your answers to the above questions give you an idea of what unfinished business you have. Most of us still have things to say and things to do. Most of us have some light unfinished business like some things yet unsaid, some business undone, some financial loose ends, some things to do, and places to see. Some folks are okay with loose ends; others will feel better tying matters up. Completing unfinished business is your business and only your business. It is not about making other people accept you. It is not about approving or forgetting. It is not about expecting anything in return from anyone else. It is between you and you. It is an important path toward peace of mind. Approaching the end of your life seems to finally give people permission to implement changes they want to make. Even if one has never before been able to "let go," this is the time, the last chance. Holding on to old hurts and trying to control things that are not controllable put you in an undesirable victim role and build tension. With forgiveness, you are no longer a victim.

Ending of unfinished business may involve forgiving yourself or another. This might be the means whereby you can finally experience peace. By no longer judging, you release a blockage of the past. Forgiving

Your best revenge is living beautifully.

means that you have learned and are no longer oppressed by this load you have been carrying. If the unfinished business you are carrying involves another person, you are in competition with that person and you are losing. You are captive in a sense and cannot move forward.

Forgiveness like the grieving process takes time and usually cannot be rushed. The exception to this is sometimes toward the end of your life when forgiveness can be rushed a bit because you know you have limited time. Sometimes long silenced "I love you's" burst free at last … but sometimes the readiness or reality is still not there. Some people have heavy unfinished business. There are instances where the anger and hurt are deeply justifiable. At some point, even in extreme cases, you need to determine whether or not to hang on to these feelings, if it is worth the energy it takes to do so. Some acts are unforgivable, and it would be a self-violation and more abuse to yourself to forgive them. Forgiving does not mean that you are a sin pardoner. You do not have any authority as a human being to forgive from a position of superiority. Often the action or cruelty itself can't be forgiven, but the person can be forgiven for having lost his/her humanity and, more importantly, you can let go and decide to free yourself from the weight of it all. It is about no longer being victimized.

Often the person hardest to forgive is you. Humans are enormously hard on themselves, usually much more merciless on themselves than they ever would be on others. People hold on to their self-hate and recrimination for decades. Had they been sent to jail for their perceived crimes, they would have been out years ago. Learn how to forgive yourself. Work on reversing the negativity. Take pride in your ability to survive, your resourcefulness, and stamina.

There is no way to get through life without making mistakes. Being hard on yourself saps energy and gets you absolutely nowhere. It is self-abuse and unfortunately many people get very good at it.

Being cruel to anyone is wrong and that includes cruelty to your self. Self-forgiveness breaks the pattern of self-abuse. You can decide to let up on yourself and feel the glorious feeling of dropping the weight of the world from your shoulders.

Forgiveness means to let go. It's not about someone else. It is about you. It is about taking charge, no longer allowing another person to hold the trump card. You cannot save him or her, but you can save yourself. You may carry with you rage, unmet expectations, fear, blame, resentment, and denial. Because of this, it is easy to block out the possibility of light and love and precious growth. Not forgiving is like punishing someone by holding your breath; you are the one who is turning blue. It's a vicious cycle. By insisting on being the victim, you become your own abuser. Ask yourself, "Who am I hurting?" If you are wasting a lot of energy hating someone, you are really handing over a victory to that person. Say to yourself, "For my own integrity and survival, I choose to no longer give away any of my energy. I choose to be the boss of my own self. I can decide to let go of this and no longer be captive." It is about being gentle with myself.

Unfinished business looms. Without resolution, it interferes with subsequent life tasks. The familiar words "don't put off saying what you have to say or doing what you have to do" are true most of the time. Whether or not to write or contact a person who is living depends on the situation. It is the ability to "let go" that allows you to finish unfinished business. Sometimes there are specific activities you can do or feel the need to do. Other times no action is necessary but quietly opening your heart is enough, releasing the toxins of the past or whatever has prevented you from liking yourself. In those instances, your finishing unfinished business is accomplished simply by changing your outlook, your attitude. Your friends and family may sense this change as evidenced by the numbers of times individuals have delightedly reported to me, "He has changed; we can see it."

This ability to be different in your relationships often happens at the end of life because you have nothing to lose, or you simply haven't the energy to be any other way. It is bittersweet that so many conversions happen at the very end of life. Had the break-through come years before, there could have been so much more quality of life. Weird family rules, fractured communication, and old hurts build up in families, separating the members like steel barriers. Then, even when there is a strong, foundational love, it is hard to penetrate the wall. Frailty often makes the powerful less threatening. The rules of my family were no touching or hugging except if you were going far away on an airplane. When my mother with Alzheimer's came to live with us her last two years, her resistance to touch was no longer there. The resistance was replaced by an eagerness to be hugged and have her back and feet rubbed—ending a lifetime of neediness on both our parts. Sometimes the path through this wall is a specific act of forgiveness. Often it is finally letting go of the past, clearing the fog, and showing a new ability to live in the present. I have heard a stated resolution, "I am a new person. Starting today, I am changed," announcing this transformation. Other times change happens slowly and is gradually observed by others. The mark of a person with no unfinished business is one who appreciates each moment and lives life so fully that "doing" takes a backseat to simply "being."

COMPLETING UNFINISHED BUSINESS

In face of life threatening illness, people I see aren't focusing on the illness at all but often have as priorities clearing up some relational matters, reconciling some estrangements, finishing some project or other issues that will make their life seem finished. They may choose to receive or offer forgiveness.

With yourself

Write your feelings down in detail.

Ask yourself, "What would it take for me to forgive me?'

Ritualize your feelings. Let them go bit by bit. The simple act of writing them on paper and burning them with a match, a candle or throwing the intention into a campfire or fireplace, saying, "It is finished!"

Let a load drop off your shoulders—savor the lightness and freedom.

With someone else

Use the "I" message. "I feel terrible that I wasn't around more when you were in your teens. I would do it differently if given another chance. "I missed out and messed up. I am sorry." This is important to do for you, not necessarily for the other. Express your feelings—especially any that will be healing. Don't blame. Don't accuse. Make your message direct and clear.

For example: Call someone you wish to see and say, "I've been diagnosed with … I don't know exactly when my time is up but would really like to see you. You don't have to think of it as a Hollywood farewell. I may be around for awhile, but I would like to spend time with you." Have no expectations of others. You are doing this for yourself. You can't count on the other person's reaction. At the very least, you can know that you attempted resolution and won't have to live with "I wish that I would have…."

Letters of reconciliation can be sent … now, or to be opened after you die. One person wrote this letter of reconciliation:

Dear _____, I've been thinking about how we hurt each other and want you to know how sorry I am for all that I did. I want to let go of my regrets about what happened and truly want you to be happy. Sincerely, _____

You need not be with the person to finish your unfinished business. It is the work you do on yourself that is important. It does not take two people to release the tension and antagonism that blocks completion. This means opening your heart, feeling the pain, and releasing it and all the encapsulated energy it holds. Only when you decide that pride and resentment are no longer worth the toll they take, will you be able to move on. To concretize this act of finishing business, you may choose to ritualize the process. Some persons set the stage by arranging a special place, gathering significant memorabilia and appropriate music to create an ambience conducive to a major event. Some go to a favorite place in nature, stretch out in a meadow, sit beside a stream, or go outside on a starry night and begin an imaginary dialogue with the particular being with whom there is unfinished business. Another woman filled a large glass bowl full of water and floated small tea lights in it. She stated regrets that she wanted to get rid of and lit a tea light for each one while saying, "May I now be free!" The lighting of the wee candles symbolized for her letting go of years of pent up anger, guilt, and regrets, freeing her energy to be used in more productive ways. This cleansing and letting go of regrets and hurts can release great tension. When resistance to whatever the pain, whether it be physical, emotional, or spiritual, is relieved, its tyranny over you is diminished and healing and balancing can occur.

Specific examples of words that have helped some to forgive and move on:

To another

- "I, (your name), ask (their name) for forgiveness for ... Please free me."
- "I would do some things differently today."
- "I wish that I had spent more time with you. I am so sorry."
- "I have learned and am wiser now. I want you to know that I have these regrets...."

To self

- "I forgive myself for my past ignorance and deeds, those that were intentional or unintentional. I want to love and care for myself and let go of the weight I carry. May this be the first moment of a new me."
- "Today, I'm recognizing that this is my only life and it is near its end. I let go of much of the blame that I aimed at myself, some deserved, but much over the top. I wish that I hadn't been so hard on myself. I am finally getting some balance on how to own and be responsible for my actions but not overdoing it. I wish that I had been able to balance better a long time ago."

Of another

- "I, (your name), let go of the pain and hurt that I have felt in this relationship. It prevents me from living my life fully in the present. I no longer want to waste my energy or allow these feelings to have any power over me. I want to be free."

Woundings and regrets are a universal human experience. Not one of us has been perfect. Not one of us has "the answer." If you have unfinished business, you can do something about it. Say whatever fits for you. One person felt better after she said to her daughter, "I have made some poor decisions in my life. I wish that I had known then what I know now. I am sorry for my poor choices. I want to move forward now and I pray that you can."

THE DYING PROCESS

It is true that there are "good—even beautiful—deaths." They are considered so when they are timely, pain-free, peaceful, and the dying one is surrounded with love. The philosophy of hospice and palliative care has greatly enhanced your chances of finishing well and most of us aspire to this. This is the ideal, however. In my experience, it is often a sad, stressful, and messy time, even when accompanied by quality health care. There are ways to maximize the odds of having the best possible death and of finishing well. My hope is that the information given here and thoughtful participation on your part will help you do what you can to make this a smooth and rich time.

Every year thousands of people die of acute illnesses, suicide, accidents, domestic violence, wars, famine, weather conditions, or a gradual petering out due to old age. Everything that gets born dies. A great percentage of Americans appear to shove that fact on to the back burner and avoid thinking about it, some sort of combination of being obsessed with death and in denial of it. We know it will happen someday but choose to make that day far away. It is typical for Americans to buy into the notion that death is a failure, that if we eat right, exercise, and pray a lot we will escape it somehow. If we get sick, we ought to be able to conquer it and be "fixed." This is a sad commentary. This inability to deal with the fact that we will die seems to be fueled by our desire for control and security. This denial, when carried to an extreme, causes us to miss out on much richness.

The time leading up to death can be a profound time full of gratitude, honesty, and intimacy. Dying people are forced to slow down, usually have no time for fluff, are as authentic as can be, and can be powerful teachers. It can be a time for pulling things together, for looking at one's journey with celebration and gratitude. I have witnessed that people who are comfortable and open about the subject of dying are able to move more peacefully through this end stage of their lives. I have seen softness, a curiosity, a fascination with the mystery of death. They are finishing well.

For me the spiritual path has always been learning how to die. That involves not just death at the end of this particular life, but all the falling apart that happens continually. The fear of death—which is also the fear of groundlessness, of insecurity, of not having it all together—seems to be the most fundamental thing that we have to work with. We have so much fear of not being in control, of not being able to hold on to things. Yet the true nature of things is that you're never in control. You're never in control. You can never hold on to anything … so my own path has been training to relax with groundlessness and the panic that accompanies it … training to die continually.
—Pema Chodron[6]

This book has talked mostly about how to live well in the later part of your life. Dying well calls for pretty much the same recipe. We have had practice by now with loss, with mini-deaths, with having to let go. If you've been with someone who has died, you become acutely aware of that mysterious tiny thread that separates life from death. Here one moment, gone the next … such a fine line. More surely than any other event, this experience of witnessing a death reawakens in many of us the awareness of the grace and wonder of being alive. Some may choose to flee back into ignoring the inevitability of death. I encourage you to join with me and take some time to look at this important last chapter of your life. It can become a rich and powerful time for you. There are better and worse ways to go through the dying process, yours or someone close to you. Facing it head on can vastly improve the chances of finishing well. Most certainly, it can make you more open to the art of living.

Death isn't, after all, some tragic mistake, a failure in the construction of the universe. Dying is not easy even though it is a natural process. Our bodies wear out and die, just like everything else in nature. Trees grow up, eventually die and new birth emerges from decay. We are part of a cycle that is time-bound and impermanent. We live in a circle, not a vertical hierarchy. Humans are not exceptions to this rule. Yet our society's norm is to fight death, and doctors too often still see death as a failure. There is a dissonance, a tension around the end of life. We are asked to accept death on the one hand and on the other, given choices about all that can be done to prolong life. It is hard to ask people to embrace death with such a push toward being able to fix whatever illness that appears. It's like death has to be negotiated. The notion that the dying time needs to be honored as a natural event has been pushed to the side.

Choice often becomes just rhetoric. It becomes the doctor's choice with the "Well, that isn't working so we have to do this now" becoming the norm. The system rolls on without the patients' involvement unless you insist.

Today four out of five Americans die in hospitals or care centers, and, until the hospice movement, family and friends were often separated from the dying person because of various institutional rules. Now the trend is rapidly returning to dying at home, or in a care center, using hospice. There is movement toward taking back personal power, and having more choices about dying in a manner you would prefer. Seven out of ten people, when polled, report that they would prefer to die at home. The hospice philosophy focuses on pain relief and enhancing the physical, emotional, and spiritual comfort of the dying person when curing the illness is no longer an option. This enlightened approach includes care for both patients and those caring for them. Check out the hospice care available in you community.

Hospice is a philosophy, not a place. Care is primarily implemented in the dying person's home, but it can be at a special free-standing hospice, or in a hospital or nursing home. Thanks to the hospice philosophy of caring for the whole person, other conventional settings where people are sick and dying appear to be embracing a more holistic approach. It's important to think about this and let your views be known so your family doesn't have to wonder what you would like if they are put in the position to make choices for you. Where would you prefer to die? In your home? In a hospital? With hospice help? How important is this to you? If you would prefer to die at home, would you accept transfer to a hospital or a hospice if it could provide more comfort for you? Or relieve the family of heavy duty?

Live long. Die quickly.

There are all sorts of views about the dying time. Probably the most popular view is the one above. The very old and the people who love them often exhibit a readiness and acceptance not felt by younger people who are understandably less likely to think that this is their time

Dying can be a time of personal introspection and meaning making. If you give up the fighting and failure approach to dying and take time to evaluate what you have learned, who you have loved and been loved by, it can be a rich time for all. If you get to a point of being comfortable with this mysterious passage, you can help other people be comfortable. Early on a favorite person said to me, "Don't feel so badly. I'm okay. I have had a good life. It's okay for me to go now. I like to think that you will remember me with love and our many precious times together." She was comforting me and teaching me an important lesson about the naturalness of this time.

Death? I rejoice in it. I love it …
If it weren't for death, life would be
unbearable.
—Malcolm Muggeridge

Accepting that we are dying is our biggest letting go. Our society doesn't even want us to grow old, much less die. It is often said that the young fear dying more than the old, but I am struck by the pervasiveness of denial of death by our young old and even the old-old.

Priest: "Every man, woman, and child
in this parish will die sometime." He
notices a man snickering in the third
pew. He inquires. The man says, "I'm not
in your parish."

Most people want to live as long as their lives have quality, which can only be determined by them, and then they move into the letting go and acceptance stage, which can be a time of awesome appreciation of all that you have learned, loved, and experienced … even if you did it with a lot of fumbling and stumbling. If you have been on a journey of making your life as good as it can be, which is being encouraged in this book, you are well on the way to finishing well also. In this final stage of life there are still opportunities for growth. It is your last chance at teaching and modeling for those around you.

Western medicine's fix-it mentality makes it difficult for us to accept death as a natural and inevitable event. In fact this fix-it way of thinking focuses so much on curing that the caring part, which is so important at this time, is way too often neglected. Dying people want to feel loved, comfortable, and at peace during this mysterious time. People who have been able to be open about the fact they are dying have modeled some of the best finishes that I have witnessed. Others simply will never feel comfortable with verbal openness, but know exactly what is happening and make those around feel at ease. Remember you are the boss of your dying. A friend requests this of visitors during her dying time:

> *To keep company with me in my last days, I ask that you be open to talking about death—at least mine. Your possible discomfort and avoidance of the subject could demean my passage and reduce the grandeur of the process. We don't need to be solemn. We can joke and laugh. I welcome your irreverence even. What I dread is your looking away, your silence, as if death is unspeakable. Let me have my understanding of death as birth. Leave me my expectation of an afterlife. See me off with wishes for a splendid journey and I will cherish your good company.*
> *—Penny*

I think that the dying process may be following the same pattern that has occurred in the childbirthing movement. In earlier days, birthing was done in the home with a visiting doctor and helpful family members. Then for quite a period doctor's dictated. Births took place in hospitals, feet up in stirrups. Mothers-to-be were kept from participating in the process and separated from their babies after their birth. Fathers were totally removed from the process and treated like walking germs. Now fathers and others are welcomed to the process and there are midwives, birthing doulas, and more births happening in homes or comfortable surroundings in a hospital. Signs point to a similar evolvement in the dying process. In the old days, dying happened at home. Then it changed radically to what we've seen in the recent decades, people dying in hospitals or nursing homes. Now, with the hospice and palliative care movement, we are seeing more deaths occurring in homes with hospices help. Hospice looks beyond what's happening physically to the emotional and spiritual aspects of dying. There is an effort to help people answer the big questions. "What has this life of mine been all about?" "Did I make a difference?"

> *Death is as natural as birth and should be talked about in a straight forward calm way*

My friend, Joyce Hutchinson, a hospice nurse in Des Moines, Iowa said "I am sure none of us wanted to be born as it was pretty comfortable in the bag of water in our mommy's womb, and we didn't want to come out into the world. I've always thought that is why we come out screaming. It is the very same thing with our dying. We may not want to think about our dying because we have never done it before. It is an unknown and seems scary.

Death is going to happen to us all, and the more we are able to comfortably incorporate it into our conversation the better chance we have of getting all the things done and discussed that will make the experience as good as it can be. Really facing the prospect of death makes life and every moment so very precious. Things get said that never get said if denial reigns. If you take refuge in false optimism, it prevents you from exploring this mysterious time and the peace that might be found. It may be a good idea for those with a lot of fear about dying to read writings that have been written about those with near-death experiences. That really helped me to give up any fear of dying. I am convinced that it is an amazing experience." Sometimes there is a "nearing death awareness" (NDE) time, when a dying person is already seemingly moving on, sees and hears people who have already died. There is a shift going on transitioning from this world to the next. Maggie Callahan and Patricia Kelley discuss this in the book *Final Gifts*.

Joyce says, over and over, how important it is to come to grips with the fact that you will absolutely die someday. "If we can sit with this thought long enough to really let it sink into the very marrow of our bones, and let it be a reality for us, we will live much more peaceful lives. If we don't do it, we always have that little dark cloud over our heads that we don't want to think about and, therefore, it becomes a burden. For some people it gives comfort to focus on all of the people who have gone before, and the possibility of seeing them again. Thinking about the fact that living forever would be awful helps. We wouldn't have any friends left and life would eventually get pretty monotonous. Our bones, heart, liver, brain, skin and all of the rest of our body is not equipped to live too much after 100, and it wouldn't be a good experience. If we can truly embrace the fact that we will die, we will be more present to the day and the moment."

Often people gasp at the suggestion of hospice and the reality of what that implies. Joyce responds to this by saying, "When we confront the business of dying, it does not mean we are eager to be dead, nor does it mean we are turning our back on life or living. In actuality, we are daring to go into the very heart of living." Joyce tells a cute story of a woman she cared for who had COPD and was on oxygen continually. She told Joyce one day about this wonderful relationship she had with her god and that she knew she would be going home and that there was going to be a wonderful hereafter. Then she hesitated a bit and looked into Joyce's eyes and said, "but I want to tell you something, deary, I am not homesick."

It doesn't matter how wonderful we might think the hereafter is, most of us still want to live as long as we can comfortably and with enough quality. People who finish well, who live fully in their dying experience peace. Finishing well is more about our capacity to love and learning lessons of gratitude, waiting, simple being, more waiting, the art of quietness and keeping watch, and prayer beyond words. It can be a healing time. As Morrie, made famous by the book *Tuesdays with Morrie*, said while being interviewed by Ted Koppel on *Nightline*, "Here is how we are different from these wonderful plants and animals. As long as we can love each other, and remember the feeling of love we had, we can die without ever really going away. All the love you created is still there. All the

> *"You won't die a day sooner on hospice, and you will have a much higher quality of life in the meantime."*

> *We don't die cured, but we can die healed.*

memories are still there. You live on—in the hearts of everyone you have touched and nurtured while you were here. Death ends a life, not a relationship."

As we have recognized throughout life, people seem to act, to really act, only a in time of crisis … when pushed to the very edge. Dying is the biggest edge we will ever face. I think that it is because of this "crisis mentality" that healing transformations happen at this time. This is it. No more putting things off. It can be a time of great peacemaking with yourself and with others in your life. I have witnessed dying persons model for those who haven't reached this part of their journey yet, a peacefulness and clarity about what is important in life. This peacefulness, this okayness with dying, has a lesson and an effect on for all around.

It is true that we are living longer in a healthy state with many more nonagenarians and centenarians. Besides wanting to live long and die quickly, most of us want quality. At some point, unless we get hit by a truck or die suddenly of a heart attack or some acute illness, most of us will gradually fizzle out with an assortment of aches and illnesses as our bodies wear out. There is usually an ambiguous time when we don't know if there is a chance to be cured and returned to an existence that we deem to have quality, and as long as there is this chance most of us go for it. At some point, the disease process becomes a dying process. Sometimes this point is made clear, sometimes not. Some people always see another option and fight their illness to the very end. How many people in our fix-it society have I heard saying up to their dying moment, "Now what shall we do?" Some of the "fighters" couple this hope for a cure with an awareness of what's happening down-deep and take care of their unfinished business at the same time—just in case. Often there is a point reached when the doctor, the patient, and the family realize there are no medical options and the dying process is at hand. How long this takes varies but if assured that you can be kept comfortable, it can be a rich time. Physical pain ought to be able to be prevented or relieved in our present health-care system the great majority of the time. I have seen people on hospice who, to be eligible, supposedly have no more than six months to live, live comfortably for years. I heard of a couple who met while in hospice, got married, and left the hospice. Miracles happen. When there are no more medical options, it is best to get on palliative care or hospice as soon as possible because of the added depth of care provided.

Hospice focuses on pain control and attends to the needs of the whole person (and the family)—the physical, emotional, and spiritual needs. It would be wonderful to have this palliative spirit throughout the health-care system. Illness always involves more than just the physical happenings. It carries with it major psychological and spiritual components and affects not only the sick person but also the people who care and love him/her. There are usually many stages and feelings to go through just like with the process of grieving—shock, denial, sadness, hopefulness, bargaining, fear of the unknown, fear of nonexistence, fear of pain, fear of being a burden, more denial, and then hopefully and gradually an acceptance.

Sometimes I think a person who knows he is going to die spends his remaining valuable time in one of three categories: (a) being alive, (b) trying to stay alive, or (c) giving up and concentrating on dying and moving on. It is your choice. If he is in category (b) he often spends his time going from hope to hope, treatment to treatment, often leaving unfinished business, things left undone or unsaid in his quest to beat this thing. Category (a) people are more likely to be thankful for their remaining time and make good use of it, enjoying what they enjoy, finishing up what they deem needs to be finished, and wanting to use this bonus time as fully as possible. This doesn't mean that they haven't pursued what there is to pursue for staying alive, but they also move to accepting that death is on the way and work on sewing up loose ends and making the most of the precious time remaining.

As long as you are alive, you are more alive than dead. This sounds a bit less than profound, but the point needs to be made over and over that many times people, nearing the end, focus only on their dying and stop trying to make the most of the potentially rich time of living they have left.

HOW TO BE WITH SOMEONE WHO IS DYING

At some point, you will probably be with someone who is very near death. Here are some practical suggestions on how to "be there." Everyone is a novice at dying and, since you only do it once, no one has any practice. You are an observer. You are an understudy. The dying person is the main actor and directs the play. Your role is to listen, be available, and offer support when called upon. It is the dying person's life and dying process.

Be there with an open heart. It is more uncomfortable for your soul to avoid being with a person, than to be there. The anticipation of discomfort is the worst part, but "being so glad I went" is the most common refrain on departure.

Don't just drop in. Call ahead and see when the best time for a visit is, and, if there's anything new about the patient's condition, it helps to know beforehand.

Ask the primary caregiver how much time you should spend there.

Give quality time. Think twice about going with several friends. It can be exhausting for the person and deprives you both of personal time together.

Let the person lead. Answer questions if asked but otherwise just be there, following his lead. If the person wants to avoid serious talk, fine. If he wants to talk or shriek about death, fine. If he wants to cry, fine. If he wants to joke around and be irreverent, fine. He is the boss of his process.

Determine, if you can, what the person does want. Present openings (Do you want to talk? Do you want to listen to music?) but don't push.

Ask what you can do and do it. (Make phone calls, read a story, answer correspondence, shop.)

If the person can't talk, assume he can hear and act accordingly.

Don't exclude the person from conversations with others.

If the person expresses anger and says seemingly irrational and hurtful things to you, depersonalize the statements. Frustrations are sometimes overwhelming at this time. Medications do funny things. Back off. Say to yourself, "This is the disease (or the meds) talking."

Say what you need to say. Don't allow your discomfort or the awkwardness you feel prevent you from taking the precious moments to let the person know how important she is to you, what particular affect she had on you, so that this person you care deeply about will know that he or she has made a difference and will be remembered.

When your dying loved one is not choosing to deal with what is going on, it can make it difficult and awkward. Chances are that she knows that she is dying

> *You matter to the last moment of your life, and we will do all we can, not only to help you die peacefully, but to live until you die.*
> *—Dame Cicely Saunders, founder of the first hospice*

> *I loved one guy's response to the question "How are you?" He replied, "Compared to somebody, I bet I'm doing great!"*

and that a simple statement or question might turn the atmosphere of respected privacy or denial around. Three examples reported to me that worked:

1. Playing on her mother's known vanity, one daughter said, "you know mom, if you should die, I bet you'd like to be wearing something else." This statement totally shot through the formerly impenetrable denial and they talked and talked.

2. A son visiting a silent dad opened the door to conversation by blurting out, "Dad, I have to get back to work now and whenever I leave you I get this terrifying thought that you might kick the bucket and I won't have even told you I love you or said all sorts of things that I wished I would have said." A precious exchange ensued.

3. Another opener is to simply ask, "Is there anything you want to say to me that would be important for me to know?"

Bring pictures for reminiscing.

Don't give advice or rattle on about your philosophy of life. This is an important, rich time for the dying person, who has her own answers.

Speak clearly but don't shout. A common error for visitors is to assume that a sick person can't hear. (Of course there's a possibility he can't hear.)

Don't patronize or talk baby talk. Use a respectful tone.

Don't give false assurances. "You'll get over this." "Nothing can get you."

Give believable assurances. "I'm going to be here with you. We'll do everything we can to make you comfortable."

Resist offering solutions and beliefs. If the person vents great fury at dying, at being robbed, and is full of "why me's?" or "why do I need to suffer like this?" The listener is often tempted to launch into expounding on solutions and beliefs. Resist this. Just listen. It is not up to you to have an answer. "I don't know" is fine. Answers need to come from the patient. Don't give unrequested advice or try to sell your beliefs. This is not your journey.

Don't take the person's defenses away. The person has a personal history, personal experiences, and personal defenses. Trust the person, in most cases, to control his or her own denial. Denial is a psychological defense mechanism that buffers pain. It usually dissolves in its own time. I am asked on occasion by family members to "break down their loved ones denial." I don't believe in doing this. I will talk with the individual, ask questions that might open the door to talking if she wants to talk…. Sometimes it's easier to talk to a stranger. Specific suggestions for words to use:

- "I'm here."
- "Are you feeling like having company?"
- "Can I help in any way?"
- "Do you want to talk about anything in particular?"
- "Do you have pain? Is there anything that I can do to help?"
- "Is there some music you would like to hear?"
- "Is there any favorite book, scripture, or poetry that I could read to you?"
- "How can I make this room as perfect as possible for you?"
- "This is a mysterious time."
- "This has got to be tough."

- "This is hard work for you; you're doing a good job."
- "Do you have any advice for me?"
- If the person wants to reminisce, say, "Looking back, tell me about some of the good times."
- "Remember the time…?"
- "What are you proudest of?"

Be an advocate. When important things are being discussed, especially with a doctor, the dying person needs another set of ears. If the person wants more information, or clarification, seek it out. Oftentimes a sick or dying person needs a bouncer, someone to let visitors know how long they can stay, how tired she is, etc. Don't say "cheer up" or "count your blessings." Don't rob a person of the right to feel bad or sad. Don't be hard on yourself if nothing seems to help. There are many things that you can do:

- Offer to pray with or for the person, with their permission.
- Provide opportunities for the person to express feelings.
- Give information the person requests.
- Offer a back rub, foot rub, or massage.

Create a healing atmosphere. If the dying person gives permission, and you can load the room with objects special or sacred to him, including memorable pictures, poems, and pictures that symbolize important relationships and memories, and spiritual or religious symbols. They can serve as interesting conversation pieces.

We always treasure feeling loved, but at the end of one's life an ideal situation is to feel surrounded by it. You or those close to you can set up this feeling of loving surroundedness by creating a love pile of pictures of people you've loved, or beauty you've witnessed, or make lists of things you've loved to do. Serve up favorite meals. Have show-time with favorite home videos. Play favorite family games like pictionary, cribbage, or scrabble. Some families sing favorite songs or hymns. Being surrounded by an atmosphere of love can't be beaten at any age or stage of life, but never is it more important for fulfillment than at this time.

When you are dying, imagine what you think would be the best possible atmosphere for you?

We like to know that our life will be remembered by things we've done or said. I spent time with a woman who was nearing death and was quite despairing. She perked up considerably when her three daughters brought in her recipe boxes and fought over her messy—because of much loving use—recipe cards. She wasn't able to speak but you could see in her eyes and her smile, the joy she was getting out of her daughters squabbling and exclaiming about her wonderful recipes and recalling particular festive times. She knew that afternoon that she, for sure, was going to live on. I read about of a woman, Hella Buchheim, who is helping families put together what she calls "family story cookbooks." She has created a DVD, called A Plate Full of Memories, that guides people in creating a family cookbook/memoir, *www.platefullofmemories.com*, believing that it is a great approach to family genealogy.

It is good to reminisce, to share memories of times spent together, to report what you have learned from him, things that will always remind you of him (objects, smells, books, music, places, etc.). On parting, say what is fitting for your relationship. Good-byes are hard. Examples:

- "Thank you for being part of my life."
- "You've been a great friend. I think you know that I love you. We have had such good times together. I will miss you terribly, but I'm going to have great memories."

If you, as a family member or close friend, think he may be hanging on just for you, it can be important to give him permission to go, to let him know that if it's time to go, don't hang on for you … that you will be okay. On the other hand, this can be carried to an extreme. One guy I visited complained that everyone who came to visit told him it was okay to go now, which punched his stubborn button. He was hanging on, by golly. There isn't any cookie-cutter way to be with someone who is near death. It is about knowing yourself and knowing the person.

Often people going to visit a person who is labeled "dying" act totally unnatural, get in a knot trying to do exactly the right thing … having contrived imaginary deep and meaningful conversations. You can't help but feel vulnerable when you walk into a situation like this, but it is best to leave your baggage at the door. Try and be as natural as possible. Try to sense the atmosphere of what's going on in the room. Is it peaceful? Is there confusion? Greet the person lovingly, whatever way represents your relationship with him/her. Maybe a hug or a kiss, if that fits for you, or maybe a statement like, "I'm so glad to be here. I've been thinking about you so much." Bring cards, amusing clippings, or columns of interest.

Humor is okay. Laughing can be wonderful. Who amongst us would not like to die laughing? I haven't seen that happen, but I do know the line between extreme emotions like laughing and crying is close, and many times there is laughter. My favorite memories during my dear friend and business partner's dying time were really pretty funny. I had been called by the hospice nurse to come to Frank's house, because they thought that he would not live through the night. Five of his chosen people gathered, and we went through a wonderful ceremony, thoughtfully put together by Frank, for this occasion—around his bed in his room. We had his chosen music; we drummed; we shared his appointed words and said our own … and then we waited. I was still with him in the wee hours of dawn when he woke up. He looked at me, shook his head in disbelief that he was still here, and said to me, "It's that dammed control issue of mine." I laughed. He smiled and shortly went off again into his quietness.

A couple of nights later, I was sitting with him, along with another friend of his, Elizabeth, a delightful nun about my age—his spiritual director. At some point, we decided to try a technique for being with a dying person called co-breathing. You follow the breathing pattern of the dying person, breathing in as he does, and with your exhalation emitting a sound that lets him know that you are there with him—loving and caring for him. I hadn't done it before but been trained in this technique, as had Elizabeth. We did it for a while. It felt good to be doing something along with "being present" with him. Then his breathing became very erratic, breathing in short gasps and then holding his breath for long periods. They didn't talk about this part in school. We were frantically trying to keep pace. I finally said, "I feel faint. I'm hyperventilating." And Elizabeth said, "Yah. They're going to find these two old broads draped over poor Frank's body!" We started to laugh, and got quite hysterical for a bit … even attracting others in the house up to the room to see what in the world was going on. *Frank smiled.* That was the last interaction any of us had with him. And so perfect.

THOUGHTS ABOUT DYING

Would you prefer dying at home? (Some people feel strongly that this is what they would prefer while others feel just as strongly that they want to go to a hospice, or would feel safer in a care center or a hospital.)

What is the best-case scenario for how you would like to die? Where? In the company of whom?

Think about what mementoes you might enjoy giving to someone you love that would always remind her of you … a way to keep you with her. What might this be?

With whom do you feel comfortable talking about death?

What experiences have you had with death so far in your life? What are you afraid of?

What do you believe happens after you die? What do you think about life-after-death? Near-death experiences?

A Harris Poll in 2003 reported that 84% of Americans believe in life after death in some form.[7] Many base this on their well-rooted religions beliefs, whether it is Christian belief in heaven and hell and reunion with deceased loved ones, in reincarnation, or infinite variations on the theme. But the religious account for only part of those who believe in life after death. Shows on TV like *Crossing Over* has the dead talking with their loved ones here on earth, and books like *Life after Life* by Raymond Moody and *The Five People You Meet in Heaven* by Mitch Albom have been best sellers and have influenced many.

Near-death experiences (NDEs) are reported by people who come close to or experience being pronounced clinically dead, having no pulse, consciousness, or ability to breathe, and then return to this world after having a glimpse of life after death. Their reports contain similar elements like a feeling of peacefulness, going through a dark tunnel into light, sometimes being welcomed by loved ones, sometimes having their life flash before their eyes, and, on return, having a noticeable change in values and attitude toward life. Books like *Life after Life: The Investigation of a Phenomenon-Survival of Bodily Death* by Raymond Moody, *Lessons from the Light: What Can We Learn from Near Death Experiences* by Kenneth Ring and Evelyn Elsaesser Valarino, *Where God Lives: The Science of the Paranormal and How our Brains Are Linked to the Universe* by Melvin Morse, MD, excite some of the religious and non-religious into looking forward to what might be next. Some dying people find certain sayings help them:

- Today, I will remember all that I am thankful for.
- Today, I don't have to carry burdens alone. I can ask for help from (my family, Jesus, Buddha, Mary, my higher power, my doctor, or a friend).
- Today, I will see every moment as a gift. I will live it with passion.
- Today, I will let others know that I value them and why I do. Examples: "I like that idea" "Remember what you recommended the other day? I tried it and you were right." "You always make me feel comfortable. I appreciate that"
- Today, I will use my energy in the most fulfilling way possible.

It is said that you finish well when your attitudinal goal shifts from fear and fighting dying to feeling gratitude for the experience of living. I have seen over and over the ever present need for hope shift from the desire to continue to live to the hope and excitement that this mysterious passage brings. Many find their religion a great source of comfort at this time, knowing that "they will soon be in the arms of their savior," or welcomed into heaven by those who have preceded them in death. Others don't know for sure what will happen after the death of their physical body, but are full of wonder about what might be next. This wonder is scary for some but an exciting time for others.

I had a client/friend who was very ready to exit this life and was totally excited and twinkly about what might be next … saying over and over that he would let me know somehow … send me a signal. On the other hand, I have witnessed people who have gone kicking, screaming, and raging into death. Even though it is hard on all those around, who is to say that this ending is not fitting, and even "finishing well" for his personality. Dying has many dimensions. The fears are being in pain, being abandoned, losing one's dignity, not liking the way they look or smell, and the familiar hating the thought of being a burden—not only physically and emotionally, but a financial strain on the family as well. In the dying process, only the controlling of physical symptoms is medical.

This chapter is not on how-to-do-dying. It remains a wonder to us all. Dying is usually complex, sad, and rarely easy. I have plenty of ideas about how I would like to be when I am dying, and have shared much of it here, but the truth is that not one of us knows how we will feel or be when we get there. It is humbling and remains a mystery. It is the final "letting go," and as my friend Frank said, it is your last battle with your control issue! As the final letting go, everything material falls away and becomes meaningless. Doing is no longer possible, and when dying is accepted, I have witnessed a new dimension of depth and peacefulness. Your "being" seems to take over.

I have had plenty of teachers … both on how I would like to be and how I don't want to be. I totally believe we can increase our chances of finishing well considerably by engaging the most reputable health team, communicating our wants and needs to our family and professional caregivers on an ongoing basis, following the suggestions in this book that have helped others, and working on our attitude of acceptance. There is no template for finishing well. It is our last learning experience.

SPIRITUAL AND MEDITATIVE PRACTICES

Many spiritual and meditative practices were included in Chapter Four when discussing how to be still and notice what is going on around you. Many of us have our own comforting form of prayer. The following practices can be used at any time of life but are decidedly effective when used by persons suffering in some way or dying.

Tonglen

I work with people of all ages who have life-threatening illnesses, and they often find it very difficult to let go of their understandably consuming thoughts and to escape even temporarily into a peaceful place. A simple and helpful meditative practice is a form of Tonglen, which I first read about in the book *Start Where You Are At* by Pema Chodrin, a delightful teacher and Buddhist monk. This practice is called a compassion meditation because it helps you calm your own suffering and further, if you choose, send healing energy to other people who are in pain also. This helps you even more because you feel less self-absorbed and isolated.

Tonglen for self

Tonglen can be used by anyone who finds themselves obsessing about something and unable to get back to the moment, when meditating or just trying to be still and relax. You pause and examine the thought that you are stuck on. What is the driving feeling behind this thought? Is it frustration, fear, worry, anxiousness, worthlessness, sadness, confusion? It is important to name the feeling and face this vulnerable place in you so that you can move toward healing. Hold this feeling gently. Feel compassion for yourself. Then think about what the opposite of this feeling is. It is usually freedom from worrying about it … wanting to lighten up, to feel liberated from the bondage of it, to feel less stressed and peaceful. Then you breathe that difficult feeling into your heart center, transform it, and breathe out the healing opposite. For example, breathe your fear into your heart center … breathe out peacefulness and love. Continue this breathing pattern for a while until the intensity of the feeling dissipates. For some people, it is more helpful to change the feeling into as sensate form such as breathing in darkness, or heaviness, or muck and breathing out clear light, gentleness, and clarity. One person I know visualizes a dark cloud coming into her heart center and meeting the sun within her, which dissolves the cloud so that she breathes out brilliant rays of compassion for herself, rays of healing love and confidence … whatever fits for you. It works best when you use your own words.

This process does not fix suffering. Fixing is about control. This process is about sending healing energy into the universe and letting go with gentleness. It is about flowing, going toward pain and sitting with it. It is a about recognizing the feeling for what it is and not backing away. Naming the feeling, learning to be open to it, reduces its intensity. Years ago, I worked with people who were having panic attacks. They were so fearful of the attacks that they desperately slammed on their brakes trying to hold them off, which unfortunately had just the opposite effect … actually increasing the effect of the next attack to tsunami proportions. They could only reduce the effect by learning how to relax, repeating phrases like, "This can't hurt me unless I let it." By understanding the chemistry behind panic and understanding that, by trying to fend off these attacks, they were only adding to their strength. They had to learn the hard lessons of how to befriend their scary feelings and only by doing that could their strength be diffused. Tonglen uses much the same principle. Name the feeling, embrace it, and then let it go … sending healing energy into the universe.

After practicing Tonglen, you can get back to being in the moment … inhaling "this moment," exhaling "only moment"… until you get stuck again. I go in and out of Tonglen depending on my state of mind any given day. You can either sandwich Tonglen into your meditation practice or do it as a separate practice making it a compassion prayer not only for yourself but for others.

Tonglen for others

Think about other people you know who are suffering, perhaps in way similar to you, or with something else. Breathe their pain into your heart center and breathe out healing energy to them. Continue this process using your heart as a source of benefit to this person. Then you can move on to other people you know. And then pray for those people you don't know personally but read about or hear about on the radio and TV. You can connect with what all humans feel. If you are familiar with a feeling in yourself, you can know the feeling in anyone. Breathe in the pain; breathe out healing energy. Another value of Tonglen is that when people get preoccupied with their problems and ailments, they get so self-involved that this self-absorption isolates them and adds another layer to their problems. Tonglen offers a way through this.

I once worked with an old, very frail woman named Lily in a nursing home whose body was almost totally unable to function but her mind was alert. She was being flipped over to prevent bedsores by staff on a regular basis, but her quality of life was miserable and she was understandably very situationally depressed. She wanted to die. I introduced her to the practice of Tonglen. She practiced it for hours each day. It reinserted meaning into her life. Besides feeling compassion for herself, it gave her a format to essentially pray for all sorts of other people, acquaintances, and people she just saw on the news on television. She became delightfully assertive with the staff, became interested in their lives, requested her favorite opera arias to be playing, and had the nurses move her bed to the window where she could watch the birds and squirrels. Being alive mattered again to her.

Spur-of-the-moment Tonglen

Whenever you feel yourself stressed, breathe in that tightness and breathe out peacefulness and calmness. It helps to connect your suffering with what all humans feel, recognizing that what you are feeling is probably being felt by many unknown others at that very moment. You are not alone. Use Tonglen whenever you witness something frightening or sad happening to others. If you see a tortured mother mistreating her child at the grocery store, breathe in the obvious pain for the mother and for the child; breathe out healing energy.

Circle of Love Meditation—Phowa (pronounced "po-wa")

This is a variation of a Buddhist practice to help us prepare for our own death. The essential practice is merging our mind with the presence of our healers. You can do it by yourself or have someone do it with you.

1. Invoke the embodiment of whatever truth you believe in, in the form of radiant light and warmth. Invoke your healers, whoever they are—maybe from your religious beliefs … Jesus,

Mary, Sophia, Buddha, KwanYin, Allah … all the grandmothers. Perhaps you have an image of your own healer-helper. I have an image of an Inuit old one who appears for me. Perhaps you have personal heroes or special friends or family who you've loved, and been loved by, who have become your healers in human form. Visualize their presence in the room with you. Feel the radiant warmth. Know that they are here with you. Feel their presence, the embodiment of their truth, wisdom, and compassion. Fill your heart with their presence. Feel loved and cared for.

2. Then focus your mind and heart, and pray … choosing one or some of "May I's" below or any fitting for you.

  a. "Through the power of your blessings and love, your grace and guidance, through the power of the light that streams from you, may I be peaceful in body and mind.

  b. May I be free of anger, fear, and worry. May all my negative thoughts and emotions and blockages be purified and removed. May I know myself forgiven for all the harm I may have thought and done. May I be wrapped in the love of all whom I've been loved by and have loved.

  c. May I be grateful for this life so full of adventure and learning.
     May I be protected from all anxiety while I wait in joyful hope.

  d. And as I leave the known behind, may I be open with excitement to the mysterious unknown that is near.

  e. May I be welcomed on the other side by…

  f. May I be returned to the earth to become part of the great cycle of life.

  g. —or whatever soothes you.

3. Now imagine that the presence of light you have invoked is moved by your sincere and heartfelt prayer, that your healers respond with loving smiles and send out love and compassion in a stream of rays of light from their hearts. As these rays touch and penetrate you, they cleanse and purify all your thoughts and emotions that are the causes of suffering. You see and feel that you are totally immersed in light and love.

4. You are now completely purified and completely healed by the light streaming from their presence, consider that your very body dissolves completely into light.

5. The body of light you are now soars up into the sky and merges, inseparably, with the blissful presence of light.

6. Remain in that state of oneness with this presence for as long as possible.

Shorter version:
   Merge your mind with the presence of your healers. For example,
"My mind and the mind of Jesus are one." "My mind and the mind of Mary are one." "May I…"
This is a powerful meditation to do with someone who is dying. You can create your own version. It can be repeated over and over so intensively that it becomes a habit.

7. AFTER-DEATH PLANNING

We all give our own meaning to every death we experience in our lifetime, including our own. Sometimes the dying process has taken a long time, and death is welcomed as a friend. Some believe that our souls live on after our body stops living; some believe in heaven and hell; some in reincarnation. Others believe that once our body dies, and that's it—our life's natural cycle is over, and will return to ashes. They see life and death as part of a cyclic process of energy, briefly taking a physical form and then dissolving back. Death is a necessary part of this constant transformation of this energy. We see this cycle modeled for us by nature's seasons. Whether we are comfortable or not with the reality that death will happen, most of us want it to happen later rather than sooner. Some are terrified of the prospect. Many are greatly comforted by their beliefs, religious or not, and others don't know what to believe but are totally intrigued by the "unknown" and the possibilities of what might be next. What do you believe about death and what happens after death?

Death is nothing at all. I have only slipped away into the next room. I am I, and you are you. Whatever we were to each other, that we still are. Call me by my old familiar name, speak to me in the easy way, which you always used to. Put no difference in your tone, wear no forced air of solemnity or sorrow. Laugh as we always laughed at the little jokes we enjoyed together. Play, smile, think of me … Let my name be ever the household word that it always was. Let it be spoken without effort, without the trace of shadow on it. Life means all that I ever meant. It is the same as it ever was; there is unbroken continuity. Why should I be out of mind because I am out of sight? All is well.
—Henry Scott Holland, Canon of St. Paul's Cathedral, 1847–1918

What do I do when the moment of death comes to a loved one?

This is a precious moment. It is a time to pause, to sit and be still. Let the wonder and mystery of what just happened soak in. Often one's adrenalin kicks into action, and you start thinking about what you should do next. It is no time to be in a hurry. There is no rush. Your loved one is at peace. There's time for you and other family and close friends to have a special thoughtful time. I speak from experience. My immediate reaction when my mother died in my home after a long illness was to rush into action. A knowing friend saved me from myself by saying, "Hey, slow down. You have time now. Make it a beautiful time." Thanks to her, we collected the family together for a time of quiet reflection and a short but most memorable service around her bed.

My mother wanted a full church funeral, which we had preplanned, but this small intimate service at bedside is especially cherished. Before we gathered, those who wished to, went one at a time into her room for some alone time with her. Then, when we all got there, we gathered, holding hands around her bedside. I said something like, "Here we all are mom … grandma. We're glad you are at peace now. We want you to know again how loved you have been … and how much we will miss you. To the group …" maybe you'd like to share something you will especially miss or something you learned from her … or just what you are learning about life and death"… and then, those who wanted to, shared. The service ended with a little prayer, "We have been blessed to have felt your love … and you have ours. We are blessed with wonderful memories that will fill us up and make us smile. You will always be with us."

Officially, at the time of death, you are to call the appropriate authority. There is more time pressure in a hospital setting or residential facility then at home, but you can still ask for time. If you have been with hospice, they need to be called, or, depending on the law of your state, you need to call your doctor, the coroner, the funeral director, or whoever is appropriate.

FUNERALS OR CELEBRATIONS OF LIFE

Funerals or celebrations of life offer a closure time, an opportunity to witness the legacy left by the deceased, a gathering where all who loved this person can do their loving, appreciating, and grieving together. You often learn valuable new information about this person from points of view other than your own. Funerals can be private family affairs or elaborate events. Some dying persons plan their funeral in great detail; some give you a general idea what they might like but leave most of the planning to those left behind. Most of the time, as is always the case in sudden death, the planning is left entirely up to family and friends. The traditional and easiest way to plan a funeral is to go to the funeral home and talk to the director or get a planning guide to answer questions and give you suggestions. Funeral directors report that one-half of the survivors they work with have no notion what kind of funeral the deceased wanted, leaving the burden to those left behind. It is such a gift to think ahead about these matters instead of being silent and leaving all decisions to your loved ones, during a time when they are grieving and under time constraints. Expenses range dramatically … another reason to research and plan your service. Cremation is becoming an increasingly popular choice. It involves decisions also, like the choice of a container and what to do with the ashes.

There is a general consensus that a service of some sort is important. It provides an opportunity to express feelings about the deceased and to get a healthy start on the grieving process. It is important that children not feel excluded, that they not be denied the expression of their grief, and that time be taken to answer their questions openly and honestly. Grandchildren can be encouraged, but not forced, to participate in the activities. They need to grieve just as adults do if they are going to accept death and not be fearful of it.

There are many ways to honor those we have loved. Many don't feel honored if they don't have a funeral in their religious tradition. It feels good when funerals or celebrations match the personality of the departed one and you find yourself thinking, "this was a perfect honoring of John," or "she would have loved this!" Kris Radish's book, *Annie Freeman's Fabulous Traveling Funeral* is a delightful book that will broaden your perspective on ways to celebrate a beloved and colorful friend.

Think about funerals you have attended. What ones did you especially like? Why?

My amazingly flamboyant dear friend and business partner, Kitty, died suddenly in a car accident along with her fiancé. She left a totally stunned swath of friends and family. Her celebration consisted of what she had planned for her up-coming wedding, with singing, dancing, breath-taking drumming by her seven children, and testimonials, and it lasted three hours because people seemed to need that much time to adjust to this mighty spirit's unexpected departure. My other business partner, dear friend, and sage teacher died slowly of AIDS and had time to plan his celebration. He collected poems and readings, carefully crafted some loving thoughts of his own for someone to read, and had the Gay Men's Chorus, which he had helped found, perform.

There seems to be a trend for individuals to plan their own Life Celebration while they are still alive, reasoning that they want to "hear all the good things folks are going to say while I can hear." They plan a party and ask all their favorite people to come, bring stories, and participate in a love-in. One acquaintance decided she wanted to do this so her friends helped her plan what she called an Awake Wake. They had a wonderful celebration, bringing together people important to her—even her old high school prom date. Attendees told great stories, and she was able to tell stories and personally thank her friends and family for their treasured friendships. She also went to a Glamour Photo's place to have her picture taken and sent many of her dearest friends a 4X4 picture of her blowing them a kiss. If you had an Awake Wake, what would you include in your plans?

Funerals and celebrations of life can be anything. Some people feel strongly about having a home funeral believing that they are more family-centered, dignified, and affordable. Home funerals are planned by the family and friends. They care for the body, usually choose not to have the deceased be autopsied, embalmed, or taken to the mortuary, and hold a memorial in the home perhaps with a home-made and decorated casket. A preplanned home funeral requires much planning and discussion. I have seen homemade coffins embellished with favorite symbols, round-the-clock vigils of friends and family, with sharing of stories, singing, tears, and laughter. For information, go to *www.finalpassages.org* or *crossings.net*, or read *Caring for the Dead, Your Final Act of Love* by Lisa Carlson, *Grave Matters* by Mark Harris, or *Last Wishes* by Lucinda Page and Michael D. Knox.

Many families and friends put together displays of art or handi-work, collages of pictures, and, with more people having hi-tech abilities, movies with music, and endless variations of creativity. Now that latex balloons are no-no's, there are businesses in Minnesota, where I live, that release doves at the end of a service or at the cemetery as a way of saying good-bye *(www.Whitedovereleases.com* and *www. whitedoveconnection.com)*.

MY WISHES

What kind of funeral/memorial/celebration of life would you like to have?

I want my funeral or celebration to be held at _____

I want _____ to officiate.

I want a time of visitation or my body to lie in honor at _____

What is your religious affiliation? _____

Name of place of worship _____

Name of clergy, or _____

Telephone #_____

At the time of death, who do you want notified? _____

I want a service that honors my beliefs, which are _____

_____

I want ❑ military ❑ Masonic ❑ other _____ rites.

I want an ❑ open casket ❑ closed casket

I prefer a ❑ traditional casket ❑ cardboard casket ❑ plain pine box

If a non-traditional casket, I would like it decorated by _____

I would like these mementos placed in the casket with my body _____

I want the pallbearers to be _____

_____

I want to wear _____

I would like to donate my body to science. ❑ Yes ❑ No

I choose to be cremated. ❑ Yes ❑ No

I would like my cremains placed in a (❑ ceramic ❑ wooden ❑ metal ❑ cloth) container.

I want to be buried at _____

I want a graveside service _____

I want my gravestone to say _____

I want my ashes scattered _____

divided up and given to _____

I want my service to include:

Favorite liturgy of my tradition_____

Favorite music_____

Favorite writings _____

These rituals _____

Story telling_____

Other_____

I would like memorials in honor of my life sent to_____

_____

The following people have copies of my funeral instructions _____

_____

What do you want included in your obituary? Would you like to write your own?)

I would hope that the above instructions will be respected and followed.

Signed _____ Dated_____

EULOGIES

If you are going to give a eulogy at a funeral for someone dear to you, it is often helpful to gather some people together and listen to their stories about the deceased. Share some memorable stories, poignant or funny or wonderfully typical, at the service. Write down what you want to say so, if you choke and feel unable to proceed, someone else can read it. You can give it to whoever may want it for posterity. It is by nature an emotional time, but people report that preparing and giving a eulogy is very healing for them. Start and end strong with words to remember. Focus on how this person made a difference to you and others. Be honest. Flaws are endearing, and false niceties are offsetting. What did this person teach you? Many people who anticipate their upcoming death write words that they want to say to those gathered and have someone read them.

What do you want to say to those you are leaving behind?

My husband heard a house wren sing shortly after his sister died suddenly of an aneurysm at thirty-nine years of age leaving four young kids. We always love when our house wren appears in the spring and remember Lynie whenever we hear its sweet call. When my mother died in our home, he saw a never-before-seen egret on our little pond, and now I never see an egret without thinking about her. After a difficult birthing of our first-born daughter, he saw the first robin of the spring on the way home from the hospital. A friend associates a piliated woodpecker with her son, who committed suicide as a young man, and is comforted and, interestingly. Frequently visited by one of those rare birds. It doesn't have to be birds or animals. I associate the wonderful smell of lilacs with my friend Lola because we made an annual visit to the arboretum to walk amongst the lilac bushes in the spring. I know several folks who associate a particular piece of music with a loved one.

Do you have symbols or associations like this?

Some people celebrate a special person who has died on a specific symbolic day every year. On the Day of the Dead in Hispanic cultures, the deceased are grandly celebrated with song and festivities. I have a friend who honors her mother annually, picnicking at graveside with her mother's favorite wine, a lobster dish in some form, and her favorite music in the background … a lovely time of remembrance. Another widow friend puts out her collection of valentines she saved from her husband on Valentine's Day and birthday cards on her birthday to remember and cherish having been so loved.

Think about ways you might want to memorialize a loved one.

What do you want in your obituary? Some of you may choose to write your own so others will be reminded of what you consider to be most significant about your life. I've heard of obit parties where women write their own and then share them! What would you like your obituary to say?

MY SPIRITUAL LEGACY/ ETHICAL WILL

Whenever you think to yourself, "I'd like to pass these lessons I've learned, write them down. Think about what you have always wished you had asked your parents (or anyone else) and never did? Can you do this for your loved ones? What do you think your children or grandchildren will want to know? A venerated Jewish custom of bequeathing a spiritual legacy to others includes leaving messages or words to live by through an ethical will. Sometimes, it is simply a love letter. Here are some suggested introductory sentences:

- I write this to you, (their name) in order to…
- I want you to know how much I love you and how grateful I am to you for…
- These were the formative events of my life…
- These are the people who most influenced me…
- These are some of my favorite possessions that I want you to have, and these are the stories that explain what makes these things so precious to me…
- Some of the scriptural passages that have meant the most to me are…
- These are the mistakes I most regret having made in my life that I hope you can learn from…
- I would like to ask your forgiveness for … and I forgive you for…
- These are some of the important lessons that I have learned in my life…
- I want you to know about a couple of events that shaped my life…
- These are some of the memories of you I cherish…
- The best advice I ever got was…

- These are some messages that I would like to leave you (friend, partner, spouse, child, grand-child, niece, nephew)…
- This is what I am grateful for…
- I won't feel comfortable leaving this world without telling you…
- These teachings have guided me…
- I want to be remembered for…
- A defining moment in my life was…
- The lesson that I have learned in my life that I most want to pass on to you is…
- I want to you to have this (gift) that I value because…

Ethical wills are usually written but, with the help of video and the Internet, this can be done orally. See Appendix B. You bequeath your material valuables in a regular will, but can bequeath your values, your lessons learned through a lifetime this way. You may choose to do this in a less formal way over time taking the opportunity to write your grandson on the occasion of a birthday or graduation words that you want say. For example:

Dear John,
Hooray! You did it. I am so proud of you. It reminds me of when I was your age and…

There is no better present for your loved ones than a written or oral gift of words or story about your life that you think would be meaningful, informative, or entertaining to them. It guarantees that you will live on.

Conclusion

. . . .

The best book for you on how to age well is the one you write. My hope is that this book helped you wake up to yourself and what life has been teaching you. I hope it precipitated reflection and gave you enough information, tools, and suggestions to help you better enjoy the valuable years before you. Nothing is more fascinating or revelatory than your own story. Everything that happens to you teaches. Your life is your best therapist. You have choices to make, and *Journeywell* aimed to broaden your perspectives of the possibilities and to provide a framework with important decision-making. Tools and techniques have been suggested to help you program your mind toward health and balance. In addition to refreshing your mind about the lessons you have learned from your own journey, you have expanded your thinking by reflecting on the stories, suggestions, and information shared in this book. This additional knowledge will enable you to get a jump-start on how you choose to live your next years.

Your self-esteem is a judgment you make about yourself. It isn't static. It is an ever-changing process, based on messages from the past. You've reviewed your past to see what those messages are so you can claim and perpetuate the positive and discard the negative. You've listed your strengths and named what you are missing. Continue to intervene and convert your negative judgments of yourself so they need not become self-fulfilling, a presumption of what you'll be in the future. Make choices that will help you like yourself more.

Journeywell has provided a roadmap to guide you toward a healthy self-regard. The criteria for raising your self-esteem are:

- Get to know yourself.
- Recognize and own your feelings.
- Recognize and focus on your strengths—the bedrock of self-esteem.
- Take responsibility for planning for what you can do or control.
- Educate yourself to existing options and choices.
- Learn how to take care of yourself.

THE 3 UPS: WAKE UP, SHOW UP, LIGHTEN UP

Wake up

Much of this book is focused on waking up, waking up to who you are now, who you want to be, and how you can best spend your remaining precious years. The first chapter took you back to your formative years to review what you experienced and to thoroughly recognize that you are still a work in progress. Your ego is the "me" that you became better acquainted with, and it is constantly changing. You were given the opportunity to recapture and marvel at some of the pleasant memories, and to remember the part of life's conditioning that wasn't helpful. If you shared your journey with a listener, it was doubly rewarding.

The second chapter asked you to look at the way your values have evolved, the differences between mid-life and later-life. It pointed out the natural and societal barriers that could make late life more difficult and what you could do to overcome them. The fast-moving, self-focused, competitive, pressured ways of the middle years have been carried to quite an extreme in our society and the gentler and softer values modeled in later life—caring, continuing to learn, being of service, working to correct the injustices in the world, being grateful, and just having a good time in the moment—are beginning to be noticed and more appreciated. We are finally looking at our fast-track society and saying, "Whoa, what are we doing? What is really important?" Our whole country seems to be paralleling this rethinking about what is really important, beginning to see that to really respect ourselves and regain the favor of the rest of the world, we need to rely on "soft power."

Global warming and globalization and economic crisis has made us aware that everything and everyone is interrelated and interdependent. The earth belongs to us all. We will join the group of the vulnerable at some point, and be part of the interdependency cycle. There is an awakening going on—a gray awakening. Being closer to the end of our lives, we have most certainly passed our physical peak, most likely our productive peak, and have

> *When we ask for a chance to live our old age in comfort, creativity, and usefulness, we ask it not for our selves alone, but for you. We are not a special interest group. We are your roots. You are our continuity. What we gain is your inheritance.*
> *—Irene Pauli[1]*

moved into the very important spiritual peaking time, which enables us to see what is important with a broader lens.

The third chapter, "How Do I Make My Life More Meaningful?" aimed directly at examining what is meaningful for you and gave information, suggestions and resources to help you see the myriads of possibilities available for getting the most out of this time of your life. Chapter four, "How Do I Make My Life as Good as It Can Be?" suggests specific techniques for working with your feelings and thoughts and suggested many approaches to self-care. It helped you see that internal rewards bring fulfillment and that being healthy has much to do with developing a tranquil spirit and a resilient attitude. Recognizing that waking up is more than what happens to your conscious self, Chapter five, "What Ways-of-Being May Lead to Being Wiser?" went a little deeper. With aging, your appreciation of the simple, the reawakening of your sense of awe and curiosity about all that you know and don't know, your increasing fascination with life's many mysteries, all indicate that unconscious archetypal universalities are seeping in, leading you to be wiser and more fulfilled, feeling connected to the bigger picture, and more at peace. In later life, there is a readiness to wake up. Your awakening has already begun. Chapter six, "What Are my Responsibilities?" helped you wake up to what quality of life means to you, to what interdependence means, and the planning that could prove helpful in the areas of health-care and housing. The last chapter was "Finishing Well." There are definitely better and worse ways to live this last part of your life. You were given information, exercises, and scenarios to help you sort out your end-of-life plans, your legacy, how to make this time as rich and satisfying as possible? Don't believe for a minute that you can no longer change and make a life for yourself that fits better for who you want to be in your remaining years. A healthy brain doesn't ossify unless you choose to let it. You have choices. This book is about you, and who you decide you want to be. *Journeywell* served as a catalyst to help you align your "being" with your "doing" self. Though people of all ages seek this alignment, it is older people who are rapidly becoming the models for attaining wholeness.

Show up

You honor life by pouring yourself into it, by showing up for every moment and noticing all the little things along the way. The point of your journey is the journey. It's about appreciating your cup of coffee or tea in the morning, marveling at the snow load on the branches in the winter or the incredible spectrum of greens when the leaves are in all their freshness in the spring. By doing what you love like gardening, reading, grandparenting, traveling, creating or appreciating the arts, or being of service in some way that is satisfying, you are making the world a little better place. When you do something congruent with your values, however tiny the action may seem, you are making a difference, and these little ripples add up to a giant wave and force for goodness. The simple act of being present with another is definitely showing up.

Showing up for life means embracing your existence by participating rather than avoiding or merely observing. Growth is optional, and not all will choose it. Growth means evolving, waking up, and then showing up, not remaining asleep in the illusion that you have it all figured out. Some will choose to sit in front of the TV and let their lives just drift or leak away. Others continue to make choices that give pleasure and make them eager to get up in the morning. Showing up means continuing to learn and grow with your heart wide open, which includes all the hurts and the pleasures. Your heart is a seasoned traveler by now. The better you take care of yourself and the more you open your heart and care about

> *Get as much playing and appreciating in your life as you can.*

others, feel passionate about a cause or a project, the more you are showing up for life. Showing up says don't just let the world happen to you. Even if you can't make something happen, you can set the stage for what you want to have happen, and have a much better chance of getting what you want. Get out there. Put yourself into circumstances where good things are more likely to happen to you. Be the architect of your future.

Lighten up

Many of the values that come with late life do lighten us up. The ways-of-being discussed in Chapter five—being authentic, comfortable with paradox, befriending mystery, appreciating the ordinary, being more humble, rediscovering our awe, being hopeful and flexible—reduce tension and stress and do a part in lightening us up. Learning how to balance between taking ourselves seriously, yet not too seriously, is key.

Having seen so many weird and unexplainable things by this time in our lives has increased our sense of the absurd, made us kind of punchy and able to laugh at ourselves. What works for one of us won't for another. Yogi Berra works for me.

> *Always go to other people's funerals, otherwise they won't come to yours.*
> *—Yogi Berra*

We learn not to judge ourselves so harshly. Just because I have a good idea about how I would like to be in my old age does not mean that I won't screw up at times. It's called being human. Our truckload of experiences has shown us that we aren't perfect but that we are survivors. The seriousness of having to prove ourselves has dissipated. Let's accept who we are, warts and all. The art of letting go of what we can't control and being able to laugh at ourselves means we are journeying well.

I hope that *Journeywell: A Guide to Quality Aging* has proven to be just that for you, a common-sense and thought-provoking guide that is helping you live this next part of your life as fully and enjoyably as possible.

Appendices

APPENDIX A: THE ART OF LISTENING

The importance of being a good listener cannot be overemphasized. A basic need of humans is to be understood. The storyteller is waiting to be discovered. You, as a listener, have an opportunity to learn. It is not altruistic listening. Ideally, you are not listening for their sake, but for your own. You are reliving another's life, empathizing with their feelings, creating a respectful atmosphere where it is safe for them to be honest.

It's a time to "be there"—not to judge, advise, or analyze. Acknowledge how important this is to you and reciprocate by sharing your own views or stories if your partner appreciates that. Let your partner set the tone. Travel with the storyteller—let him or her take you along on the journey. Your listening is a gift of time. Be gentle. Don't push. Let your partner pick and choose what he or she wants to reflect upon. If you are the initiator of this exploration:

- Explain why you want to do this.
- Ask for permission. If granted, set a time. Pick a place that minimizes interruptions.
- Be aware that interviewing can be tiring and stop before exhaustion.
- Agree on a future time and place.

Listen to another as you would want him/her to listen to you.

There is an art to listening well. It is an act of love. It is an action, not passive. You are demonstrating by your listening that you care. The simple act of listening is far more powerful than words. It says, "I am interested in you as a person. I think what you feel is important. I'm just listening. I am not judging or evaluating you. I want to understand."

Pay Attention

Concentrate on the person. Let go of all other thoughts for now. You are not here to deal with your fears or problems. Maintain eye contact. Speak distinctly. Get rid of any avoidable outside distractions such as television, radio, visitors.

Let Speaker Know You Are Listening

Encourage the speaker to keep talking. Check out what you think you are hearing by periodically repeating what you hear.

Ask for Clarification

If it's not clear to you what the speaker is saying, don't assume anything or let it pass. Check it out. Say, "Am I hearing you correctly?" Don't assume that your solution to a problem is the speaker's solution.

Be Empathetic

Aim to understand the speaker's point of view. This means "getting in his or her shoes" and looking at the world from that perspective. Listen for meaning and feeling. If the story is sad, you could say, "You are really a survivor." Encourage description of feelings.

Be Supportive

Communicate your concern and caring in an atmosphere of warmth and acceptance. Keep aside any judgmentalism that you may feel. Most of the time being supportive will be very natural, but, even if you are unable to agree with the speaker's point of view, you can always be supportive with comments such as "this has been hard for you" or "it's good that you're talking about these things." Look for parallels of agreement. Support does not mean "I'll solve your problems for you" or that you necessarily agree with the speaker.

Limit Your Own Talking

Keep the focus on the speaker and off yourself and your opinions. This is his or her time. Your role is to ask appropriate questions in order to help you both become more aware of the speaker's values, feelings, or wants. An exception to this occurs if you have agreed that this is to be an exchange of stories instead of a one-way exploration.

Don't Give Advice

The objective of active listening is to help the speaker figure out how he or she feels or what he or she wants to do. You are a facilitator in this process. You may point out options or express your opinions if requested. It is not your responsibility to tell the speaker what to do, to fix the speaker, or to make him or her happy. The speaker may distort stories. Listening without fixing or correcting can be very difficult. But if you truly listen, he or she will probably come closer to the truth.

> *If you're talking, you aren't listening ... or learning.*

Be Respectful

You are modeling respect for yourself, for others, and the storyteller. Be prompt, reliable, and able to set limits. Tell the speaker how much time you have to spend and when you can do it again.

Encourage Recognition and Expression of Feelings

Focusing on feelings is a core ingredient to effective active listening. A goal is to create an atmosphere of acceptance of feelings—any feelings—without judgment. Bringing feelings into awareness is the first step in a process of change or acceptance. Don't invalidate the speaker's feelings by false cheerfulness. Tell the speaker what you are learning. Help the speaker find proof of his or her own competence.

Don't Demand 'Truth'

Remember this is the speaker's story—not yours. A story is a person's interpretation of an event. Storytelling isn't a science. When you listen to another's story, you are viewing the experiences as the speaker sees them. Listening is caring, not judging.

Empower Them

The deepest act of love is to help persons love themselves. Your purpose is to help them help themselves. By active listening you are saying: "I am interested in you as a person and respect your thoughts. I am not here to change or evaluate you. You are worth my time. You can trust me. I think what you feel is important."

> *There are three truths: My truth, Your truth and The truth.*
> —*Chinese Proverb*

APPENDIX B: GUIDELINES FOR RECORDING YOUR STORY

The oral tradition, handing down family wisdom, humor, and history, has been carried on since the beginning of humankind.

Etiquette if you are recording another's story:

1. Ask for permission if recording another.
2. Set a special time/sequence of times.
3. Give the storyteller some lead-time so he or she can look over this book and decide what areas are of interest. If you are the initiator, have questions ready.
4. In addition to the book, you might bring along props to trigger memories (photos, old newspaper headlines, articles, etc.).
5. Check your equipment thoroughly so the flow isn't interrupted. (Technology is moving too fast to predict what equipment you may choose to use.)
6. Find a quiet, suitable place for recording with as little outside interference as possible. Take the phone off the hook.
7. Introduce the session with the date, place, occasion, name(s) of those speaking.

8. Set a time limit and be aware of the storyteller's energy level. Make an appointment for the next interview time, if desired.

Getting Started on Family History

It all begins with stories. If you want to pursue in more depth your genealogy and family history, start with stories. Then add photos, letters, written records, yearbooks, and more stories. The Internet is an amazing resource for helping in this project. Here are a few websites to get you started: familysearch.org, Rootsweg.com, Ancestry.com/save/charts/ (library has this for free), genealogy.com, and geneology today.com. Whether you have Jewish, Scandinavian, Polish, Italian roots … it's on the Internet.

Self-Record Your Own Story.

Give it as a gift, your legacy.* Interview another. This can be either totally other-oriented or it can be an agreed upon interaction between the storyteller and one other or the storyteller with a bunch of family/ friends asking questions recording the hubbub, laughter of a group occasion. A fun relatively new idea for passing on your stories is to do a legacy video, telling your story on camera so your family and friends can actually witness the actual you, hear your voice, see your expressions, and enjoy your laugh. It is getting easier and easier with new tools springing into existence every day. If you are unfamiliar with the new technology, get lessons (perhaps you have a grandchild who can help).

Interesting Family History Websites:
(Some with $ sign cost money)

COLLABORATIVE WEBSITES:
www.ancientfaces.com

www.rootsweb.com

www. geneanet.org

www.mytrees.com

HISTORY AND REFERENCE
www.americancivilwar.info

INTERNATIONAL AND IMMIGRATION FOR TRACING ANCESTORS JOURNEYS
www.Ellisisland.org

www.imigrantships.net

www.worldgenweb.org

www.origins.net

RECORDS
www.usgenweb.com

rootsweb.com

Ancestry.com $ * (free at libraries)

Geneology.com $

Familysearch.org (Mormon)*

Findagrave.com
www.census-online.com
www.accessgenelogy.com
uscitydirectories.com

APPENDIX C: ADDITIONAL QUESTIONS FOR LIFE REVIEW

FAMILY OF ORIGIN

Where did you live growing up? What was your childhood like? Do you remember your bedroom? Tell me about your hobbies. Pets? Friends? Clubs? Favorite possessions? Do you remember special birthday parties? Halloweens? Games you played? Other traditions? What sort of community did you grow up in? How did you fit in? What did you do for fun?

Did your family laugh a lot? Can you remember any particularly funny times? What parts did music, dance, or art play in your life? What songs did you sing as a child? Could you sing one? Did you play any musical instruments? Were there any special talents you were known for? Who were your favorite relatives? Neighbors? Friends? Describe a smell or a sound that you associate with your childhood. What messages about life did you acquire from your childhood? Overall, what was life like for you as a child? Tell me about your grandparents. Do you know how they met? Do you remember any stories about them that they or others told you? Who were your favorite relatives? Why? Tell me about your brother(s) and sisters(s). What was your birth rank? How did you and your siblings get along growing up? How do you think your ordinal position in the family affected your life? What stories about your family stick out in your mind?

Favorites:

Describe a favorite place where you lived. Did you have a favorite spot in the house? Was it traumatic for you to leave home? What neighbors were particularly memorable? Why? What about other favorites? Foods? Pets? Can you sing a favorite song that you learned as a kid?

YOUR ADULTHOOD
Work

If you did not work outside the home, was it a choice? How did you feel about it? How much were you influenced by need for money? Did you work too hard, not hard enough, or about the right amount? Did you like your work? Who was your favorite boss? Least favorite? Did you prefer working alone or with others? Did you prefer working for yourself or for others? Do you have any regrets about choices not taken? Paths not pursued? How would you describe your earning power, your financial status over the years? Do you have any favorite work tale? Funny? Horrible? Unfair? Tell me about some of your proudest moments, your hardest decisions, your best decisions.

Clothes

Did you tend to be conservative or flashy? If you went some place where no one knew you, what kind of clothing might you wear? What's your favorite kind of outfit? What was your fanciest dress-up outing? How have fashions changed? Do you remember a particularly foolish clothing purchase?

Firsts

Do you remember the first time you saw a television? When? What early programs do you remember? Do you remember your first plane or train ride? How many modes of transportation have you used? What was your first major hurt? Sadness? When did you first see the ocean? Swim in it? Water-ski? What was your first experience earning money? How much did you earn? When was the first time you felt "on your own" or lived alone? Who was your first boyfriend or girlfriend? When was your first kiss? What do you remember about the first time you made love?

APPENDIX D: MARKETPLACE OF OPPORTUNITIES, RESOURCES, POSSIBILITIES[1,2]

Not all of these will be available in your community, but they give you an idea of all that's out there. Check out any that look interesting to you.

AARP (*www.aarp.org/money/careers/findingajob*) is a non-profit membership organization offering resources, advocacy, and community service opportunities 888-687-2277.

Allliance for Retired Americans (*www.retiredamericans.org*) is a progressive organization allied with the AFL-CIO that presses for action on retiree issues 202-974-8222.

America's Promise (*www.americapromise.org*) is dedicated to mobilizing volunteers to build the character and competence of youth by serving as a mentor, tutor, or coach during after school hours. General Colin Powell leads it.

Civic Ventures (*www.civicventures.org*) provides retirees with options for applying their experience to new kinds of work.

Corporation for National Service (CNS) (*www.cns.gov*) is the umbrella organization for national service programs such as AmeriCorps, VISTA, Learn and Serve America, National Senior Service Corps, which operates Seniors for Schools and the Experience Corps for Independent Living, National Senior Service Corps, which includes Foster Grandparents, Senior Companion Program and the Retired and Senior Volunteer Program operating in all 50 states.

Craigslist (*www.craigslist.com*) lists local jobs and volunteer opportunities.

Earthelders (www.*secondjourney.org/elders/*) care about older people and the earth and explore ways to connect the generations within communities.

Elderhostel (*www.elderhostel.org*) offer educational trips, college and university-based institutes for learning, and service programs.(Life long learning while traveling.)

Elders Share the Arts (*www.elderssharethearts.org*)

Environmental Alliance for Senior Involvement (*www.easi.org*) older people and elementary schoolers get together and practice organic gardening, reducing use of pesticides and herbicides, water quality monitoring, and groundwater protection.

Essential Grandparent (*www.essentialgrandparent.com*) provides resources for grandparents seeking information about grandparenting.

Executive Service Corps (*www.esscus.org*) is made up of retired business persons who volunteer their time to consult with public service and nonprofit agencies.

Faith in Action (*www.fiavolunteers.org*) helps homebound elderly with everyday activities allowing them to remain independent.

Foster Grandparents (*www.fostergrandparents.org*) serves children with care and emotional support, tutoring and mentoring.

Global Volunteers (*www.globalvolunteer.org*) organizes short-term volunteer service programs teaching conversational English, and service projects around the world.

Grandkids and me (*www.grandkidsandme.com*) offers seasonal camps for grandparents to go with grandchildren.

Gray Panthers (*www.graypanthers.org*) actively works on social problems such as peace, housing, healthcare, and jobs 800-280-5362.

Habitat for Humanity International (*www.habitat.org*) is a nonprofit, ecumenical housing ministry dedicated to eliminating substandard housing and homelessness by building houses using volunteers.

Habitat for Humanity (*www. habitat.org*) is a nonprofit, ecumenical Christian ministry dedicated to providing housing for families in need.

Hosteling International-USA (*www. hiayh.org*) once reserved for the young but is expanding. Provides inexpensive, safe, and clean housing.

International Home Exchange (*www.ihen.com*) shares your home or vacation spot in exchange for experiencing other parts of the world.

ᴛship Caregivers Association (*www.mkca.org*) gives information on grandparent support groups especially around legal issues.

ᴇ of Woman Voters (*www.lwv.org*) is a multi-issue, grassroots organization of volunteers working to better understand and influence civic issues.

ᴇgacy Works is a project under Elders Share the Arts (*www.elderssharehearts*) where artists teach teens skills of interviewing and making collages and the match them with homebound elders.

Little Brother-Friends of the Elderly (*www.littlebrothers.org*) is a national, nonprofit organization committed to relieving isolation and loneliness among the elderly. Volunteers provide companionship, occasional driving, and help set up events.

Older Women's League (OWL) (*www.owl-national*) is a national grassroots organization that works on older women's concerns through research, education, and advocacy.

Peace Corps (*www.peace.corps.gov*) recruits older people for service around the world. Take couples and singles working in many skill sectors but primarily education and business.

Points of Light Foundation (*www.pointsoflight*) works in communities throughout the United States promoting community service and volunteering.

Raging Grannies (*www.raginggrannies.com*) protests injustices and has a lot of fun doing it. Dressing up, singing, satirizing evil-doing in public and getting everyone singing.

Red Cross Volunteers (*www.redcross.org*) provides volunteer opportunities in transportation, disaster aid, health and safety.

SCORE (*www.score.org*) has retired professionals giving free and confidential small business advice to want-to-be entrepreneurs.

Seniors Vacation and Home Exchange (*www.seniorshomeexchange.com*) must be over 50.

Small Business Administration (*www.sba.gov*) is an independent agency of the federal government that counsels, helps Americans start and grow businesses.

Spiritual Eldering Institute (*www.spiriualeldering.org*) is a multi-faith organization that promotes educational programs and leadership training, and workshops 303-449-724.

U.S. Department of Labor (*www.careervoyages.gov/careerchangers-main.cfm*, *RetirementJobs.com*) lists job opportunities for those over fifty.

Vital Aging Network (*www.van.umn.edu*) promotes the self-determination, community involvement, and personal enrichment for and with older adults through education and advocacy.

Volunteers in Medicine Clinics (VIM) provides free medical and dental service to individuals who otherwise would have no access to service staffed by retired medical professionals.

Wilderness Inquiry (*www.wisdernessinquiry.org*) provides outdoor adventure for people of all ages and abilities and use volunteers to assist them.

APPENDIX E: HEALTH-CARE, LEGAL, AND ETHICAL TERMS[1]

*Note: States have slightly varying definitions of some of these terms. Check with authorities in your state for accuracy.

Advance directives - Legal documents in which competent individuals can retain some control over their health-care decisions in the event they are no longer able to do so for themselves. A living will ar durable power of attorney for health care are the most common examples.

Assisted suicide - Occurs when a patient kills him-or herself after having been given information or assisted by another in gaining access to the means for committing suicide.

Competent (in medical context) - A person able to make decisions for himself or herself. Legally, a patient i. considered competent to make a decision if he or she has the ability to understand relevant information about the medical problem and the consequences of the decisions about treatment.

Complementary and Alternative Medicine (CAM) - A group of diverse medical and health-care practices that are *not* presently considered to be part of conventional medicine. Complementary medicine (examples would be acupuncture, aromatherapy, acupressure) is used together with conventional medicine, and alternative medicine is used in place of conventional medicine.

Conservatorship - When a person is determined to be unable to make his or her own decisions and has not previously designated a surrogate decisions-maker in a DPAHC or living will, a court can appoint an individual, or a corporation with trusteepowers, to manage the financial affairs You may plan for this situation by pre-designating a conservator. Some states give a conservator only rights to make financial decisions, other states give conservator right to make health and personal care decisions.

Conventional medicine or Western medicine - The medicine practiced in the United States by holders of a M.D. (medical doctor) degree or D.O. (doctor of osteopathy) and by other allied professionals such as psychologists, physical therapists, and registered nurses. Holders of an M.D. are referred to as allopathic physicians, while those with a D.O. are known as osteopathic physicians.

Death - Flat EEGs over forty-eight-hour period

Do not hospitalize (DNH) order - When care center residents for whom the experience of hospitalization would be more confusing and painful than therapeutic gain, DNH orders are established by prior agreement of the resident or decision-maker.

Do not intubate (DNI) order - Declares that the patient should not be given artificial nutrition or hydration through tubes.

Durable power of attorney for health care (DPAHC) - A legal document that appoints another person to make health-related decisions for you in case you are unable to do so. This extends the authority beyond death, thus making it "durable." It is an important and cheaper alternative to guardianship and conservatorship.

Euthanasia - Active killing of a suffering patient.

Guardianship - The most extreme form of surrogate decision-making. If a person is declared incompetent to make his or her own decisions, a guardian can be appointed by the court to make all decisions, including health care.

Hospice care - A philosophy of caring for terminally ill people that provides symptom and pain relief, emotional and spiritual support for the patient and his or her family and friends. It is based on the belief that every person has the right to die pain-free and with dignity in the company of family and friends. It is a physician-directed, nurse-coordinated team approach that may take place in the home, hospice center, nursing home, or hospital. Care is individually designed to deal with dying, death, and grief in the last phases of a terminal illness. To be paid for by the Medicare Hospice Benefit, you are to have an expectancy of less than six months to live in the judgment of the patient's attending physician and the hospice medical director.

(In Case of Emergency) - ICE is a campaign encouraging people to enter an emergency contact number in their cell phone's memory under the heading of ICE in order for paramedics and police to be able to contact a designated person in case of emergency. In an emergency like a car accident or heart attack, officials will be able to locate your next of kin if you have a cell phone handy.

Integrative medicine - An approach to medicine that combines treatments from conventional medicine and complementary medicine for which there is some high-quality evidence of safety and effectiveness.

Kidney dialysis - A process used to remove unwanted fluid and waste products from the body when the kidneys are unable to do so. The blood is purified by being pumped from a patient's artery through a kidney machine and returned through a vein.

Life-prolonging measures - Treatment that is likely only to prolong the natural process of dying when there is no significant hope of functional recovery. Examples could include resuscitation or artificially administered nutrition.

Limited time trial - The use of medical measures for a specified period of time to determine whether benefits will outweigh the burdens.

Living will - A written statement, which is a legal document in many states, in which a person who is still able to make competent decisions can state his or her wishes and instructions about the kind of medical treatment she would want if terminally ill.

Palliative care - The focus is on quality of life, pain relief, treating the patient and family as the unit of care as in hospice, but it is different than hospice because you don't need to be "terminal" and it is not covered by the Hospice Medicare Benefit.

Persistent vegetative state (PVS) - When a person's higher brain is dead but the brain stem still functions. A person in this state is awake but unaware, requires artificial food and nutrition but often does not require a respirator for breathing. A person can live for a long time in this state (thirty-seven years is the record).

Proxy - A person legally named to make decisions for another.

Respirator/ventilator - Mechanical breathing machine that assists a patient's breathing when he or she is partially or totally unable to do so on his or her own.

Total or palliative sedation - When symptoms are considered to be intractable and every other intervention has failed, enough sedation is given to put the dying person in a state of unconsciousness. 800-247-7421 (*caringfriends@endoflifechoices.org*).

Terminal illness - A terminal condition is an incurable or irreversible condition for which the administration of medical treatment will only prolong the dying process.

Will - A legal document that designates what happens to one's property and assets when one dies (does not involve health-care decisions).

APPENDIX F: CARDIOPULMONARY RESUSCITATION (CPR) AND ARTIFICIAL FEEDING AND HYDRATION

Cardiopulmonary resuscitation (CPR) - In the event that the heart, blood pressure, and breathing fail to the extent that death is expected within minutes or seconds, rescue measures are taken su[...] pounding on the chest, inserting a breathing tube into the windpipe, and administering medica[...] tions and electrical shocks.

Do not resuscitate (DNR) - A request that resuscitation (CPR) measures not be initiated because the patien[...] and family in consultation with a physician have requested such an order is on the patient's chart. A statement about resuscitation is often required for patients with a terminal condition in which resuscitation may serve only to prolong the dying process. The order can be reversed at any time and should be reviewed regularly to determine if the DNR order should remain.

Artificial feeding and hydration (food and fluids) - In situations where a person is unable to take in food or fluids by mouth or swallow or eat in a manner adequate to sustain life, a tube may be inserted into a vein (hyperalimentation), through the nose (nasogastric), or directly into the stomach (gastrostomy) for purposes of providing liquid nutrition and hydration on an ongoing basis.

RESUSCITATION

Cardiopulmonary resuscitation (CPR) is an emergency intervention designed to restore heartbeat and breathing. Procedures range from simple chest compression to help the blood keep circulating to sophisticated electrical defibrillation. It is now being recognized that although CPR is successful sometimes, there are often poor outcomes and CPR should not be universally administered. Medical and gerontological journals repeatedly report grim statistics on the use of CPR with frail elderly persons. Even when life is technically saved, patients are often reduced to a poor quality of life, confined to intensive care units or nursing homes, requiring constant care.

CPR is routinely administered in most situations when someone experiences cardiac or respiratory arrest. There is a presumption favoring the preservation of life in this country, regardless of a person's general physical condition, and a corresponding legal presumption that assumes patient consent to CPR. It is important to realize that CPR occurs automatically in emergency situations unless there is a DNR order in place. Many people in foreign countries are staggered by the fact that we automatically give CPR to such poor prospects. Persons receiving CPR fall into three categories:

a. CPR should be given to patients who overdose, who have ventricular arrhythmias, heart attacks, anesthesia complications, or given to any basically healthy person who suffers an unexpected trauma. Resuscitation is most effective where the collapse is observed and effective resuscitation is commenced immediately.

b. Poor results are generally seen in persons over seventy who receive CPR and who suffer from advanced chronic diseases such as cerebral vascular disease, cirrhosis, chronic lung disease, and so on. This group shows a poor statistical probability of ultimate survival (less than 10%). Persons in this category should discuss DNR orders with those close to them and with their doctor. The physician needs to outline explicitly the pros and cons of treatment options, so that the best possible decision can be made about the patient's future.

For persons with irreversible illness, patients who suffer with multiple organ failure or unresponsive metastatic cancer, CPR should not be given or even considered. The family should be advised of its futility and a DNR order should be written.

The public seriously overestimates CPR's effectiveness, perhaps because how the success rate is portrayed on TV. A 1996 study of 97 episodes of *ER*, *Chicago Hope*, and *Rescue 911* in which CPR was depicted showed 75% surviving in the short term and 67% percent in the long term. In reality very few survive in the third frail category and on average the percentage of people who survive in the non-frail category is only 20%[1]

DNR orders should be carefully discussed. Only by questioning your physician will you get enough information to make a well-informed decision. If DNR is decided upon, orders should be placed in the person's medical record and hospital chart. The DNR order should be part of the care plan with specific, written instructions on what should and should not be done. These decisions should be discussed with key caregivers. Nurses should not only know what to do but also the rationale for the decision so that they can answer questions and ease worries that the patient or family may have. DNR orders should be reviewed on a regular basis in case there is any pertinent change in health status or the patient or family has any qualms that need to be addressed.

A major concern is that a DNR order might mean that the patient will be abandoned, ignored, or receive less care. Special attention needs to be given to alleviate this fear. Patients with DNR orders need to understand that they will receive comfort care and that every effort will be made to minimize suffering. A DNR order does not mean that other therapies will be withheld. We all need to remember that fear of abandonment and fear of dying doesn't just go away. An individual's fears need to be verbalized, questions need to be asked, and therapeutic options need to be thoroughly discussed. It is critical to alleviate these fears and for the patient to understand that he or she will be kept comfortable.

EMTs and paramedics who come when 911 is called will automatically resuscitate unless we have a DNR order signed and dated by our physician in hand for them to see. Some states call this document a POLST (Physician Orders for Life-Sustaining Treatment). It lets emergency personnel withhold resuscitation.

ARTIFICIAL FOOD AND HYDRATION

Laws regarding this subject vary from state to state. It is best if we state definitively in our advance directive how we feel about this matter. It is important to distinguish between artificial food and hydration and eating and drinking. The food and liquid that we put in our mouth are eating and drinking. Prepared products artificially put into our system are considered medical treatment and can extend our life, depending on the circumstance, for many years.

Artificial nutrition and hydration can only be given with a doctor's order and the consent of the patient or the patient's surrogate. It is an extremely beneficial treatment in the recovery of some but considered by many an unnecessary treatment for persons with no hope of recovery … when it only extends the dying process. Keep in mind that life-support discussions occur only when further treatment is considered futile and the patient is unable to make his or her own decisions. According to researchers Joanne Lynn[2] and James Childress, patients who are allowed to die without artificial hydration and nutrition may sometimes die more comfortably than those who receive it. Someti when a serious or life-threatening accident involves a formerly active, healthy person, artificial fo and hydration are given on a time-limited basis. This enables an adequate assessment of the medica condition, can help the family adjust to the suddenness of the need for decision-making, and decide whether the situation is indeed futile.

In 1986, the American Medical Association[3] issued a major opinion: "It is not unethical to discontinue all means of life-prolonging medical treatment. Life-prolonging medical treatment includes medication and artificially or technologically supplied respiration, nutrition and hydration." The question of the morality of discontinuing artificial food and hydration continues. Thousands of Americans who exist in a persistent vegetative state (PVS) are maintained by tube feedings. One woman remained in a vegetative state for thirty-seven years at great cost to tax payers. Despite one court ruling after another stating that artificial feeding and hydration are medical procedures similar to artificial breathing by means of a respirator, feelings about this particular set of life-prolonging measures are varied and intense. It is important to determine how we feel about this issue, that our surrogate decision-maker knows our feelings, and that we have chosen a doctor who will follow our wishes.[4]

Eating and drinking symbolize love and caring to many people. Many cannot make the distinction between eating and drinking and artificial nutrition and hydration. If this is a person's belief, it is important that it be stated. Many people also recall their own experiences of hunger or thirst and imagine that dying from malnutrition and dehydration must be pure agony, no matter what they are told to the contrary. Kidney dialysis machines and respirators are equally foreign technology, but they simply do not engender the same value-laden, emotional response as giving or withholding artificial food and hydration.

APPENDIX G: HOME SERVICES

Emergency response systems. Electronic monitors are available that activate an attachment on your telephone that is tied into the emergency room of the hospital, police department, emergency squads. It allows older adults to live alone but never be out of contact with help in case of an emergency. The older adult who lives alone wears or carries in a pocket a small wireless help button that, when pushed, calls an emergency number. When the call comes in, a trained listener immediately calls the sender to see what the problem is and then, if the sender does not answer, calls one of the designated responders, who could be a neighbor or a family member, to go to the home immediately. It is an inexpensive service, and one that stretches the freedom of the person living alone. This service has different names (Lifeline, Alert USA).

Friendly visiting /peer counseling/Stephen ministers. Volunteers working under the umbrella of senior service organizations, hospitals, churches, and synagogues listen, do errands, write letters, and provide companionship.

Meals on Wheels. Volunteers bring one hot meal a day to the home-bound. Fees vary.

Home health-care agencies. They provide a spectrum of care from occupational and physical therapy and homemaker services to advanced skilled nursing services with mobile technology such as ventilators and oxygen. Medicaid often covers it. The degree to which private insurance cover these services vary widely. Check the yellow pages or your local area agency on aging for information.

Homemakers/aides. Aides do light housekeeping and assist in personal care such as bathing and dressing. Sometimes, if under supervision, they can monitor medication.

Chore service helpers. Helpers clean, shop, wash clothes, cook, and sometimes make small repairs in the house and do yard work.

Transportation services. Transportation services vary from community to community. Many have reduced fares for seniors on public transportation, medical vehicles from hospitals, non-medical transports for medical appointments, senior center buses, and special taxi rates. Learn how to access these services. Delivery services, dry cleaners, food markets, catalogue retailers, and pharmacies that deliver are springing up. Cable television offers shop-at-home services.

Escort services. Volunteer and paid escort services are available in some communities.

Libraries. Libraries offer special services to the homebound. Books can be delivered or mailed along with "talking books" services. Call your local library or national office at 800-424-8567.

Non-Medical Home Care. These providers can usually be found under Home Health Care Services in the yellow pages. They do errands, housecleaning, serve as companions, and respite helpers. These services are springing up and come under an assortment of names.

Adult Day Care. Adult day care provides social and rehabilitative activities to older adults during the day in a community facility. Participants can attend one to five days a week. It is often a perfect solution for all involved in situations where adult children or a spouse who works during the day or needs relief from caregiving responsibilities at home can have a safe, stimulating place for a loved one during the day.

Legal Assistance. Legal assistance may be available for those who need help with wills, taxes, public program benefits, protection services, disability care. Inquire through lawyer information and referral services, legal aid society, or legal counsel for the elderly.

Mental Health Services. Mental health services for addiction and abuse problems as well as everyday life transitions and adjustment to loss are available through community mental health agencies and sometimes through senior service agencies and senior centers.

Respite Care for Caregivers. Respite care is available in some communities. This service allows persons who care for another in their home full-time to get some rest and re-energize.

Telephone Reassurance or Communicare. Telephone reassurance is a program available in some communities where homebound elderly are called (or may call in) daily by a volunteer to assure that all is well.

"Golden Age" Banking Services. These banking services offer a discounted brokerage service, direct deposit of social security checks, free traveler's checks, no service charge, and payment of utility bills as inducements for older adults.

Geriatric Case Managers. These individuals assess the needs of an individual and match him or her with services locally or far away. For a care manager locater arranged by geographical area, go to *www.caremanager.org* (520-881-8008). Hospital social workers and discharge planners, and senior centers can recommend care managers.

Congregate Dining. Congregate dining offers nutritionally balanced meals to older people in a social setting such as a senior center, church, or school. A donation is requested, but the meals are subsidized. Weatherization and fuel assistance. Federal and state aid, which varies from state to state, are available to low-income households for weatherization and fuel assistance, sometimes including free energy audits, insulation, and the cost of labor.

> *Note: There is a confusion or overlap in the definition of many terms (homemakers/aides, chore services, home health care, home improvement, and personal care services). Different parts of the country label the helper categories differently. Ask the Area Agency on Aging for clarification and information and referral numbers in your community. Obtain a resource directory for your area. Order a Silver Pages telephone directory at 800-252-6060. Use yellow pages to find transportation, nutrition services, home health care, and societies for persons with vision or hearing impairments, and local senior centers.*

CAREGIVER SERVICES

For those with Internet access, there is a virtual community of resources and companionship available from your living room. You can ask for suggestions and help on chat rooms and hear how others are coping with your particular query. Numbers to call and websites:

- National Association of Area Agencies on Aging
- Eldercare Locator (800-677-1116. *www.n4a.org*)
- ElderCare Online (*www.ec-online*)
- National Family Caregivers Association (800-896-3650, *www.nfcaccares.org*)
- The Well Spouse Foundation (800-838-0879, *www.wellspouse.org*)
- U.S. Administration on Aging's National Family Caregiver Support Program (*aoa.gov/prof/ aoaprog/caregiver/carefam/carefam.asp*) *Caregivershome.com/newsletter/newnews.cfm*
- Caregiver's Home Companion Spousal Caregiving pages (*caregiveshome.com/spousal/spousal .cfm*)

APPENDIX H: HOUSING OPTIONS

Accessory apartments. One converts an area of one's house into an apartment for a family member or rents it out for additional income or moves into it and rents the bulk of the house.

Share-a-home. For reduced rent, an older person with a home shares it with another person who helps with household chores.

Intentional communities. A planned residential community designed to promote a high degree of social interaction usually with a common social, political, or spiritual vision. They also share responsibilities and resources. Intentional communities include co-housing, residential land trusts, eco-villages, communes, housing cooperatives.

Reverse mortgage/home equity. Home equity allows older persons to remain in their own homes and receive set payments from their home's equity for a predetermined number of years. Basically, it means selling your house but continuing to live in it. It allows you to convert your home equity to liquid assets, enabling you to continue living there. Check out the variations in your area.

[Condo]miniums. Individually owned units in a complex where common property is jointly owned. This is often a first step for independent older adults who no longer want a large home, want less maintenance responsibility, and want more security.

Co-housing. A kind of intentional community composed of private homes with full kitchens, supplemented by extensive common facilities. A co-housing community is planned, owned, and managed by the residents. Common facilities vary but usually include a large kitchen and dining room where residents can take turns cooking for the community. Other communal facilities may include a library, laundry, recreation facilities, offices, Internet access, game room, TV room, workshop etc.

Cooperatives. These are multi-unit developments where residents own shares in the whole enterprise versus owning individual units.

ECHO (Elder Cottage Housing Opportunity). Housing where seniors occupy a second family living unit or apartment with a separate entrance often called granny apartments. Senior citizen apartment communities. These feature private living quarters with easy access to transportation, social activities, housekeeping services, and sometimes a meal a day.

Rental housing. This includes single-family homes, apartments, and town houses. Costs range from government-subsidized to expensive.

Adult care homes. Sometimes called foster homes, these generally provide meals and personal care and some degree of supervision in a private home. They are not considered medical facilities but medical help is available.

Boarding homes. These tend to serve a particular category of residents—older persons and those with mental or physical disabilities. They provide room, board, and personal assistance.

Life care communities. Sometimes called continuing care retirement communities (CCRCs), these types of communities provide a full range of services from apartments for independent living to skilled nursing care. They generally require monthly payments plus an entrance fee that is sometimes refundable at death. Prices and contractual agreements vary. Some are luxury high-rises with communal living resembling fancy restaurants; others look more like college dining halls, serving cafeteria-style meals.

Assisted living. This offers services, usually non-medical, to residents whom need some help but want to live in their own private living units. It is similar to Congregate Housing where you live in your individual space and can choose whether to join others in social activities or not. Sometimes you pay monthly and sometimes you can buy a unit.

Care centers. Nursing homes and retirement centers provide twenty-four-hour access to skilled care or intermediate custodial care. Medicare pays only for skilled and acute care. It does not pay for care for chronic illnesses such as Alzheimer's or bedridden stroke victims. Quality homes often have waiting lists. It is smart and responsible to investigate the homes in your area and put yourself on a waiting list. You are under no obligation to go into the facility when your name rises to the top of the list, but it is wonderful insurance to know the option is available when you're ready. Care centers can be the best alternative for many reasons: if you need more medical attention than you can receive elsewhere, if you need short-term care after a hospital stay, if you worry about being a burden or your care-giver is wearing down, if you require so much nursing care in your home that the costs exceed your ability to pay, if you feel isolated in your own house and choose to have more social (if this is the only reason, there are probably other alternatives).

END-NOTES

Introduction

1. Lars Tornstam *Gerotranscendence: A Developmental Theory of Positive Aging* 2005.
2. Abraham Maslow *Motivation and Personality* 1970.

Chapter One

1. Vaclav Havel *International Herald Tribune* 21 February 1990.
2. Erik Erikson and Helen Kivnick *Childhood and Society* New York, Norton, 1963.
3. John Brantner Keynote talk Fall Conference for Minnesota Gerontological Society, 1985.

Chapter Two

1. May Sarton *Encore: A Journal of the Eightieth Year* 1993.
2. Ellen Langer and J. Rodin "The effects of enhanced personal responsibility for the aged: A field experiment in and institutional setting." pp. 191–98.
3. Nicholas Perricone *The Wrinkle Cream* p. 2.
4. Nora Epfron *I Feel Bad About My Neck: And Other Thoughts on Being a Woman* p. 55.
5. May Sarton "Friend or Enemy" *Coming into Eighty: New Poems* 1994.
6. Malcolm Cowley *The View from Eighty*. New York: Penguin Books, 1982 p. 8.
7. Nora Epfron *I Feel Bad About My Neck: And Other Thoughts on Being a Woman* 2006.
8. Stevie Ray "Is Faster Better?" First published in American City Business Newspapers, Stevie Ray's Improv Company, Minneapolis, MN (date not archived)
9. Ken Keyes, Jr. *The Hundredth Monkey* 1981.
10. Margaret Mead "Courtesy of The Institute for Intercultural Studies, Inc., New York."

Chapter Three

1. Victor Frankl *The Will to Meaning: Foundations and Applications of Logotherapy* p. 48.
2. Steve Reilly *Simple Psychology: Simple Living in a Complicated World* p. 21.
3. Nancy Paddock "Lie Down" *Trust the Wild Heart,* p. 80.
4. Mary Oliver "At Blackwater Pond" 1992. p. 226.
5. Mary Jean Iron "Normal Day" ThinkExist.com Quotations Online 1 Sep. 2008.
6. Daniel H Pink. *A Whole New Mind: Moving from the information Age to the Conceptual Age,* p.61
7. Florida Scott-Maxwell *The Measure of My Days,* p. 142.
8. Stephnie L. Brown et al "Providing social support may be more beneficial than receiving it," pp. 320–327.
    Sam Harris *The End of Faith* p. 171.

ter Four

Ethyl M. Sternberg *The Balance Within: The Science Connecting Health and Emotions* p. 208.
    ibid p. 209.
3. Jerome Ellison *Life's Second Half: The Pleasures of Aging,* p. 48.
4. Ellen E. Langer *Mindfulness,* pp. 102–113.
5. Candace Pert "The Wisdom of the Receptors: Neuropeptides, the Emotions, and Bodymind" p. 8.
6. S. Kobasa and M. Puccetti "Personality and Social Resources in Stress Resistance" p. 45.
7. Bruce Lipton *The Biology of Belief: Unleashing the Power of Consciousness, Matter and Miracles* 2005.
8. Joseph Fabry *Guideposts to Meaning: Discovering What Really Matters.* p. 16.
9. John Brantner Keynote talk Fall Conference for Minnesota Gerontolgical Society, 1985.
10. Nossrat *Peseschkian In Search of Meaning: A Psychotherapy of Small Steps* 1985.
11. Rachel Naomi Remen quoted by Anne Lamott in "Scattering the Present" Salon.com.
12. Joan Didion *The Year of Magical Thinking* p. 188.
13. Robert Veninga *The Gift of Hope,* p. 41.
14. Meridel LeSeuer *Ripenings: Selected Works, 1927–1980* 1982.

15. Candace Pert "The Wisdom of the Receptors: Neuropeptides, the Emotions, and Bodymind" pp. 8–16.

16. Mimi Guaneri Speech at The Marsh, Minnetonka, MN April 27, 2006.

17. Salim Yusuf "Interheart: A Global Case-Control.Study of Risk Factors for Acute Myocardial Infarction" September 2004.

18. Tammy Felton "We Must find Peace" Reprinted from *Images: Women in Transition* p. 111.

19. May Sarton *At Seventy*, p. 10.

20. Matthew Sanford *Waking:A Memoir of Trauma and Transcendence* 2005.

21. Dr. Miriam E. Nelson quoted by Jane Brody *New York Times*, June 24, 2008 p. D7.

22. Lyn Freeman *Mosbey's Complementary and Alternative Medicine: A Research based Approach* 2004.

23. Nancy Manahan and Becky Bohan *Living Consciously, Dying Gracefully: A Journey with Cancer and Beyond* 2007.

24. Parker Palmer *Let Your Life Speak* p. 29.

Chapter Five

1. Margery Williams *The Velveteen Rabbit* 1922.

2. Florida Scott Maxwell *The Measure of my Days*, pp. 17–18.

3. Wendy Lustbader. *What's Worth Knowing* 2001.

4. May Sarton *At Seventy*, p. 37.

5. Denise Chen "Heavenly Scent" *New Science Magazine*, June 1999.

6. Vaclav Havel *Disturbing the Peace*, p. 181.

Chapter Six

1. Joan Chittister *Scared by Struggle: Transformed by Hope*, p. 19.

2. Norman Cousins "The Right to Die" *Saturday Review*, June 1975.

3. Warren Wolfe "Man would refuse to take wife off respirator" *Minneapolis-St. Paul StarTribune*, May 2 1991.

4. Margaret Battin "Euthanasia: The Way We Do It, the Way They Do It" 1991.

5. James M. Hoefler *Managing Death* 1997.

6. *Compassion and Choices Magazine* "Eight Years after Kevorkian" p. 14.

7. G. Scofield "Privacy (or Liberty) and Assisted Suicide" July 5, 1991.

Chapter Seven

1. Gail Sheehy "How Can We Help Our Nation's Caregivers" p. 6.

2. Henri *Nouwen Reaching Out: The Three Movements of Spiritual Life.* p. 68.

3. Janet Peterson "Fine Tuning" *A Book of Yes* 1982.

4. William J.Worden *Grief Counseling and Grief Therapy: A Handbook for the Mental Health Professional*, 1992.

5. Donna Swanson "Minnie Remembers" *Images: Women in Transition* compiled by Janice Grana, (http://www.upperroom.org/bookstore) pp.118–19.

6. Pema Chodron "The Wisdom of Hopelessness" from an interview in *Utne Reader* May–June 1997.

7. Rebecca O'Connor (Editor) *Is There Life after Death?* p. 8.

Conclusion

1. Irene Pauli "Everyone's studying us: The Ironies of Aging in the Pepsi Generation" quoted in *Women and Aging: An Anthology by Women* Jo Alexander, ed. p. 47.

Appendix D: Market Place of Options

1. Mark Skeie and Janet Skeie, Julie Roles (eds.*) Mapping Your Retirement: A Personal Guide to Maintaining Your Health, Managing Your Money, and Living Well* 2007.
2. Marc Freedman *Prime Time: How Baby Boomers will revolutionize retirement and transform America* 1999.

Appendix E: Health-Care, Legal and Ethical Terms

1. Jean Orsello, Jean K. "Planning for Incapacity" 1990.

Appendix F: Resuscitation Artificial feeding and Hydration

1. Susan J. Diem, John Lantos, and James Tulsky "Cardiopulmonary Resuscitation on Television: Miracles and Misinformation" p. 1578.
2. Joanne Lynn and James F. Childress. "Must Patients Always Be Given Food and Water?" pp. 17–21.
3. American Medical Association "Opinion of the AMA Council on Ethical and Judicial Affairs" 1986.
4. J. V. Zerwekh "The Dehydration Question" pp. 41–51.

BIBLIOGRAPHY

American Medical Association. "Opinion of the AMA Council on Ethical and Judicial Affairs," Chicago, IL, 15 March 1986.

Baum, P. S. and L.H. Roth. "Clinical Issues in the Assessment of Competency" *American Journal of Psychiatry* 138 pp. 1462–67, 1981.

Battin Margaret P. "Euthanasia: The Way We Do It, the Way They Do It" *Journal of Pain and Symptom Management* 6, no. 5 July 1991.

Brantner, John. Keynote to Senior Workers Association Minneapolis, Minnesota, 1981.

Brown, Stephnie L. et. al "Providing social support may be more beneficial than receiving it," *Psychological Science* Vol. 14 Issue 4, 2003 pp. 320–327.

Butler, Robert N., and Myrna Lewis. *Aging and Mental Health: Positive Psychosocial Approaches.* Saint Louis: C. V. Mosby, 1977.

Callahan, Maggie, and Patricia Kelley. *Final Gifts: Understanding the Special Awareness, Needs, and Communication of the Dying* New York: Bantam Books 1997.

Carlson, Lisa. *Caring For Your Own Dead: Your Final Act of Love* Hinesburg, VT: Upper Access Books, 1998.

Chittister, Joan. *Scared by Struggle: Transformed by Hope* Cambridge, MA: Wm. B. Eerdmans Publishing Co, 2003.

Chodron, Pema. *When Things Fall Apart: Heart Advice for Difficult Times* Boston: .Shambhala Dragon Productions: A Guide to Compassionate Living 1997.

Copper, Baba. "Voices: On Becoming Old Women" in *Women and Aging: An Anthology by Women* Corvallis, OR: Calyx Books 1993.

Compassion and Choices Magazine. "Eight Years after Kevorkian" Summer 2007 Vol. 6 No 2.

Cousins, Norman. "The Right to Die." *Saturday Review,* June 14, 1975.

Cowley, Malcolm. *The View from Eighty* New York: Penguin Books, 1982.

Dass, Ram. *Still Here* Riverhead Books Penquin Group: (USA) 2000.

Didion, Joan. *The Year of Magical Thinking* New York: Alfred A. Knopf, 2005, pp. 188–9.

Diem, Susan J., John Lantos, and James Tulsky "Cardiopulmonary Resuscitation on Television: Miracles and Misinformation" *The New England Journal of Medicine,* June 13, 1996.

Ellison, Jerome. *Life's Second Half: The Pleasure of Aging.* Greenwich, Conn.: Devin-Adair Co., 1978.

Ephron, Nora. *I Feel Bad About My Neck: And Other Thoughts on Being a Woman* NY: Random House 2006.

Erikson, Erik, and Helen Kivnick. *Childhood and Society.* New York: Norton, 1963.

Evans, A.L., and B.A. Brody. "The Do-Not-Resuscitate Order in Teaching Hospitals. *Journal of American Medical Association* 253, no 15, April 19, 1985 pp. 2236–39.

Fabry, Joseph. *Guideposts to Meaning: Discovering What Really Matters.* Oakland, CA: New Harbinger Publications, 1988.

Felton, Tammy Felton. "We Must find Peace" Reprinted from *Images: Women in Transition*compiled by Janice Grana Hinesburg, VT Upper Room Books 1975.

Frankl, Victor. *Foundations and Applications of Logotherapy The Will to Meaning.* NewYork: New American Library, 1969.

Freedman, Marc. *Prime Time: How Baby Boomers will revolutionize retirement and transform America* Published by Public-Affairs, 1999.

Freeman, L.W. *Mosby's Complementary and Alternative Medicine: A Research based approach.* St. Louis, MO: Mosby, 2004.

Grana, Janice. *Images: Women in Transition* Los Angeles: Acton House, 1975.

Guarneri, Mimi. *The Heart Speaks: A Cardiologist Reveals the Secret Language of Healing* New York, Simon and Schuster, 2006.

Harris, Mark. *Grave Matters: A Journey Through the Modern Funeral Industry to a Natural Way of Burial* New York: Scribner Press, January 2007.

Harris, Sam. *The End of Faith,* New York W.W. Norton and Co., 2005.

Havel, Vaclav. *Disturbing the Peace,* New York: Alfred A. Knopt, 1990.

Herbert, Trish. *The Vintage Journey: A Guide to Artful Aging,* Cleveland, Ohio: United Church Press, 1995.

———. "The Most Courageous of All" Minnesota Sun Publications, February 16, 1987.

Hoefler, James M. *Managing Death* Boulder, CO: Westview Press, 1997.

Humphrey, Derek. *Final Exit* Secaucus, N.J.: Carol Publishing, 1991.

Jung, Carl Gustav. *Modern Man in Search of a Soul* Orlando, FL: Harcourt, Inc. 1933.

Kanin, Garson. *It Takes a Long Time to Become Young* New York: Doubleday 1978.

Keyes, Ken, Jr. *The Hundredth Monkey* St. Mary, Kentucky: Vision Books 1981.

Kobasa, S., and M. Puccetti. "Personality and Social Resources in Stress Resistance" *Journal of Personality and Social Psychology* 45, no. 4. 1983.

Langer, Ellen, and Rodin, J. "The effects of enhanced personal responsibility for the aged: A field experiment in and institutional setting." *Journal of Personality and Social Psychology*, 34, 1976 191–98.

Langer, Ellen. *Mindfulness* Reading, MA: Addison-Wesley 1989.

LeSeuer, Meridel. *Ripenings: Selected Works, 1927–1980.* Old Westbury, NY: The Feminist Press 1982.

Lipton, Bruce. *The Biology of Belief: Unleashing the Power of Consciousness, Matter and Miracles* 2005.

Luks, Allan, and Peggy Payne. *The Healing Power of Doing Good* New York: Fawcett Columbine 1991.

Lustblader, Wendy. *What's Worth Knowing* New York Tarcher/Penquin, 2001.

Lynn, Joanne, and James F. Childress. "Must Patients Always Be Given Food and Water?" The Hastings Center Report 13, no. 5): October 17–21, 1983.

Lynch, James. *A Cry Unheard: New Insights into the Medical Consequences of Loneliness* Baltimore, MD: Bancroft Press, 2000.

Manahan, Nancy, and Becky Bohan. Living *Consciously, Dying Gracefully: A Journey with Cancer and Beyond* Edina, Beaver's Pond Press 2007.

Maslow, A. H. *Motivation and Personality* (2nd ed.). New York: Harper and Row. 1970.

Nagel, E. L. "Complications of CPR" *Critical Care Medicine* 9, no. 5: 424 1981.

Nouwen, Henri. *Reaching Out: The Three Movements of Spiritual Life.* Garden City, NY: Doubleday, 1975.

O'Connor, Rebecca (Editor), *Is There Life after Death?* Farmington Hills, MI: Greenhaven Press, ThomsonGale, 2005.

Oliver, Mary. *New and Selected Poems* Boston, MA: Beacon Press 1992.

Oliver, *Mary. New and Selected Poems, Volume Two* Boston, MA: Beacon Press 2005.

Orsello, Jean K. "Planning for Incapacity" St. Paul: Minnesota Adult Protection Coalition, 1990.

Paddock, Nancy. *Trust the Wild Heart*, Redwing, MN Red Dragonfly Press, 2006.

Palmer, Parker. *Let Your Life Speak:Listening for the Voice of Vocation* New York, Jossey-Bass 1999.

Paul, Irene. "Everyone's studying us: The Ironies of Aging in the Pepsi Generation" *Women and Aging: An Anthology by Women* edited by Alexander Corvallis, OR: Calyx Books, 1991.

Perricone, N V. *The Wrinkle Cream.* Emmaus, PA: Rodale Books, 2000.

Pert, Candice B. "The Wisdom of the Receptors: Neuropeptides, the Emotions, and the Bodymind," Advances: Institute for Advancement of Health 3, no 3) 8–16. Summer 1986.

Peseschkian, Nossrat. *In Search of Meaning: A Psychotherapy of Small Steps.* New York: Springer-Verlag, Bellins, 1985.

Peterson, Janet. "Fine Tuning," *A Book of Yes* Niles, Ill. Argus Communication 1982.

Pink, Daniel H. *A Whole New Mind: Moving from the information Age to the Conceptual Age* Riverhead Books, New York 2005.

President's Commission for the Study of Ethical Problems in Medicine and Biomedical and Behavioral Research 'Defining Death' Washington, D.C.: GPO, 1981.

Remen, Rachel Naomi. *Kitchen Table Wisdom: Stories that Heal* New York, Riverhead Books, 1996.

Reilly, Steve. *Simple Psychology: Simple Living in a Complicated World* Columbia, MO Motivation Press, 1996.

Rossi, Ernest. *The Psychobiology of Mind-Body Healing* New York: W. W. Norton, 1986.

Sanford, Matthew. *Waking: A Memoir of Trauma and Transcendence* New York: Rodale, 2006.

Sarton, May. *Coming into Eighty: New Poems* New York: Norton, 1994.

———. *At seventy: a Journal* [1st ed.] New York: W.W. Norton, 1984.

———. *Encore: a journal of the eightieth year.* New York: W.W. Norton & Co. 1993.

Scofield, G. "Privacy (or Liberty) and Assisted Suicide." *Journal of Pain and Symptom Management* 6, no. 5 July 1991.

Scott-Maxwell, Florida. *The Measure of My Days*, New York: Penquin Books, 1968.

Sheehy, Gail. "How Can We Help Our Nation's Caregivers" *Parade Magazine*, September 9, 2007.

Skeie, Mark, and Janet and Julie Roles (Eds.) *Mapping Your Retirement: A Personal Guide to Maintaining Your Health, Managing Your Money, and Living Well* Minneapolis, Minnesota MYR Publications, 2007.

Slovut, Gordon. "They'd Give High Doses of Pain-killers to Dying, Doctors Say. *Minneapolis StarTribune*, April 26, 1990.

Sternberg, Ethyl M. *The Balance Within: The Science Connecting Health and Emotions*, New York: WH Freeman and Company, 2000.

Swanson, Donna. "Minnie Remembers" *Images: Women in Transition* compiled by Janice Grana, 1975.

Tornstam, Lars. *Gerotranscendence: A Developmental Theory of Positive Aging* New York: Springer Publishing Company, 2005.

Veninga, Robert L. *The gift of Hope* New York: Ballentine Books, 1985.

Wallis, Velma. *Two Old Women* New York: HarperCollins 1993.

Williams, Margery *The Velveteen Rabbit* New York, Doubleday & Company, Inc. 1922.

Wolfe, Warren. "Man Would Refuse Ruling to Take Wife Off Respirator." *Minneapolis StarTribune*, May 29, 1991.

Worden, J. William. *Grief Counseling and Grief Therapy: A Handbook for the Mental Health Professional*, New York: Springer Publishing Company, 1992.

Yusuf, S., and S. Hawken Ounpuu. Report of INTERHEART The Lancet. September 2004.

Zerwekh, J. V. "The Dehydration Question" *Nursing*, January, 41–51.1983.